Maestro of Crystal

# MAESTRO OF CRYSTAL

## The Story of Miroslav Havel

How a young man from a small village in Czechoslovakia became
the design genius behind Ireland's celebrated Waterford Crystal

Brian F. Havel

CURRACH
PRESS

First published in 2005 by
CURRACH PRESS
55A Spruce Avenue, Stillorgan Industrial Park, Blackrock, Co Dublin

www.currach.ie


Cover by Slick Fish Design
Cover photograph (main) by Terry Murphy
Origination by Currach Press
Printed by ScandBook AB, Sweden


The author has asserted his moral rights.


ISBN 1-85607-930-9

# CONTENTS

# KDE DOMOV MŮJ? (Where is My Home?)

Kde domov můj, kde domov můj?
Voda hučí po lučinách,
Bory šumí po skalinách,
V sadě skví se jara květ,
Zemský ráj to na pohled!
A to je ta krásná země,
Země česká, domov můj,
Země česká, domov můj!


Where is my home, where is my home?
Water rushing across the meadows,
Pinewoods rush o'er rocky hills,
Orchards where spring blossom gleams,
Paradise on earth it seems!
And this is that beautiful land,
The Czech land, [here is] my home,
The Czech land, [here is] my home!

(Czech Republic National Anthem)

# Acknowledgements and Dedication

I am grateful to a number of people who assisted me in my research and writing tasks. I owe a great debt of gratitude to Brian Lynch, publisher of Currach Press, who encouraged me on the basis of his review of a short book treatment to complete the task of writing the finished manuscript. I am thankful to Mairead Dunlevy, one of Ireland's foremost writers and experts in the decorative arts, for doing me the honour of contributing such a beautiful foreword to the book. My thanks extend also to Emer Ryan, my editor, for her efforts to improve the text, and to Tomáš Ritter, my sister Julie's Czech-born boyfriend, for his help in translating documents and letters. My brother Mirek provided complete access to his personal collection of my father's designs and was helpful in explaining some of the technical aspects of glass-making. I am grateful to Terry Murphy, for many years Waterford Crystal's official photographer, for his generosity in allowing me to use several of his excellent photographs as illustrations in the book (including the colour photograph that graces the front cover), and to John Foley, chief executive of Waterford Crystal, for his graciousness in providing the necessary copyright permissions. Chicago artist John David

Mooney, who collaborated with my father on a spectacular crystal-and-steel sculpture at the University of Chicago, has been a constant source of inspiration. My friend and former schoolmate at Waterpark College, Kieran Walsh, editor of the *Munster Express*, supported the project from the beginning and has generated many good ideas based on his unrivalled knowledge of Waterford City and its history. I am indebted also to my friend Alice Rudolph in Chicago for her peerless proofreading skills. Finally, I want to thank my parents, who patiently co-operated in responding to questions, in dredging up old documents and photographs, and in allowing me the freedom to write the story as I wanted it to be written.

This book is dedicated to my parents, Miroslav and Betty, to my brothers and sisters and their spouses who have all given me their full support and encouragement during the writing process – John and Deirdre, Mirek and Marie, Liz and Brian, Clodagh and James, and Julie, as well as to Miroslav and Betty's eleven grandchildren (John, Mark, Karl, Katie, Ben, Anninka, Louisa, Laura, Mirek Jr, Jimmy and Rory). For their support over the years, I also dedicate the book to Betty's sister, Margaret Cooke, and her husband Donie, and to her late sister, Angela Fitzgerald, and her husband John. For their personal support in this and other writing projects, I am pleased to include in this dedication the Dinwoodie and Kane families of Prestwick, Scotland and Crouch End, London (David, Isa, Graeme, Christine, Davy and Maya). I would also like to offer a special dedication to the late Dick Kervick of The Vinery, Summerville Avenue, who was the first person to suggest to me, during a conversation on Grange Park Road, Waterford, that took place many, many years ago, that I should write Miroslav Havel's story. Lastly, this book is dedicated to all of the people of Waterford Crystal – past, present and future.

Brian Havel
Chicago
1 September 2005

# Foreword

The arts which depend on design have been thought the greatest ornaments in society (because) design is the child of genius – the principle of it must exist in the soul and can be called forth only by education and improved by practice.
– John Gwyn, *An Essay on Design, Including Proposals for Erecting a Public Academy to be supported by Voluntary Subscription* (Dublin, 1749)

Although written about two hundred years before Miroslav Havel arrived in Ireland, the above quotation encapsulates his strongly held belief, one that was not shared enthusiastically by many in Ireland at the time. Waterford Crystal would have been an entirely different product were it not for Havel, its first designer and the man who trained generations of its glassmakers and artists. His personal glass collection, selected from the creative work of contemporary artists in Belgium, Czechoslovakia, Sweden, Venice, the United States and elsewhere, shows his enjoyment of and passion for the discipline of glass form, use of colour, understanding of refractions, and design finishes. That exuberance was no less passionate when he designed commercially but there his approach to style and decoration was controlled by concerns of price, quality and market demand. A talented but practical enthusiast, his commitment to the development of his friend Charles Bačik's glass factory at Waterford meant that he involved himself in everything from building glass furnaces and supervising the development of machinery to packing finished glasses in boxes. Always a pioneer, he overcame the difficulties of the fledgling factory by, for example, overseeing the production of simply-cut soda glass to initiate new employment in Waterford, and using such imaginative but traditional techniques as throwing potatoes and turnips into melted glass to improve the crystal quality.

The establishment of a glass factory at Waterford in 1947 could be attributed to the drive of the entrepreneur Charles Bačik, who was proud of the quality of hand-cut crystal produced in his various glasshouses in Czechoslovakia. When one of them was taken over by Communists in October 1945, he feared that development of his factories would be retarded and so he left his homeland the following year. Selecting an Ireland that was neutral during the war and where many spoke of 'centuries of oppression' may have had resonances for a Czechoslovak with his war-torn land existing under the shadow of its powerful neighbours. But Ireland was weak after the period called the Emergency (1939-45) and the Irish, with limited buying power, were expected to be content with 'frugal comfort'. Politically astute, Bačik saw the problems of inflation, emigration and underdeveloped agriculture but he also recognised that in 1946-7, Seán Lemass as Minister for Industry and Commerce had aspirations to develop efficient industries, some of which would target a more sophisticated market. Bačik was encouraged and supported by Bernard J. Fitzpatrick, a Dublin manufacturing jeweller. The initial plan was to open in Carlow because of the similarity in name to Bačik's successful glasshouse, Karlov. But it was the lore associated with the early Waterford glass works along with the demand for that glass in antique shops internationally that proved irresistible. Few spoke of the fact that the term had become such a synonym for the antique cut glass of the late eighteenth/early nineteenth centuries, that glass from many Irish and British factories was commonly attributed to 'Waterford'.

For this new venture Bačik needed skilled workers and so, in an ingenious manner, he recruited Miroslav Havel, a gifted student who was doing his internship at the Karlov factory. Havel's motivation for travel was to improve his glass-making and decorating skills. Disappointed on arrival in 1947 to discover that Waterford's glass factory closed a century earlier, it was his loyalty to Bačik and his commitment to working in Ireland for a few months that made him stay initially. Havel was unique in Ireland at the time as he had formal training in glass design and manufacture. His training followed the enlightened educational system of mid-eighteenth century France, Austria and Germany. In those countries it was believed that to become a commercial designer one needed years of training in drawing and the liberal arts, alongside practical training in the workplace in all aspects of production, an understanding of the machinery used, and an awareness of market forces. Havel enrolled at the Železny Brod glass school when he was sixteen years of age. There he spent three days a week learning art, business and the German language, with the other days spent in practical training in workshops. In 1940 he was admitted to the Academy of Art and Industrial Design at the Charles University of Prague. There, glass chemistry and techniques, along with engraving and sculpture, were added to the curriculum. In his subsequent internship with Bačik's factory, he continued to develop other techniques such as cutting. Attracting Havel to Ireland because of his expertise followed in the tradition whereby, at least from the seventeenth century, many industries were developed in Ireland with the support of foreign specialists. As craft workers were mobile it is true, too, that Irish workers sought employment abroad when their skills were in demand. It is hardly surprising, therefore, that in that tradition, Havel travelled extensively in Denmark, Germany and Sweden to recruit experts for Waterford in crystal production, stem-production, handles, moulds and so on.

His own role was pivotal as he enthusiastically experimented in production and design. Of major importance was the introduction of a training system similar to that in Czechoslovakia where apprentices in the factory were given tuition in design and art at the local technical college. Hardly surprisingly, one of the after-hours teachers there was Havel. Novel and successful ideas in marketing at this time included the provision of trophy awards in engraved cut crystal and the identification of the potential of the US market. There was an irony though, in that the cut glass designs which were being promoted were in part derived from those of the late eighteenth/early nineteenth century period when Ireland was the European leader in glass design – before Bohemia took that leadership!

Bačik, Fitzpatrick and Havel were hampered by the lack of venture capital, but injection of money came in 1950 with the major involvement of Joseph McGrath, Joseph Griffin and their families. Then it was possible to build a new factory to produce and decorate the finest quality crystal using new technologies and to develop a modern business. The sales department, with its remarkable manager Con Dooley, promoted this quality hand-cut crystal by associating it with Ireland's proud past. Working with John Miller of New York, Dooley and others developed a sophisticated brand loyalty in the United States. An important element was the new trademark, which was based on elements of Waterford City's coat of arms. Havel designed that mark to symbolise Waterford, excellence and Ireland.

Brian Havel has told the story of his father, a Czechoslovak/ Irish man, with humour and sympathy. His is a story of a generous, enthusiastic man whose love of Betty made him partially forget the sorrows of leaving home. It is the story of transplanting and then 'nationalising' a major glass factory, but overall it is a story of commitment, pride, ambition, romance, deprivation, creativity, curiosity, tireless energy and sheer hard work.

This early immigrant has served his adopted country well. It can truly be said, 'Ní bheidh a leithéid arís ann.'

Mairead Dunlevy
Keeper Emeritus
National Museum of Ireland

# Preface

Waterford Glass. A world-famous hand-blown lead crystal manufactured in the city of Waterford. The enterprise was established by [English] Quaker brothers, George and William Penrose, in 1783. Their glass won several gold medals at the Great London Exhibition of 1851, and the brand was revived in 1950 ... as a symbol of craftsmanship and beauty. The most popular and best-selling stemware pattern in the world is Waterford's Lismore range, introduced to the market in October 1952. It was created by Mirek Havel, who emigrated from Czechoslovakia in 1947 and became chief designer at the factory. In 1967 Jacqueline Kennedy toured the factory while staying nearby, and ordered Waterford Glass chandeliers for the Kennedy Centre in [Washington, DC]. This association cemented the product's popularity among Irish-Americans, who account for a large proportion of sales both in Ireland and the USA.

– Brewer's *Dictionary of Irish Phrase & Fable* (2004)

This book originated in December 2002 when I read in the *Irish Independent* newspaper an article by Mary Kenny about the importance of recording the memories of the oldest generations still among us. She urged readers to 'purchase a routine, inexpensive tape recorder, place in it an ordinary cassette tape ...[a]nd then just get them to talk, talk, talk.'

In the winter of 2002 and 2003, I took Kenny's advice and recorded many hours of conversations with my father, Miroslav Havel, the chief designer of Waterford Crystal until his retirement in 1990. ('Mirek', as he is called in the above extract, is a more familiar shortening of Miroslav.) This book is, in principal part, the product of those conversations, but it also reflects conversations with people who worked with my father. In addition, I have used many surviving documents (including some of his original designs) that I have been able to access.

However, the book remains primarily a record of my father's own recollections of his remarkable personal and working life. For that reason, I often quote him directly or refer to his thoughts and have tried not to replace him as the primary witness to his own experiences. His is a life of the twentieth century that I hope readers will enjoy remembering with him. When I quote my father, the reader should bear in mind that he was, after all, brought up speaking Czech, and this fact, compounded by a lifetime of hearing problems, means that his English has always had an eccentric and often semi-grammatical twist that makes him sometimes hard to understand but always easy to appreciate.

Throughout the book, I take the liberty of referring to my father by his first name, Miroslav. I have never actually addressed him by his first name. But I am taking this liberty here, and feel comfortable doing so, simply because Miroslav has been the way his nurses and doctors in Waterford have addressed him with perfect Czech pronunciation when helping him with his successful rehabilitation from the broken femur he sustained in his eighty-first year (ironically, on stepping into his doctor's surgery). Miroslav Havel, born in Czechoslovakia but a native son of Ireland; this is the paradox of my father's life, and this is my father's story.

The book is divided into two parts. The first part, 'Czechoslovakia', gives a flavour of my father's childhood and early adulthood in the country in which he was born. It shows the development of his artistic skills against the charged background of world war and Nazi occupation. The second part, 'Ireland', takes the story to the country where he has spent most of his adult life. It tells the intertwining story of his experiences as a transplanted Czech in a country of which he knew hardly anything when he arrived for a three-month stay in 1947, his contribution to the success of Waterford Crystal for the next forty years, after the Communists seized power in Prague and he was unable to return to his homeland. At the end of this part, there is a chapter which presents some of my father's work as both studio artist and industrial designer in his four decades with Waterford Crystal. Most of the pieces discussed in this chapter are illustrated in a series of photographs contained in the book.

The book is not intended to offer a detailed technical account of how my father produced his designs or of the technical complexities of the manufacture of high-grade lead crystal. I am only too aware, as a novice in these matters, how much of his talent must consequently remain unexpressed in this account of his life. Just to give one example, his long-time associate in the engraving department, Jim Burke, recently told me about my father's ingenuity in creating larger-scale versions of drinking-glass patterns to fit the vases and decanters in a particular Waterford Crystal suite. To represent that skill accurately would require a collection of engineering drawings and detailed explanatory mathematical and geometric notes. I have seen some of these symbols of higher mathematics scribbled on the margins of my father's design work.

However, that kind of detail would stray from my purpose in writing this book, which is to show my father's life in a way that I hope the reader will find stimulating but not too obsessed with technical matters. I have discussed the technical aspects of glass-making and decorating in a way that I myself, as someone with no prior training in this field, could understand, and that approach, I believe, serves the book's purpose best.

Having denied any obsession with technicalities, I must nevertheless add a little note on the pronunciation of some of the Czech names that appear throughout the book. The reader will often see the little symbol 'v' over the letter 'c' (as in *Babička*, the Czech for 'grandmother'). This simply means that the letter 'c' is pronounced as if it were written as the 'ch' in 'chick' or 'China'. The name 'Bačik', for example, which appears frequently in the book, is pronounced 'Ba-chick'. When the 'v' is over the 's', as in František (the name of my grandfather), the letter 's' is pronounced 'sh' as in 'shoot' (thus, Fran-ti-shek). When the 'v' is over the letter 'z' (as in my father's home village of Držkov), or over the letters 'e' or 'r', it is best for the non-Czech speaker to ignore the symbol and just move on.

Finally, the main title of this book, *Maestro of Crystal*, is borrowed from the description used to introduce my father in Waterford Crystal's film documentary of its manufacturing process, *Celebration of Light*. Transatlantic air travellers will recall this film as a staple on many Aer Lingus flights from the United States to Ireland over the past couple of decades.

Crystal glass is an astonishingly difficult medium to master. Whether the glass was in its molten form as it came streaming out of a hot clay pot at temperatures exceeding 1,500° centigrade, or was stone-cold and being decorated with spinning metal wheels, Miroslav Havel had a command of each part of the manufacturing process, and this, in conjunction with his mastery of design, truly earned him the title of 'maestro'. Indeed, his success as a designer was intimately connected with his unsurpassed skills in cutting, engraving, and polishing, his ability to sculpt beauty from solid blocks of crystal, his familiarity with the blower's and the mould-maker's arts, and his immersion in every aspect of the art and craft and science of glass-making.

'Throughout the years, Havel has been our chief designer,' Noel Griffin, the late general manager of Waterford Crystal, wrote in 1981. 'He's a genius. He can blow, cut, sculpt, paint, and engrave as well as design. We still have this very superior man, and we have some good Irish designers who have learned from him.' In an appreciation of Miroslav Havel's career, featured in the 1997 Yearbook of the *Irish Arts Review*, Mairead Dunlevy, Keeper Emeritus, the National Museum of Ireland, dubbed him 'Designer Extraordinary'. These were nice compliments, and I hope that the reader will find enough evidence in this book to justify their inclusion in this preface.

# Part One

# CZECHOSLOVAKIA

# A Bohemian Life

My father, Miroslav Patrick Havel (the strange mixture of a Czech first name and an Irish middle name will be explained later) was born in a tiny village of six hundred people, Držkov, nestled beneath a great mountain in what was then the Bohemian region of the free and independent Republic of Czechoslovakia, on 26 May 1922. The phrase *Drž kov*, as two words in Czech, means 'hold the metal', although what that means (or ever was intended to mean) is anybody's guess.

The story begins, at least from my point of view, in the mists of the beginning decades of another century and in a country that I can hardly imagine and that no longer exists. Miroslav was the only child of František Havel and Anna Klubelova. By the time he was born, his parents were well-established business people in the little village, and they were able to give their adored son what he now calls 'very, very nice young days'. They did everything in their power to make their son's life a happy one – a natural consequence, according to Miroslav, of his status as an only child.

However, they also delegated a lot of his upbringing to others. Their costume jewellery manufacturing business, in fact, kept them so busy that Miroslav's early years were spent mostly under the care of his grandmother, Božena, his father's mother, to whom he referred in traditional Czech parlance as his *Babička*. Božena owned and lived in a big old house next door to an empty property which František later bought and on which he built his own family home. Miroslav was actually born in his grandmother's house, way up in the top-floor attic and occasional birthing room.

With his grandmother so much involved in his early upbringing, Miroslav enjoyed much freedom during his childhood, making him (in his own words) sometimes 'an odd little fellow', probably spending a lot of time on his own, as only children often do. However, he used that time wisely, cultivating a natural gift for drawing, and spending countless hours upstairs in the room where he was born, doodling and sketching and making little portraits of his family and school friends. His artistic skills came quickly to the attention of his teachers at the village school, which was only a short ten-minute walk from his home. He was prevailed upon to spend many pleasant hours after class painting the scenery for the school's pride and joy, its little puppet theatre.

Miroslav was happy to help out in this way, because it helped him shake off some of what he refers to as his 'oddness', and to emerge from the sheltered existence in which he had spent a lot of his time under the sometimes too-embracing protection of his beloved grandmother. He gradually learned to be more sociable and developed a knack for winning friends that would stand him in good stead years later when he would find himself, through a most unusual series of circumstances, alone and uncertain in a distant foreign country. When Miroslav was twelve, he started going a little further afield to school, to the nearby village of Zásada, just fifteen minutes away in winter when he travelled on his sturdy cross-country skis.

In those days, children in Czechoslovakia rarely inquired, and were not encouraged to inquire, about the circumstances of their parents' meeting. However, he does know that František and Anna grew up about 200 kilometres apart. František was a native of Držkov, located about a hundred kilometres north of Prague, hard on the Polish-German border, and a couple of hundred kilometres west of the birthplace of the late Pope John Paul II. Indeed, Miroslav's heavily accented English makes him sound very like John Paul, or at least like John Paul when he spoke English.

The Klubela family of Anna, Miroslav's mother, lived on a farm in the southern province of Moravia. Miroslav recalls the gentleness of his mother's nature and that of her family. 'She was an angel,' he says. Anna, who was named after her mother, was the youngest of ten children, nine girls and one boy. Miroslav knew his mother's family and their farm fairly well. As a child, his mother had sent him for three months to a school in Rohožna, the local town, because she and her husband were on bad terms with each other. Anna felt it would be best for Miroslav if he were away for a while. The school was Roman Catholic, even though neither Anna nor her husband was a Catholic, and Miroslav was surprised to be at a school where public prayers were said fifteen or twenty times a day.

Later, in his teens, Miroslav visited the old farm several times, making the long journey down to Moravia on his trusty motorbike. The Klubela farm was in one of the most inaccessible parts of the countryside, and the area around the farm was known as Zadní Pole, which means 'back field'. In fact, the farm comprised not alone a back field, but a patchwork of many connected fields. It was a huge and sprawling property, roughly a square shape when you looked at the whole thing, with three big stables in the middle which were filled with what Miroslav recalls as 'oxen', and of course with the stench of manure. On one trip, his cousins even persuaded him to join them in ploughing with some of the biggest of the oxen, a very different experience from the motorised tractors he had seen up north.

František, also a man of the countryside, was hewn from much rougher stuff than his gentle wife, more than a bit of a devil to her angel. His father's name, interestingly, was Václav Havel, and there is reportedly a distant-cousin connection with former Czechoslovak President Havel, whose family hails from the same region of Bohemia. František was one of three children, including a brother, Miloslav, after whom he claimed he had named his son, in spite of the difference in spelling of the two names.

For his own name, František preferred 'Franta', rather than his rather cumbersome first name. He was first and foremost a shrewd and persistent, if not always lucky, entrepreneur – a gene that would completely bypass his only son and be transmitted intact to his second grandson, John, now a successful businessman in Dublin. The nature of Franta's various businesses, however, could never easily be expressed in a single thought. In 1918, he had come into possession of an oil and petrol agency for Držkov and its region, and was travelling around selling these commodities to local filling stations. He was making decent money, but he was looking for something even more lucrative.

Meanwhile, as part of a brood of ten children, and with the traditional priority given to the only son, Anna Klubela was unable to remain on the family farm. She went in search of a job, and got some nursing experience at a local hospital. When the First World War began, she was assigned to a military hospital in Vienna. Her future husband served with the balloonist corps of the Czechoslovak Army, one of the most hazardous assignments at a time when aviation was scarcely past the Wright Brothers era. Franta injured his right leg during a dangerous landing and ended up under Anna's care in Vienna toward the end of the war. Six-foot-three and ruggedly handsome, with an almost Celtic charm and sense of mischief, Franta exploited his ballooning injury to win Anna's sympathy and then her affections.

According to Miroslav, Franta never liked to talk about his war service, or about his confinement in Vienna. The few details he knows about his parents' meeting and marriage were disclosed to him when he was already in his twenties. He is reasonably certain that Franta and Anna got married in Držkov in 1918 after a very brief courtship. But what month in 1918, who the guests were, or any of the usual details that modern life finds so indispensable, are completely lacking. There is no surviving photograph of the event. The earliest photographs Miroslav has of his parents are a wartime army photograph of his father and a picture taken with his mother and father when he was about four years old.

Sometime in the mid-1920s, and it is hard to know exactly

when because no records remain, Franta decided to enter the *bijouterie* business, specialising in artificial or costume jewellery for women. His oil and gas agency had put him in contact with ethnic Germans and Jews in Bohemia who dominated the costume jewellery trade. Their products, a variety of brooches, necklaces, pendants, bracelets, earrings and similar stuff made from stringing together tiny coloured glass beads, were in constant demand in much the same way that 'bling' has a certain fashion cachet today. Franta obtained the basic glass beads through his contacts in the regional capital, Jablonec, and persuaded a local glass-maker, a veteran soldier who had lost a leg in the war, to add the colour. Franta conscripted his wife to make sample designs, and she proved naturally good at it.

Franta himself never lacked self-confidence, and was certain that his 'bad' knowledge of German (Miroslav's recollection) would be enough to allow him to conduct the necessary negotiations for getting his products into the marketplace. He even ventured beyond costume jewellery, asking Anna to produce samples also of table decorations, including fancy placemats.

As it turned out, Franta's business skills quickly propelled him ahead of all of his regional competitors. Indulging himself, he eventually used his growing prosperity to build a large new residence only ten metres from the front door of his mother's house, the house where Miroslav had been born and where Franta and Anna lived on the top floor during the first decade or so of their marriage. According to Miroslav, the new house was one of the finest in the village (see photograph 1).

Franta's costume jewellery business was a masterpiece of efficient decentralisation and low input costs. He recruited over three hundred families from towns and villages within a fifty-kilometre radius of Držkov to assemble hundreds of thousands of coloured beads into hundreds of items of low fashion. Držkov, in fact, proved to be a good base from which Franta could attack, almost by stealth, the bigger surrounding towns and markets, especially the regional capital of Jablonec. Being local also helped Franta to execute his clever plan to tap into the craft skills of his country neighbours.

Anna helped in recruiting the families and in negotiating deals that would keep costs as low as possible. She often worked twenty-hour days to keep the business going. Most of the families involved were farmers, and they did the work at night-time. It was perfect work, really, for the long winter evenings (another shrewd reason why Franta insisted on a village-based business). The women, in particular, had a native knack for the patient and precise needlework required to string the glass beads together through a tiny hole in the middle of each bead. According to Miroslav, the women could start production of a new sample after only about two days of training. Their effort was all the more remarkable given that they were ordinary villagers with no special expertise other than their inherited ability to do folk crafts.

Once his cottage industry of bead-deliverers and assemblers was put together, Franta typically gave his families fourteen days to string each shipment of beads and then he arranged collection and delivery of the finished products to his German and Jewish distributors in Jablonec and over the border in Germany. He shipped the boxes of finished jewellery by car or sometimes, in winter, by a sleigh pulled by two big horses. Although Franta had relationships with three or four big companies in Jablonec, he never entered into any written agreements or anything as fancy as a 'contract'; all of his business, with his suppliers, his families of willing bead-stringers, and his distributors, was done by word-of-mouth understandings.

It was a risky business, too, partly because of Franta's personal behaviour. On one occasion, Miroslav recalls, Franta arrived home without a penny, despite having collected ten or fifteen thousand Czechoslovak crowns in Jablonec. He had gambled and drunk it away, leaving no money to pay his assemblers. Anna, always resourceful, managed to lean on a local neighbour to help out, on the promise that the money would be repaid in a week.

A more serious risk, however, was that the industry was notoriously subject to changes in fashion taste. Franta had to make sure he had the services of a few designers who could keep up with (and even set) trends in costume jewellery. Actually, he was too cheap to use real designers very much, and most often he just corralled Anna into coming up with clever new designs. Anna was particularly good at designing patterns for brooches, which were assembled by mounting the beads on a metal plate with a layer of cotton wool between the beads and the plate to give more dimension and depth to the brooch. The idea of a 'designer' of a consumer product was intriguing to the artistic Miroslav, who sometimes helped in the intricate but tedious task of stringing the beads together.

Franta, meanwhile, had become a sort of a generic businessman, using his income stream from the jewellery business and the petrol agency to fund other ventures as opportunities came up. He was a high spender, and along the way he made many bad investments. 'He would go into anything,' according to Miroslav. His part-ownership of a tile factory, located about fifty kilometres from Držkov, produced lots of money for a while. Franta kept only a distant eye on the business, and then his partner disappeared and the venture collapsed. Miroslav suspects that not all of Franta's activities were above board, especially given his father's propensity to hang around with the rogues he ran into in bars. But some of his investments clearly paid off. He bought a lovely villa in the spa town of Luhacovice, still one of the most popular resorts in South Moravia, and sold it two years later for a handsome profit.

In fact, Franta's oddball business connections could bring unusual treats. When he sold the villa, he managed to persuade the buyer to reserve free rooms for himself and his family every summer. He was always looking for hard-to-get things, like a regular supply of bananas, then a highly prized exotic food. Franta would sometimes march through the village flaunting these extras, whether it was a big bunch of ripe bananas or maybe an impressive specimen of the traditional Bohemian Christmas fish, the carp.

Even though his parents' business meant that he spent more time with his grandmother, Miroslav certainly enjoyed a very prosperous upbringing in those early years in Držkov. Christmas, in particular, was celebrated lavishly with the exchange of gifts on Christmas Eve, followed by the eating of carp and goose on Christmas Day.

Christmas trees were everywhere. Since the surrounding mountains were studded with vast pine forests, Miroslav and his father simply strapped on their snow boots, marched up one of the mountain trails, and cut down a large tree to put beside the fireplace.

However, in that era, even prosperous times carried strong lessons from past deprivation. Miroslav's parents, who lived through two world wars, had a strong sense of thrift and efficiency. When the Christmas goose was brought home (minus its head, as was the traditional way of selling it), Anna carefully plucked its feathers to make pillows and the sumptuous feather-filled eiderdowns that made all that snow and cold so deliciously bearable in the long winter evenings and nights. Any visitor to a Czech home, even today, will enjoy these enormous bed covers, known in Czech as *peřina*, which are hand-made by the nimble fingers of at least two or three women. They are so big and body-hugging that they hermetically seal the sleeper. But they are not found in hotels because they are difficult to wash and clean. For Miroslav, *peřina* are a treasured memory of the bitingly cold winter evenings in his homeland.

Franta, who was not always the most attentive or patient father, could nevertheless be very generous to his only child. When Miroslav was nine, his father gave him a beautiful ice-hockey stick which was the envy of Miroslav's village pals. It was a precious gift because the kids at the time were playing ice hockey without ice or skates or proper hockey sticks, or even a puck – just hitting around a weighted tin cup with sticks made from tree branches. Miroslav played the game with his new hockey stick, but was always just a bit anxious about the consequences if he happened to break it.

When Miroslav turned ten, Franta gave him a pair of handmade hickory skis. Miroslav loved winter sports. He loved all sports, but he thought no other form of athletics could come close to skiing. For him, it was a sport of beauty, out on his own, surrounded only by snow. He had modest success in competitive skiing, but mostly he used his splendid skis for cross-country treks to and from his high school in nearby Zásada. His skis were the kind used in competitive racing – light and graceful – and the heavily packed snow allowed him to glide in almost a straight line, without zigzagging, across the gleaming white fields separating Držkov and Zásada (see photograph 2). Cross-country was really his most beloved ski activity, and although he did some jumping, he never attempted the trickier feats of the downhill slalom.

Miroslav's hickory skis were much too light for any kind of serious jumping, but he did once make the mistake of entering a jumping competition with them. As he came off the ramp, the breeze immediately blew his skis sideways, and Miroslav came down with a thump, breaking one of the skis. He started to cry, thinking only of his father's likely reaction to the broken ski. Franta, however, surprised his son by taking a sportsmanlike approach to the disaster. Franta himself liked competitive sports and he was just disappointed that Miroslav came from the race without a cup or a medal to show for all that effort.

Still, Miroslav did once enjoy a gift from the gods – a victory in cross-country that saw him passing everyone in sight, even drawing gasps from the crowds as he sailed past. According to his victory diploma, just before his eighteenth birthday he did the nine-kilometre run in slightly under fifty-six minutes. He attributes his success that day to how he applied the wax to the bottom of his hickory skis, a technique that is well-known in the sport. Science combines with art to determine the consistency of the wax, which must be applied with an eye to the weather, the wetness of the snow, the brightness of the day and the undulations of the course. Much depends also on how much the wax is gently heated up, sometimes just by the breath of the skier. Ordinary beeswax can be just as effective as professional waxes. Somehow, Miroslav mixed the ingredients brilliantly that day, and a 'miracle' resulted. Franta, too, was overjoyed.

Miroslav's sports activities included being part of the Czechoslovak national youth sports organisation, Sokol. Sokol's biggest event came once a year at the Strahov Stadium in Prague, when 280,000 competitors performed athletic exercises before 200,000 spectators. This huge celebration of youth began in innocent pre-Fascist days but was, rather curiously, abolished by the Nazis. Each town and village had its local equivalent of the big Sokol demonstration. In Držkov, Miroslav put on his special Sokol outfit, which with its military regalia was even a little bit Fascist in its inspiration.

Wearing his black leather Sokol jacket and boots, Miroslav walked in the parade to the local sports centre at the top of the village for a festival of table tennis, volleyball and gymnastics. Swimming and soccer were not included. Swimming was impossible without a pool (no municipal pool would be built for another thirty years), and splashing around in the river did not teach Miroslav or most of his schoolmates how to swim. The older Sokol members (those aged forty and up) also walked in the parade and were allowed to wear a special ceremonial Sokol boot that came up rather uncomfortably above the knees. Because his life would take an unexpected turn, Miroslav would never get to wear those ceremonial boots.

When Miroslav was only twelve years of age, his father gave him an even more extraordinary gift – a motorbike. 'This is for you,' Franta announced to his startled son when he wheeled the motorcycle into the front yard. As Miroslav recalls, however, the gift was really to help Franta's business because he ordered Miroslav to use the motorcycle to deliver beads to the families who were assembling jewellery. Miroslav headed off each morning, an hour before school, to make these deliveries. On the other hand, Miroslav always thought, he did have his own motorcycle, a pretty unusual possession for a twelve-year-old boy even by today's materialistic standards.

Miroslav's youth and upbringing had something of an idyllic quality. Setting aside Franta's occasional fits of temper, little disturbed the young man's progress into adulthood. His grandmother doted on him, telling Franta that she would rather look after Miroslav than work (as he had persuaded Anna to do) in his 'damn business'. Miroslav remembers the marvellous and contented routine of the Bohemian seasons. He recalls so much snow in those winters, snow blanketing row after row of pine trees, and indeed he thinks of his childhood and youth as almost always being winter, because that is the season he most loved. No Christmas ever came without a heavy blanket of snow, as opposed to a solitary Christmas snowfall in the six decades he has lived in Ireland.

Evidently, Miroslav had a lucky childhood as well as a generally happy one. When he was nine, a huge midsummer fire broke out in the forests surrounding Držkov, only about two kilometres from the family home. The fire brigade hoses were full of holes, and lots of helpers were recruited to keep their fingers on the holes as the fires were sprayed. Young Miroslav was one of the helpers. The fire caused a mad exodus of all manner of forest creatures. Miroslav doesn't remember when or how, but suddenly he had a small snake on his right hand, biting into his skin. The snake, known in Czech as a *zmía*, has a venom that is harmless if removed immediately but deadly poison if left untreated. Miroslav had no idea about the bite's fatal potential, so he threw off the snake, stamped it to death and then went off to boast to his pals about his conquest and his obvious snake-bite.

Anna sent him down to the local doctor, Marek, who simply poured lots of water over the bite-mark. There was no pain but Miroslav's hand was trembling pretty violently. Next morning, the hand had swollen up into the shape and size of a boxing glove. The doctor was called again. Finally understanding how bad things were, he told Franta to take the boy by car to the regional hospital at Tanvald. Miroslav's hand was operated on straight away. The doctors told Franta that waiting one more day would have cost Miroslav his hand, if not also his life. Miroslav returned to Držkov a hero to his school friends, the slayer of the *zmía*.

A few years later, Miroslav had another brush with death. It was around when he turned twelve and he almost paid a terrible price for his failure to learn how to swim. He went down to the frozen river with his friends, hoping to play some ice hockey. They found a section of the river that was solid ice and were enjoying a relaxing game, just banging around with sticks and a puck. Miroslav veered off toward the edge of the river, where the ice is thinnest, and suddenly one of his skates cut through the surface. His ankle twisted quickly, cracking a hole in the ice which he instantly fell through. Miroslav found himself trapped underneath, just managing to keep his head out of the water to breathe, in the space between the surface of the water and the bottom of the ice cover. His friends heard his frantic shouting, but could not see him.

Like in a scene from a Hans Christian Andersen fairytale, a local woodcutter happened to be working near the riverbank, heard the screaming, spotted the terrified victim, and ran to get a hatchet. He hacked away at the ice surrounding the hole, narrowly missing Miroslav on a couple of occasions. The worst part of the experience was getting home in the frigid cold, sneezing and coughing, but the compensation was three days out of school.

Aside from such life-threatening incidents, Miroslav's young life was peppered by his father's occasional falls from grace. Franta's misfortune, according to his son, was that he was overly keen on alcohol. 'When you talk about drinking, he really was bad,' according to Miroslav. On the compensating side, Franta's voracious appetites also included food, and so he managed to balance out his drinking by eating heartily. Even when he was drunk, therefore, he could be quite sober in a way – a 'sober drunk', as Miroslav puts it.

What this meant for his son, however, was that when he turned his attention to Miroslav's behaviour, which was rare, he could be quick to anger. Miroslav tells many stories of his father's high-spirited behaviour. Some of these stories concern his father's occasionally temperamental treatment of his only son. But one story ends with Franta himself locked behind bars, and another with his narrow escape from what could have been a terrible tragedy.

Miroslav remembers sitting in the family kitchen one evening when Franta came in, a little boozed and very upset about something that Miroslav had done. Miroslav was then about twelve years old, just before the gift of the motorcycle, and was growing addicted to a game machine in one of the village shops. For a crown coin, he got to manipulate a needle that punched any one of sixty-four holes on a large square of cardboard. Each punched hole revealed a prize underneath. If he ended up punching all sixty-four holes on this primitive Play Station, he would win a real football. Miroslav, obsessed with winning this much-desired prize, had discovered that

Franta had the habit, before going to bed, of carefully sliding the crown coins he won at poker sideways into big socks. He began to steal crown coins from his father's socks to fund his own little 'gambling' habit once he ran out of his regular pocket money. The first time he did it, Miroslav realised that Franta didn't notice, so he got the courage to do it a second time.

His father, the more senior gambler, heard from the shopkeeper, who happened to be a friend of his, that Miroslav had only four holes left to conquer before winning the football. Then Franta must have figured out that his careful piles of coins were getting a little unsteady.

'Why did you steal that money?' Franta roared at his shocked son as he entered the kitchen that evening. Before Miroslav could reply, Franta had rushed out of the house, past Anna who was watching nervously at the kitchen door, and grabbed a bunch of branches from a tree. Miroslav, knowing that a thrashing was in prospect, raced out of the kitchen with his father in hot pursuit.

Franta got the upper hand, and at one point actually managed to hit Miroslav in the face with the branches. The son's face was puffy and sore and lined with the marks of the branches. Anna, enraged, ordered her husband out of the house. She told Miroslav that he could not go to school with such a bruised face. Franta, returning defiantly to the house, would not tolerate an absence from school. 'I will not forgive what he did but I will write him a note for school,' he declared. The note, of course, was anything but the truth. Miroslav, Franta wrote, had been running in the local forest when he tried to push aside some low-hanging branches which snapped back and hit him in the face. 'It's a much simpler explanation,' Franta announced.

Miroslav admits that his father was strict, at least on those rare occasions when he showed interest in Miroslav's conduct, but explains it charitably as part of Franta's business background. 'Business needs strict thinking,' Miroslav says, 'so he naturally took this into the family.'

On another occasion, Franta's tough side was on display to his son at the Christmas dinner table. Normally, Christmas was a happy, plentiful occasion in the Havel family. But Miroslav remembers being about ten years of age and clashing with his father on the eating of the traditional Czechoslovak carp and goose. Turkey was never an option, which is one reason why Miroslav much prefers Christmas dinner in Ireland.

Anna always took home a live carp, which is a lake fish in Bohemia and is often sold still thrashing, and Miroslav had to hold the fish down on the butcher's block table while Anna smashed its head with a hammer. The fish flapped and fought, and sometimes would be impossible to hold as it careened in a nervous twitch around the kitchen. Anna's generation did this sort of thing without flinching, but Miroslav hated it. So much so, in fact, that over the years he grew to despise the Christmas carp. He was even more reluctant to eat the prime Christmas dish, goose, although it did not involve a similar bloody sacrifice ritual. He just hated the taste and fatty texture.

On this particular Christmas Day, Anna, Franta and Miroslav sat down to dinner. Franta was already 'having a little in the head', Miroslav's way of saying that his father was more than a little drunk, when Anna brought in a huge plate on which sat the carp and the cooked goose, dripping fat. Franta stood up and grandly carved the goose and put several thick slices on each plate. He knew that Miroslav didn't like it and that he was terrified to eat it.

'Eat!' roared the big man.

'Dad, I cannot eat it,' came the sorrowful reply.

Anna tried as usual to intervene: 'Franta, he won't eat it, so don't bother getting upset – he can have the fish and then some cakes.'

But Franta would not be appeased. He stood up, went behind Miroslav, grabbed the boy by the back of the head and shoved his face into the goose and the horrible fat. It was a really bad start to Christmas, Miroslav remembers. However, Franta was not an entirely unreasonable man. He never repeated the incident, and on every Christmas after that he did not carve any goose for Miroslav, who got by with a little of the carp.

Still, these outbursts were few and far between, and mostly Franta left his son in peace. Franta's public conduct, on the other hand, produced enough mildly embarrassing or downright dangerous episodes to cause Miroslav much concern that his father would get himself into serious trouble.

Franta and Anna were members of what was called the Czechoslovak Church. Miroslav remembers this church as an offspring of the Catholic Church, with similar rites and services except for open confession at mass instead of private visits to the confessional. Anna was observant only at Christmas and Franta exposed himself to organised religion mainly to amuse himself. Notorious for marathon round-the-clock poker games and an accompanying consumption of beer, he occasionally showed up with his card-playing cronies (all of them grown men in their forties and fifties) at the door of the church to interrupt the service in progress.

Miroslav recalls his father making one of these unholy interruptions on Christmas Eve, when the impact and notoriety of showing up drunk at the traditional midnight mass was likely to be greatest. With Anna and Miroslav watching in deep shame, a commotion took place at the back of the church as Franta and his two comrades, just out of a long night and day of cards and booze, shouted, 'Let us in, we love God!' down the middle of the nave. Anna, a popular and hard-working figure in the village, was mortified. Dinner on Christmas Day was always quite late in the evening, because Franta would need most of the day to sleep off his merriment.

Franta also disliked all breeds of the political animal, his inclination always being to ridicule rather than respect the powers who sought to influence his existence. Three years before the Germans arrived, there was one final free election in the doomed Czechoslovak Republic. Franta was blunt and outspoken, a businessman before anything else. But he did like to meddle a little in politics. He put some money into a party led locally by a rich Russian who had a lovely villa in the mountains where Franta was sometimes a drinking guest. The man genuinely believed in social progress, and the party had a distinctly anti-Russian cast as a result of his bitter experiences with Communism in his native country. One of the party's candidates actually stayed at Franta's house during the election, using it as a base from which to tour the region. After his guest left, Franta was called to the office of the mayor. He was told only that he had done something very wrong and would have to attend a court hearing fifty kilometres away in the regional judicial capital of Mláda Boleslav. Franta refused to go to court, and was taken there involuntarily under police escort.

Only when he appeared in the courtroom did he find out the nature of these mysterious charges. The candidate who had been staying under his protection had informed local officials that Mr František Havel had a picture of the President of the Republic in a not very sacred place – namely, plastered to the wall above the toilet bowl in the bathroom. Under the picture was a legend indicating that 'the above picture should help you go more easily'. Evidently, this coarse display of the presidential visage offended some ordinance against political blasphemy. Franta was put on trial before a judge. Amazingly, on the testimony of his ungrateful guest, he was convicted of 'dishonouring' the President. The first thing Miroslav learned about the situation was that his father had been sentenced to ninety days in prison, with no leave to appeal.

So Franta went to jail in Mláda Boleslav, wearing a classic striped prison outfit. Anna was left to take care of the business on her own. When she and Miroslav went to visit him about two weeks after he was incarcerated, they found a humiliated and terrified man: 'His eyes were half-way out of their sockets,' Miroslav recalls.

Franta, too, seemed to have caught the meaning of his predicament – however unjustified or ridiculous the charges against him, he was actually in prison. People would remember such a thing and it would not do him any good at all. And people would remember that he had been accused by a 'big shot' who was running for the national parliament. He did not even have the consolation of being in Prague's Pankrac prison, regarded as the high-status penitentiary for political prisoners (including, much later, the future President Václav Havel). Franta was disappointed in the candidate who had reported him, although not angry, but he certainly never spoke to him again.

Franta sat disconsolately on the other side of the glass partition that separated him from his wife and son. It was just a glass panel which had enough free space beneath it to allow them to shake hands and was thin enough that they could converse audibly to each other without shouting. Anna had smuggled in a pack of a hundred cigarettes, concealed inside her salami-filled food basket. But the visit was being watched and she didn't have the courage to pass the cigarettes to him until the second visit. The idea of the big man detained in prison was both startling and in some way amusing to his wife and son, because his usual bluster was nowhere in evidence. Miroslav recalls that his father showed 'no courage at all' in his confinement.

Of course, Franta quickly found a way to ease the severity of his situation. On their third or fourth visit, Anna and Miroslav went to the little office at the prison which issued visitor cards and asked for the usual permission to see the family convict. They were told that 'Mr Havel is in the town, attending the dentist.' The visitors got the name and address of the dentist and went to his office immediately. They were told there that, yes, Mr Havel had an appointment and his teeth had been checked, but that he had left with his guard some time ago. He had said something about a local restaurant, they were told.

It didn't take long to track Franta down to a nearby hostelry, where he and his guard (who had willingly accepted a small bribe) were drinking vodka and engaging in the harmless and primitive practice of clay bowling – nine-pin bowling on a rough surface. Harmless, but Franta managed to make it harmful to himself. One of the players threw a ball and knocked down everything except the middle pin. Franta shouted at the top of his voice, 'Hitler is still standing!'

Obviously, he had recovered from his earlier fright and forgotten any lessons he learned from the reason for his jail sentence. His loud behaviour, as usual, attracted unfavourable attention, this time from watching Germans.

Franta was a man under suspicion long before the nation fell to Nazism. But he did pull the dentist trick (and similar ruses) several more times before he finally left prison, and he spent about as much time out and about in the town as he did within the prison walls.

Miroslav thinks that Franta was unlucky psychologically, given that he was such an obviously bright and resourceful man, not to have had any intellectual company in his life. His schooling was rudimentary. Like Anna, he attended a village school until the age of fourteen but had no further education after that. Anna did take a few nursing courses in Vienna, but nothing else. Franta fell into fairly rough company – nice people, but a rough crowd, according to his son.

There was a restaurant in Držkov, right across from the village church and just at the turn in the road coming down from Zásada, where Franta held court for many years: 'That was his throne,' Miroslav says. 'He was the boss there.' This was one of the places where he worked his special deals – for example, arranging for supplies of meat from his connections with the butchering trade, even during wartime shortages when there was no meat to be found anywhere. Two of his butcher friends would end up being executed by the Germans.

Miroslav describes his father as having a 'farmer's brain', perhaps a kind of backhanded compliment to the Irish agricultural community. The phrase, he claims, refers to someone who does well no matter what circumstances occur. Franta was not the kind of man who picked fights or was violent, except for his occasional outbursts at home. His high spirits, particularly in bars, never produced any bar fights. As Miroslav points out, he always paid for everybody's drinks. Fighting him would just cut off the free supply.

On one particular weekend, Miroslav recalls, Franta did not come home from his business meetings in Jablonec on Friday evening, and not on Saturday or on Sunday either. Given his unpredictable patterns of behaviour, Anna and Miroslav did not panic, assuming that he was sleeping off a drunken escapade somewhere in a nearby village or town. But by Sunday evening they had grown very concerned and initiated a search. Somebody eventually got the word to Anna that her husband had shown up in the village restaurant, occupying his usual corner spot, and that he had quite a story to tell. When Anna and Miroslav reached the restaurant, Franta was wrapped in a blanket and was deep into a huge mug of coffee.

He had indeed been drinking on Friday evening, he told them, and had made himself nearly unconscious from alcohol. Still, he got into his car and was driving across the bridge in the small town of Velké Hamry when he lost control, rammed through two of the guard pillars on the left-hand side of the bridge, and plunged into the river. As the car sank, the water pressure against the doors made pushing them open a physical impossibility. Luckily, the car had a canvas roof and Franta, despite his intoxication, had enough presence of mind to free himself by breaking through the roof with his powerful fists and pushing himself up through the opening. He spent the night somewhere – he wasn't entirely sure where – but next day he couldn't remember where he had left the car.

The remains of the canvas roof, as it happened, had floated several kilometres downstream to Plavy, where some of the locals recognised it as the top of Havel's car. With that information, Franta was somehow able to piece together the sequence of events. Anna, of course, was appalled at her husband's typically reckless behaviour, not to mention the total loss of the family car.

Fast driving had always been one of Franta's favourite activities. He befriended a race-car driver who had a fabulous custom race-car with six exhausts on the side, a very American souped-up vehicle. Franta managed on several occasions to borrow the car, put on a pair of racing goggles, and take the car screaming through Držkov and the surrounding villages, disturbing the tranquil country environment but always waving in a friendly way to his neighbours who looked on in consternation.

His father's larger-than-life personality encouraged the much quieter Miroslav, who took after his mother in personality, to continue to spend many hours in the calm of his grandmother's house. This remained true even when Franta built the big new house next door. Franta's brother, Miloslav, also lived with his wife and son in some of the upper rooms in the grandmother's house. Miroslav still has no idea how his grandmother made any money or how she even made ends meet, but her house was always heaving with good food and she cooked incessantly.

Not unusually in those post-war days, Miroslav's grandmother had been married twice, first to Franta's biological father, Václav Havel, who had been killed in the First World War, and then to another Václav with the last name of Sourek. She had a daughter by Sourek, who was Franta's half-sister and Miroslav's aunt. The daughter died of tuberculosis, a common and very dangerous disease at the time, while Miroslav was a child. She lived her entire life in yet another one of the upstairs rooms, never leaving the house, and Miroslav hardly knew her.

Miroslav has no memory of his real grandfather, but he did have great affection for his step-grandfather, Václav Sourek, whom he often joined on excursions to pick forest mushrooms at their best time, five in the morning. Sourek was something of an expert in knowing where to find non-poisonous mushrooms,.

Miroslav's first cousin, František, his uncle's only child, was called after Franta, in exchange for Miroslav supposedly having been called after Franta's brother, Miloslav. This František, whom everyone addressed as Frank, was born in the same year as Miroslav. Frank's passion was horses and he abandoned school in order to spend his time looking after horses on the local farms. As Miroslav recalls, Frank often slept in the stables with the horses because he could not bear to leave them. These were not fancy racehorses, but ordinary farm horses which pulled wagons and sleighs, yet Frank adored them. He spent a hard life with his horses, delivering coal and other necessities to the remote mountain villages of the region around Držkov.

Frank was much bigger physically than Miroslav, and always stood up for his smaller cousin. Once, at a village 'tea dance', Miroslav was being physically threatened by a group of boys from another village, who were incensed that he was spending time with one of the girls from their village, the lovely Olga. Frank, who took after his uncle in his fondness for alcohol, pushed the boys aside, yelling, 'I am here to defend my cousin.' He then jumped up on the platform and smashed the band's drums in a gesture of supreme defiance. The attackers, startled by his display, retreated.

Frank went on to have three daughters. The eldest, Miluška, died very young. The younger daughters are Ludiška, who still lives in Držkov with her family, and Hedvička, who lives deep in the Bohemian countryside not far from Mláda Boleslav. They are the last two remaining links that Miroslav has to his original family. Frank died suddenly in November 1970, at only forty-eight years of age, having suffered a brain haemorrhage while sitting on a bench about fifty metres from his father's house in Držkov. Miroslav remembers Frank fondly as a younger version of his own father – not just because he liked to drink but also in his large-hearted view of life.

Miroslav has fond memories of his teenage summers with his parents at the spa town of Luhacovice. They always stayed in the villa that Franta had sold but in which he retained complimentary room rights for his family. However, one 'difficult' memory for him, he says, concerns his father's often raucous shenanigans at the spa. 'Daddy was having a party of his own there,' he recalls. He and Anna pretty much made their own plans, because Franta was usually busy with his poker and drinking buddies. One shocking but also amusing example of his father's misbehaviour at the spa still sticks in Miroslav's mind. Again, it involved political misjudgement, but this time Franta seems to have avoided any serious consequences.

The Republic's Minister for Finance, Emanuel Moravec, was also a regular visitor to Luhacovice. He had heard about the foolish antics of Franta and his fellow drinkers, and decided that he would like to join in the fun. Franta was delighted to perform this public service for the Minister. He and his friends pushed a dozen or more big vodkas into Moravec during a long evening at the villa, and then one of the gang went outside and found a donkey. They put the stupefied Minister for Finance on the back of the startled donkey and sent man and animal staggering down the main street of Luhacovice. The wonder for all who witnessed the late-evening spectacle was that the Minister somehow managed to hang on by the hairs on the back of the donkey's neck.

Moravec, however, was not at all pleased when he recovered and realised that he had played the role of a drunken Don Quixote for the entire town. He could easily have initiated some kind of criminal action, but, being a corrupt Communist, he was content to take a large envelope of cash from his tormentors. In fact, a few years later, just before the Communists themselves booted Moravec out of the party, he joined Franta and his friends for another night of carousing in Luhacovice – no donkey was involved this time.

Still, despite his father's unmanageable behaviour, Miroslav remembers those long summers at Luhacovice as 'a beautiful time'. He is especially proud of a photograph of himself with his parents walking out together confidently on the promenade on a sunny morning in July 1938, in those balmy days just before the war (see photograph 3). This is one of the few surviving pictures of a youthful Miroslav with his parents, and it shows the Havel family at the height of Franta's prosperity. It was also the high point for the prosperity of the Czechoslovak Republic, which boasted an industrial output at the time that was greater than that of France.

The three promenaders are dressed in tailored suits, models of fashionable elegance. Franta is wearing a summer overcoat and Miroslav is carrying a similar one. The coats, which were in fashion at the time, were made from the same cloth that would later be used to construct parachutes during the war. Franta is grinning mischievously, no doubt still relishing his service to Minister Moravec. Anna has the upright bearing of a true lady. And Miroslav is resplendent in his coming-of-age double-breasted white suit and white shoes. Three debutantes of an optimistic age, wholly unaware (the picture suggests) of a world hurtling toward cataclysm and changes that history would never reverse.

By the age of sixteen, just before that picture in Luhacovice was taken, Miroslav had achieved excellent results in his final examinations at the Zásada school and was wondering what to do next with his life. He dreamed of the life he would lead in his native country. Like any young Czechoslovak growing up in the 1920s and 1930s, he would have had little awareness of the stirrings of the war and destruction to come – what Winston Churchill would later describe (thinking precisely of the fate of the Republic of Czechoslovakia) as a 'gathering storm'.

In the long pre-war years of Miroslav's youth, he certainly knew that many ethnic Germans and Jews lived in the western fringes of the Republic, the so-called Sudetenland. But neither he nor his contemporaries could imagine that the German leadership would eventually move to incorporate not only the Sudetenland, but all of their country, into the Third Reich.

# An Artistic Education in
# Železny Brod

In 1938, Miroslav was focusing not on the great political events of the day but on his life after Zásada high school. Under the Republic's law, education was compulsory until the age of sixteen and he had now almost reached that point of transition. For young people in Držkov, a number of possibilities existed. Many of them would work on the family farms surrounding the village. Tanvald, a prosperous commercial town a few kilometres north near the Polish border, offered plenty of jobs in its textile factories. Despite a few trips to his mother's family farm, a life in agriculture held no appeal for Miroslav and he was not interested in factory life.

Meanwhile, Miroslav saw no way to collaborate with his unpredictable, independent-minded, domineering father in running a business. With his motorbike, he had done a lot of work on the delivery and collection routes for Franta's bead-making families, but he had never enjoyed the work and certainly did not anticipate making a career of it. Franta would probably have been delighted to send him down into the high-paying uranium or coal mines, where he himself was eventually to make his living when times turned bad, although he said exactly the opposite when asked.

For someone of Miroslav's artistic temperament, Bohemia's fame

44

as a centre of fine arts offered a number of higher education opportunities, such as the beautiful bijouterie technical school in the major regional city of Jablonec and the specialised fine arts colleges in the even bigger provincial capital of Liberec. None of the art schools was part of a university, but they were all highly regarded training institutions for one of the key engines of the Bohemian economy. And Miroslav, just a little bit influenced by his father's business flair, also thought about attending a well-regarded business college in Liberec.

Much depended on what Miroslav calls 'the quality of the paper' a student received from secondary school – 'They made their minds up about your stupidness,' he says frankly. Miroslav had done well enough in the Zásada secondary school to consider going on to third-level education. He had gained a high score in the national academic points system and in his final oral examinations. While Franta showed little interest in what Miroslav might do, Anna was quietly hoping that her only son would follow in the footsteps of several members of her side of the family by becoming a teacher. As he thought about the matter, he looked seriously at the possibility of going to a teacher-training school. He even subjected himself to violin lessons, not something he enjoyed, to prepare for the requirements of the entrance examination.

However, it was not surprising that Miroslav would at least have thought about a life in crystal glass. As he told an Irish television interviewer in 1991, Bohemia had a thousand-year-old tradition of glass-making. As part of the Austro-Hungarian Empire, it was the first continental location outside Venice to start making and decorating high-quality crystal. The predominant techniques of decoration in Bohemia were cutting and engraving. Hundreds of small cutting shops (with at most five or six craftspeople working in each of them) were scattered throughout the independent Bohemia of Miroslav's youth. As he says, 'It was a common kind of thing to become a cutter' – meaning that it happened frequently, not that it was looked down upon. But it was much rarer for someone to be trained as an engraver.

One morning in the late summer of 1938, Miroslav and his Zásada schoolmate, Mrva Tom, were idly chatting about what they might do next. Mrva mentioned that he had heard about an examination scheduled that afternoon for admission to the well-regarded glass school in Železny Brod, only about eleven kilometres down the mountains from Držkov. The school had opened in 1920 as part of the Czechoslovak Republic's emphasis on glass artistry as a symbol of the new state's cultural and commercial ambitions.

Mrva, too, had been good at art in the Zásada school, but he mainly wanted to persuade Miroslav to head down to Železny Brod to sample some of the town's famous cakes and pastries after they completed the exam. The two lads hopped on their motorbikes and went down to 'Brod' to have a go at the exam. Miroslav had no intention of attending glass school. At this point in his life, he did not have an inclination toward anything in particular, although he retained some guilty desire to comply with Anna's hopes.

However, he did have a sense that his artistic talent might prevent him from having an embarrassing experience before he tucked into the cakes. Good food having always been a priority for Miroslav, he was also thinking, at least in the back of his mind, that going to school in Brod would mean that he could come home for a cooked dinner every day. The exams for the teaching college, which would mean a move to Prague, were still several months away.

The exam was not the only event at the Brod school that day. Miroslav and Mrva joined the other applicants in a tour of the school facility, with its separate cutting and engraving and fine arts sections, and found the whole operation very impressive. 'I was not normally interested in glass, but when I saw this place, something hit me inside,' he remembers. After finishing the exam, Miroslav and Mrva also filled out questionnaires from the Brod school, asking them to identify the section of the glass school to which they would prefer to be admitted. Miroslav had always enjoyed drawing so much that he thought the engraving section would make sense, but he had no real priority because he felt that he was doing this mainly because Mrva wanted a trip down to Brod.

The exams were reviewed by three well-known professors who were not experts in glass-making as such (one of them, in fact, was an architect who designed big displays of 'architectural' glass and had acquired a good reputation for this highly specialised art form). Three days later, when the exam results were posted, Miroslav discovered that he and Mrva had both been accepted at the school. Miroslav had secured the top grade in the drawing component and almost the top grade in every other subject. He was awarded one of only four places in engraving, with a scholarship, while Mrva was accepted into the cutting department. The school was a veritable academy of fine arts, also offering training courses in glass-blowing, in painting, in clay and marble sculpture, and even in jewellery-making.

Anna, however, was not pleased with this unexpected turn of events. She had never even heard of the glass school in Železny Brod, which had yet to achieve the renown that it would in later years when it became a world-class institution. She softened a little though when she saw some link, although a vague one, between Miroslav's motorbike escapades picking up beads and delivering jewellery and the kinds of activities he might pursue in the glass school.

In any event, on the first day of September, in 1938, Miroslav and his friend Mrva began their careers in crystal glass. Miroslav spent the years from 1938 to 1940 in Železny Brod, his sixteenth to eighteenth years, under the tutelage of the Brod school's assortment of good professors. Unlike during his later wartime studies in Prague, he often felt rather carefree while at Brod. He left home at seven in the morning, travelled by bus, started school at eight, and caught the bus back at five in the afternoon. In his second year, a rail connection opened between Držkov and Železny Brod, with a little railway stop next to the river in Držkov, and he made even better time, as well as adding the fun of more social interaction with his fellow passengers. He liked living at home but having the flexibility to be away all day. He loved the long holidays and occasionally defying Anna's stern instructions by wasting his lunch money on more of the local cakes and pastries he and Mrva had enjoyed on that summer afternoon when they had taken the entrance examination together. The years in Brod were also the beginnings of an incurable sweet tooth that Miroslav would always have.

But Miroslav found that he also really enjoyed being a student of glass. The school specialised in a re-interpretation of traditional Bohemian cutting and engraving styles to emphasise the importance of relating decoration to form. Glass-making and decoration were taught in the studios of such well-regarded craftsmen as Ladislav Přenosil and Jaroslav Brychta. Two days a week, Miroslav was in their studios, studying engraving and also doing some cutting. He also received training in the art of glass polishing, using a tiny brush and wooden or lead wheels to brighten the accents in an unpolished engraving design.

Miroslav's professional course in engraving was untypical. Most glass artisans in the region did not attend special training schools; they apprenticed to one of the cutting shops and eventually graduated to the status of master cutter. Only masters could open their own glass-making and decorating shops. The Americans never had that rule, Miroslav recalls. It was said in Czechoslovakia at the time that the American freedom to open a glass business regardless of training provided a large measure of freedom to go bankrupt. Spots for trainee engravers in the local shops were hard to get, however, and even in the school only a handful of students trained in engraving. Miroslav was one of those students.

The art of cutting had been revived in Prague at the beginning of the seventeenth century. Its chief aim is to bring light into dull glass. A cutter uses the edge of a spinning carborundum or diamond wheel, which can be up to two feet in diameter, to grind away the surface of the glass. These incisions create prisms and facets that refract and deflect the rays of light, instead of letting them pass directly through the glass.

Cutting is a freehand skill which requires the artist to support the glass by resting both elbows on the bench in front of the wheel. Since the wheel is below the cutting blank, much of the work has to be done by looking through the glass to the bottom surface of the glass on the other side. And the cutter must be careful about the effect of changing light as the piece is turned, since differing angles of light can give a misleading sense of depth.

Because the cutting wheels are so large, there is very little pictorial or representational cutting. That is the role of engraving. Wheel engraving, the art of inscribing designs on glass by removing part of its surface, arrived in Bohemia around the early 1600s. It uses smaller copper wheels which are rotated in a small lathe at a much slower pace than cutting wheels. The lathe and wheel project sideways over the glass to be engraved. The wheel is smeared with an abrasive paste of linseed oil and carborundum powder. Because copper is more porous than ordinary metal, the paste adheres to and almost bonds with the copper. In this way, the copper wheel only directs the paste, but it is the paste itself which causes the engraving marks to be made on the glass.

Again, copper-wheel engraving is a freehand skill. The article to be engraved is pressed against the underside of the wheel (which means it is out of direct eye range) and requires only the slightest touch against the rotating wheel to leave a greyish-white mark on the surface of the glass. Unlike cutting, engraving presents the top surface of the glass to the artist. To complicate the skill, the part of the surface on which the engraver is working is always covered by the abrasive material as it grinds the glass. The artist must continually rub off the abrasive paste with a thumb or finger to see the result, alternating this movement with pressing the glass to the wheel. For an experienced engraver, these movements are so rapid that the glass seems to be continuously on the wheel.

Engraving has been compared to taking a pencil and paper, securing the pencil in a clamp, and then moving the paper around the pencil to create a drawing. As an art, it offers greater scope for artistic expression than, for example, drawing or painting, because it operates also in the third dimension of depth. The engraver makes constant artistic decisions on the depth of the engraved lines, as well as on which parts of the design will be left dull or polished. Not surprisingly it takes more than a decade to become a master engraver.

As Miroslav worked in his professors' studios, his eyes and hands became his primary engraving tools. He learned how to carry a pattern in his mind and to work directly on the glass without any markings or outlines drawn in advance on the surface. He discovered how the coarseness of the abrasive paste affected the roughness of the cut, and how the size of the wheel affected the depth and width of the cut.

Using only an old-fashioned foot-powered engraving machine, he enjoyed experimenting with different consistencies of paste and with a range of over two hundred copper wheels, the smallest only the diameter of a pinhead. He would later transfer these exceptional skills he learned at Železny Brod and his ability to perform them at a speed appropriate to industrial production, to Irish engraving experts at Waterford Glass, like Tommy Wall and Tommy Hayes.

The other three days at Brod involved courses in glass arts, business and the German language. The school kept the usual holiday periods, including the long summer vacation, and Miroslav started to look around for out-of-term work in one of the many glass shops and larger factories in the region. There were plenty to choose from, and he visited several large and small facilities to observe their operations. He didn't actually start doing serious work until he turned eighteen, in his third year, because the Republic's law did not allow insurance coverage for factory employees until they reached eighteen.

Miroslav heard from one of his fellow students at Brod that there was a 'nice' glass-cutting shop in the picturesque town of Mála Skála, about seventeen kilometres south-west of Držkov. The name *Mála Skála* means 'small rock', although paradoxically its most famous and inspirational feature is a natural formation of colossal granite rocks, tall and sheer, which forms a stunning physical backdrop to the town. The shop ('factory' would be too grand a name for a facility that was only one of the hundreds of small glass studios that dotted Bohemia at the time) was owned by Frank Bouček. It had an excellent reputation for glass cutting and a small amount of engraving, although no glass was actually blown there.

Miroslav instantly liked the work atmosphere in Bouček's shop, where there were only half a dozen cutters and two engravers. Here also he met his lifelong friend, Anna Pačesova, whom he describes now affectionately as 'that nice girl in the office'. Bouček was a pleasant man, but a demanding one, who constantly asked Miroslav to come back to the shop to do more work. Bouček himself suffered from epilepsy (for which no repressing drugs then existed) and one of Miroslav's first and most unnerving instructions was to act quickly to switch off his boss's cutting machine at moments when a fit seemed imminent.

During school holidays, Miroslav was at his cutting machine from six in the morning to five in the evening, virtually without a break, and began to like this regimented existence very much. He became accustomed to a factory routine during this period, and perhaps discovered that he was temperamentally much less like an academic with a very unstructured life than he sometimes imagined himself to be. Although most of his work involved production cutting, whenever he could he would grab an opportunity to work on one of the engraving machines at the Bouček shop.

While nothing survives of what we might grandly call Miroslav's artistic 'juvenilia' or early-career production, in the case of the Mála Skála shop this may be a disguised blessing. He recalls a number of disasters from that period, as he tackled more and more difficult projects. One in particular was an attempt to engrave two angelic cherubs, of the kind favoured by the nineteenth-century Czech painter Josef Manes, on a large crystal vase. This happened about a month after he joined the shop.

He laboured for four days on engraving these naked baby angels with wings, but found it almost impossible to reproduce the unmarked features of the classical cherub. When he showed the results to Bouček, the proprietor exclaimed, 'Oh my God, Miroslav, you made nice little angels but you gave them faces older than my grandmother's!' The debacle sticks with him, a lesson in the need for constant effort, doing and re-doing everything that crystal engraving demands. In fact, he didn't conquer his unease with engraving children and cherubs, with their unmarked faces, until more than three decades later when he did an engraved reproduction of the faces of Irish comedian Maureen Potter's two young sons. Ms Potter was honoured with the piece by presenter Gay Byrne on an Irish television special.

Franta left Miroslav largely alone during the Brod years, not really sure why his son was suddenly so captivated by glass-making, but too busy to bother interfering. But that didn't mean that Franta couldn't make use of his only offspring whenever one of his business schemes demanded it. In one episode, involving contraband salami, he even conscripted his own mother.

After the Nazi takeover of the Sudetenland in September 1938 and of the rest of Czechoslovakia in March 1939, the Germans imposed strict controls on the manufacture and transport of certain food products, including all kinds of salami, across the new border between the Sudetenland and what was now the Protectorate of Bohemia and Moravia (Slovakia was shorn off as a nominally independent state). For that very reason, Franta became obsessed with getting (and sometimes selling) good salami. His contact was a food dealer, Mrtlov, who was also a saxophonist with a jazz band in the nearby town of Velké Hamry. Mrtlov was a totally unreliable man when it came to money, and had once paid a debt to Franta by presenting him with a beautiful new saxophone. Franta promptly gave the instrument to Miroslav with an imperious order to learn how to play it.

One morning, as Miroslav was getting ready to catch the bus to Železny Brod, Franta approached him in a conspiratorial mood. 'Mirek, somebody in Brod will give you a small suitcase, and you must put it somewhere on the bus so that nobody will see it, and bring it home,' Franta told his son. Miroslav dutifully accepted the case from a short bald man at the Brod bus station, boarded the bus with it as instructed and shoved it under his seat. The whole bus reeked of salami during the journey to Držkov, but no fingers were pointed at Miroslav. When the bus stopped, everyone tumbled out, and Miroslav retrieved the case and followed them. However, Franta was nowhere to be seen, despite his assurance that he would be there, so Miroslav walked back to the house, carrying the case.

When Franta eventually opened the mysterious case, Miroslav

was amazed to see that it was stuffed with every possible size and shape of salami, the product of illegal slaughtering of animals that had taken place near Hamry. Anna, of course, was furious that Franta had put Miroslav at such terrible risk – trafficking in foodstuffs could carry the death penalty under German regulations. But Franta's scheme wasn't finished yet. What Anna didn't know was that Franta had arranged for his own mother to take the salamis across the customs control point at the Sudetenland border. To do this, Franta had arranged for poor Božena to wear a specially-made skirt with about ten deep pockets into which bunches of salamis could be inserted. On two separate occasions, Miroslav's little grandmother bravely walked through the Sudetenland customs checkpoint with the hope that the heavy weight of the salamis would not cause her skirt to collapse around her ankles at the wrong moment. Miroslav still cannot forgive his father for enrolling his own mother – never mind his only son – in his outrageous salami smuggling.

After graduating from the Železny Brod school in 1940, Miroslav was now, to use one of his favourite English idioms, 'at sixes and sevens' about his future. He had become a qualified glass engraver, although not yet a master, and could probably have worked in one of the engraving and cutting shops for which Brod and its region were well-known. His friend, Mrva, did exactly that, and Miroslav also decided to postpone any thoughts about further studies until he picked up a little more practical experience. It was a chance to earn some money outside Franta's orbit, although the cutting shops were not known for paying good wages. He decided to stay full-time for almost another year, from mid-1940 to mid-1941, at the Mála Skála shop.

Sometimes, Miroslav chatted casually with Bouček about how he might develop a career in glass-making. Bouček was well connected with a professor at one of the Republic's most prestigious institutions for advanced study in art and design, Vysoká Umělecká Průmyslová Škola, the Academy of Art and Industrial Design in Prague. The Academy's popular name was an acronym which links parts of the second and third words of its name as 'Umprum'.

Umprum was (and is) a nationally recognised institution of higher education in the industrial arts, and part of the renowned Charles University. The Academy had only eight places available each year in glass engraving, and, one day, Bouček said that he would have a word with his professor contact to see if he could assist Miroslav's admission. Bouček's connection to Umprum extended to offering internships to students there – two of Miroslav's fellow cutters during his 'gap year' were students at the school. Umprum was very happy with Bouček's internships, because he insisted on making the students complete an independent exercise in glass decoration before they returned to the school. The two students were very helpful to Miroslav in persuading him of the professional advantages of attending Umprum.

To Miroslav's astonishment, Franta, too, had an unexpected but not inconsiderable role to play in this process. As one of his many sideline investments, Franta had bought a little tourist restaurant up in the Krkonoše mountains on the Polish border. On one of his weekend visits there, and no doubt fuelled by a few libations, he was chatting with a well-dressed Prague visitor and the conversation worked its way around to Miroslav and his future ambitions.

Franta remembered that Miroslav had once expressed an interest in Umprum. 'You are talking to the right man – don't you worry, I'll take care of it!' said the visitor, who by coincidence happened to be an education supervisor in Prague with some input into Umprum's admission process. No doubt the visitor thought better of his rash promise when his hangover subsided, but he kept his word to Franta and gave what assistance he could to Miroslav.

Perhaps some of these contacts were helpful in getting his name into play, but Miroslav still had to compete in a rigorous entrance examination for Umprum. The exam had three parts – drawing, life modelling and a free association exercise which allowed the candidate to submit any kind of artwork on a supplied theme.

Miroslav describes his drawing effort as 'not the worst'. The life modelling, however, was a different matter. His model was a woman sitting with a full-grown goose in her arms. Animals and birds, like cherubs, were not Miroslav's favourite subjects. His goose, after many revisions, was pretty sad. Nor could he make it look as though the woman was simply holding the goose as opposed to throttling it. Despite doing well in the third part, he thought to himself that he had reached the end of his journey.

Perhaps Franta's drunken companion helped, perhaps Bouček's professor friend helped, perhaps Miroslav's goose was not as bad as he feared, but in any event he won one of the coveted places in engraving at Umprum. The young man was starting to show some serious ambition.

However, it must also have been on his mind that his career in industrial design could now lead, through Charles University, to an academic posting, and perhaps even to a professorship in the industrial arts or in some aspect of the applied arts. How appealing that would have seemed to him – an opportunity to pursue his marvellous artistic talents and also to teach, the very thing that Anna had always hoped he would do.

# Art and War in Prague

Franta, perhaps feeling responsible for Miroslav's success, initially took a rather unexpected interest in his son's time at Umprum. Not long after Miroslav left for Prague, Franta made his way to the Umprum building in the centre of the city and asked the porter at the lobby reception kiosk where he might find his son. The porter, overawed by the large well-dressed figure standing sternly before him, broke the rules and gave Franta the number of a classroom where Miroslav might be in class. Franta marched upstairs to the classroom, threw open the door, and saw his son, wearing a white laboratory coat, busily making a sketch of a naked woman model.

Franta's penetrating eyes popped in disbelief. 'What is that woman doing there?' he shouted at Miroslav and his eight or nine fellow life-modelling students. Miroslav stammered out an explanation that she was the class drawing model. His father bellowed back, to Miroslav's mortification, 'What kind of school is this? This is a disgrace!' Miroslav had to lead his outraged father to the rector's office, by which time Franta had composed himself enough to urge the head of the school to ensure that Miroslav would take courses in which he would be exposed to graphic design rather than nude models.

This story had some wry echoes some sixty-five years later when Miroslav's son, John, in so many ways the genetic successor to

Franta, infiltrated the Dublin Business School, his own son John's chosen college, to introduce himself to John junior's professors. The son's outrage may have matched Miroslav's own startled surprise when his father appeared without warning at the classroom door.

Franta, after that spectacular foray into Umprum, was not much in evidence during these years, although Miroslav tapped him from a distance when cash became short. In any event, Miroslav's courses at Umprum were the result not of his father's meddling, but of his own artistic temperament. He took required courses in German, mathematics, glass-making techniques, glass chemistry and technical drawing. But he constructed his optional courses to include an artist's palette of design, calligraphy, free drawing, drawing from nature and life modelling. Drawing from nature was always a Czech specialty, because so many of the early Bohemian engravers were also painters.

Miroslav, however, proved most adept at free drawing and life modelling. Foundational graphic talent can never be dispensed with, especially if an artist is going to become a trailblazer. Miroslav was, above all, a gifted artist, and that is ultimately how he became a great artist in glass. In 1941, however, he was not producing great works of art glass. He recalls that his life-drawing experiments included more women clutching unruly geese, clearly a staple of Umprum's life-modelling classes. And, in those days of great political incorrectness, he was also asked to sketch a number of disabled people. None of these early masterworks survives.

From his experiences both in Prague and Málá Skála, Miroslav was lucky enough to find himself in the company of some very talented artists. His mentor at Umprum was Professor Karel Štipl, a noted glass sculptor whose career flourished both before and after the Communist takeover. Glass sculpture is the shaping of representational and abstract forms from solid blocks of high-density crystal. It uses the same copper-wheel technology as engraving, and sometimes uses even larger cutting wheels, but is as different from engraving as drawing is from sculpture. For Miroslav, glass sculpting was the highest achievement in crystal, and he aspired to specialise as a sculptor in the way that Štipl was doing.

Karel Štipl was a seminal figure at Umprum. He established a department at the school that was dedicated specifically to the improvement of design in the Czechoslovak glass industry. He was a strong critic of the industry, which he thought lacked flair and imagination and was stuck doing the same thing over and over again. He was also chief of the engraving department at Umprum, in which Miroslav was spending twenty hours a week by his third year.

Štipl made sure that all of his student engravers were trained also in the special techniques of glass sculpture. He had two assistant professors working with him, Ladislav Havlas and Václav Vele. Both Havlas and Vele were master engravers, and helped Štipl in the day-to-day supervision of student work. Vele had a strong family background in glass-making. His brother was head of the largest crystal glass works in Železny Brod. Havlas and Miroslav remained personal friends, and they had several happy meetings when Miroslav was finally able to return to Czechoslovakia, until Havlas died in 1995.

At Umprum, Miroslav continued to raise his performance levels in both engraving and glass sculpture. Along the way, he discovered another gap in his skills as a draftsman – a gap that he was never able to correct entirely – the drawing of animals. Numerous sessions in front of the tiger cages at Prague Zoo produced a very disappointing product. 'If I hadn't written "tiger" under it, you would never have known,' he says. His sculptural studies were enhanced also through working in stone and marble. For this, the students travelled to the outskirts of Prague where a former Umprum professor had set up a stonemason's studio, equipped with every tool and chisel imaginable.

This period produced some frustrating grades for Miroslav. In a range of 9 to 15 points for sculpture, with 11 as a minimum for passing, he scored between 11 and 12 over several exams. He felt that he was 'fiddling around'. Disappointed, he stopped drawing tigers and returned again and again to his favourite subject, the human head. To do this, he studied anatomy and the shapes of the skull. He produced a skull in clay and got 13 points for this creation. 'You cannot really create a face if you do not understand the skull,' he insists. His breakthrough piece, as he recalls it, was a head he created of a Catholic saint and founder of a religious order. The model from which the students worked was oversized, and they were asked to reduce the model to actual size for an assignment which required working in stone. Miroslav spent a lot of time modelling the blessed head in clay before switching to stone. After two and a half months of intense application, his final effort earned 14 points. He was astounded by his score, the best in the class.

However, even as he progressed at Umprum, national and international events were beginning to cast a long shadow over Miroslav's student life. He grew up in a region that had very strong ties to Germany and a very powerful German influence. Just a few kilometres north, on the very edge of the border with Poland, was the town of Tanvald. Tanvald, Miroslav recalls, was 'practically German'. From there westwards to the border with Germany, many of the towns had German names that were used alongside, and often instead of, their Czech equivalents. The post offices, a reliable indicator of place-name convention, recognised Jablonec also as Gablonz, Liberec also as Reichenberg, and Nový Bor as Neustadt. Even Držkov was rendered in German as the equally unpronounceable Drschke. No matter what services the Germans needed in the region, whether the post office or the local markets or the education or health systems, they could expect to speak their language and to be perfectly understood.

As Miroslav recalls, the three million or so Germans simply considered themselves to be as Czech as the ethnic Slavs of the region. In fact, before the war, the so-called 'German-Czechs' were in the majority along the corridor running from Karlovy Vary (Karlsbad) near the Bavarian border all the way north-east to Jablonec and Liberec. Their presence was a legacy of the common home they shared before 1918 with the Czechs and Slovaks within the Austro-Hungarian Empire of the Habsburgs. The independent Republic of Czechoslovakia itself was a relatively recent invention, formed in 1918 as part of the post-war resettlement of Europe's borders.

The German-Czechs even had their own organised political party, the strongest in the Czechoslovak parliament, but the party was never invited into any of the several multi-party governments of the Republic. The German-Czechs, Miroslav recalls, were largely content with their lives in their accidental Republic. Among other things, after all, they got to do a lot of business with Franta.

However, things darkened in the mid-1930s, when the Nazi government launched a propaganda war that stirred emotions within the German-Czech population about reuniting with the Fatherland. This was exactly the same kind of *Heim ins Reich* ('home into the realm') propaganda that the Nazis were directing at another relic of the Habsburg monarchy, Austria. Hitler began to speak of his desire to be united with 'our brothers and sisters in Czechoslovakia', creating a growing unease among the non-German population in the Republic.

The government began to take dramatic defensive precautions, massing forces on the German border and building fortresses packed with firearms and cannons. The Republic had a very good army and one of the best air forces for a country of its size. Far from having the expected deterrent effect, however, the strength of the Czechoslovak armed forces and armaments simply encouraged Hitler to pursue his conquest.

In September 1938, Britain, France and Italy signed the Munich Pact with Nazi Germany which gave Hitler the right to invade the Sudetenland. France ignored its treaty with the Czechoslovak Republic, requiring assistance in the event of military aggression. This was a terrible betrayal, the treaty having resulted from the fact that for the first two years of the Republic's existence, its army had actually been part of the French armed forces. After Munich, too, British premier Neville Chamberlain made his notorious remark that the Czechs were 'a people of whom we know nothing'. Like many of his contemporaries, Miroslav remembers the phrase used by Chamberlain more colloquially as 'Who are the Czechs?' And he also recalls the bitter catchphrase by which the Munich Pact was interpreted in his country: *o nás bez nás*, meaning 'about us, without us'.

As soon as the Munich Pact was signed, Hitler sent a message to the Czechoslovak President, Edward Beneš, that the German Army would immediately occupy the Sudetenland. For Miroslav, it was tragic to see the national armed forces moving back from the border with Germany without firing a single shot in defence of their country and abandoning all of their arms and munitions. 'They didn't move one cannon to defend us,' he remembers. Once Hitler occupied the Sudetenland, it was only a matter of time before the rest of the nation would fall. The takeover, just as in Austria, was bloodless. No shot was fired. On 15 March 1939, Germany simply absorbed Czechoslovakia. Bohemia and Moravia became a German protectorate, and Slovakia was placed under a puppet government.

After the annexation, Franta's costume jewellery business went into a swift decline. It was a strange time for the Havel family. For as long as Miroslav could remember, he had lived in a prosperous, independent country, and his father had enjoyed a share of that national prosperity. The economy of Czechoslovakia even managed to bounce back from a low point in 1933, when unemployment spiked upwards, but after 1938 the gathering storm could not be averted. Franta weathered the 1933 crisis pretty well, and actually built his new house in that year, but it was hard for anyone to dodge the unravelling economic conditions of five years later, particularly the exchange crisis that forced the Czech crown to be heavily devalued against the Reichsmark. This reversal of fortune cost Franta a great deal of money as his markets in Germany became more and more expensive and he scrambled to build his store of Reichsmarks. Later on, even more perniciously, all bank accounts held in Czech crowns were frozen by the Nazi administration. To survive, people had to rely entirely on their weekly pay-packets, paid in the form of the only acceptable currency, the 'new' Czech crown.

Franta was forced to scale back his allowance to his son in Prague. Luckily for Miroslav, he also had the continued support of his grandmother in Držkov. She continued to send him a regular supply of new Czechoslovak bills. He never found out where her money came from, but she kept a regular monthly income even after the switch to the new currency. Miroslav thinks that she was able to convert a certain amount of old money, which gave her enough to live on. But the young did not ask such questions of their elders.

According to Miroslav, Franta had 'colossal' bank accounts in Czech crowns, but they were suddenly useless to him. Still, his general mood continued to be one of enjoying life. Other than recurrent headaches which were easily explained by his taste for vodka and similar remedies, Franta's health was good. Somehow he managed to have three cars – a range of Opels from small to large. Miroslav jokes that perhaps Franta was out holding up banks at gunpoint to keep this standard of living going in troubled times. In any event, both Franta and his mother seemed good at finding money where little was to be found.

Franta, whose commercial philosophy was always to do business with whomever would do business with him, began to notice that his Jewish customers and suppliers were scaling back or even disappearing. As well as feeling the effects of reduced demand as the country went on a war footing, Jewish businesses in Czechoslovakia were suffering from the anti-Semitism being stoked by the Nazis across the border. Without his steadiest customers and suppliers, Franta's costume jewellery business was in deepening trouble.

However, he was never a man to be afraid of any kind of hard work, including hard physical effort, and he looked around for ways to generate a more steady income. There wasn't a lot on offer, but one reliable opportunity, especially in wartime, was coal and uranium mining. Franta liked money, and he really was prepared to try anything. He despised the ration-card system which was introduced between 1941 and 1942, but cigarettes also became a kind of substitute currency with which shrewd operators like Franta could get extra supplies of rationed goods.

First, he went to Železny Brod, where for a time he unloaded coal from train wagons, but this wasn't much of a money-maker. Next, he voluntarily showed up at a uranium mine near the town of Most, about a hundred kilometres west of Držkov. 'Nobody wants to work in the mines,' he loudly proclaimed to Anna when he informed her of his decision. 'But they pay good money and I need good money, so I'm going to the blasted uranium mine.' He stayed at Most for five years, but was eventually discharged because he failed a medical test.

By the end of that time, Franta already had trace deposits of uranium in his lungs. Uranium mining, however, was extremely well paid, and he insisted on staying in the mining community. The town of Most also had coal mines, and he showed up for work at those mines almost as soon as he failed his medical test at the uranium mine. Franta's big personality and dominating physique made him a natural leader. After only a year underground in the coal mine, he became the union organiser, which really meant that he was the chief operating official at the coalface.

Franta would continue working at the Most coal mine long after the war ended. He refused to go back home because he liked being able to earn plenty of ready cash and to make full use of opportunities for overtime and weekend pay. Even though the jewellery business was effectively dead without his presence, he came back to the village only once a month or so. Working in the mine also allowed him to beat the post-war rationing system by getting a steady supply of free coal for the family home in Držkov, akin to his earlier success at keeping Anna and Miroslav well-stocked with bananas. His odd combination of union mineworker and costume-jewellery entrepreneur certainly puzzled the Communists immediately after the war. Despite his union activities, because of his past as an entrepreneur they identified him as a member of the despised 'bourgeoisie'. And, because of the Communists, Franta eventually had no choice but to stay in the coal mines, as he was never allowed to do anything else during the remainder of his working life.

For Miroslav, a young man in the capital city in the historical year of 1941, it was initially a time of good friends, girlfriends, studies and the prospect of a significant qualification. Once again, as in Železny Brod just a few years before, he was aware of the swirl of public events more from the newspapers than from his actual experiences. Franta gave him enough money to pay for a decent flat and food, and he frequently caught the packed Friday evening train north to Držkov to enjoy Anna's home cooking. Prague had always been a cosmopolitan place, full of good restaurants, and (with Budapest and Vienna) it was one of the three great imperial capitals of the Habsburgs.

However, Miroslav remembers becoming gradually aware that the German occupation was changing the character of the city and of his own life there. Once the Germans came in, he says, Prague went 'under the clouds'. The Nazis established a ruthless dictatorship in the new Protectorate of Bohemia and Moravia. Miroslav was issued a 'Deutsches Reich' Kennkarte or identity card, made out of a peculiar soft fabric, with the Swastika prominently displayed on the cover. He noticed how people kept very much to themselves, as social life in the capital came to a standstill. Conditions were nerve-wracking, and became even more so as the Czechoslovak people realised that the Nazi machine had crushed the Russians and the French in their home countries. 'The Germans were on top,' Miroslav recalls. 'And they did not give a damn for anybody else.'

The Umprum students became wary, whenever possible travelling together in groups. They didn't go to any bars or clubs, fearing that they would be watched, and chose to socialise almost entirely among themselves. Their paranoia was probably wise. The German military, Miroslav says, did not have any respect for life, and randomly shot and killed people for the smallest infraction.

Posters in the Czech language, signed by the Nazi commander General Blaskowitz, informed the citizens of Prague that they would be shot on sight if they violated the new Nazi curfew law or were caught listening to a foreign radio broadcast. German propaganda dominated the streets and the airwaves, the Sondergerichten (special army courts) were imposing death sentences on civilians in a few hours without any possibility of appeal, and opposition leaders were being arrested and executed. There were reportedly twenty-five to thirty political executions every day. All the street names were changed, and Miroslav remembers such absurdities as having the street where he lived, known in Czech as *Francouská Ulice* ('French Street'), suddenly becoming the German *Bismarckstrasse* ('Bismarck Street').

Looking back sixty-five years, we know how Nazi anti-Semitism became a contagion. The scene in Prague was no different. Jewish shops and businesses were attacked and closed. The Jews themselves became an object of persecution in Prague after 1938. Many Jews spent virtually the entire period of the war in shabby hiding places, including underground in the mausoleums and graves of the city's Jewish cemetery. Umprum was located only fifty metres from the Jewish cemetery and Miroslav and his fellow students had heard rumours of the hiding-places in the cemetery. And they saw plenty of evidence of the new, open anti-Semitism. It was considered socially appropriate to order Jewish people, known now by yellow stars on their clothing, to move seats even on a nearly empty tram, or to get to the back of a queue in a shop. Miroslav remembers that Czechs, not necessarily German-Czechs, were part of this anti-Jewish mania.

The contagion spread outside Prague into the provinces. In Mála Skála, Frank Bouček found himself taking the kind of personal risk that is today honoured by Yad Vashem, the Jewish organisation that celebrates non-Jews who made sacrifices to help their Jewish neighbours during Nazism. In the town, there was a well-known Jewish family, the Feinbergs, who owned a wine shop. Word was already circulating in 1939 that Hitler was persecuting Jews in Poland. Late in the year, Mr Feinberg asked Bouček if he could take care of his son, aged about thirteen, for just a few weeks. Bouček agreed without asking why. Working with his secretary, Miroslav's friend, Anna Pačesova, he set up a small room over the cutting shop and hid the child there. All of the family suddenly disappeared, and Bouček and Anna took care of the Feinberg boy for the rest of the war. Each night, they spirited the child to Bouček's house for dinner.

Many people in the town apparently had knowledge of what Bouček was doing but nobody betrayed the truth to the Germans. Nevertheless, as Miroslav remembers, Bouček and Anna were playing 'a very dangerous game', but they never flinched from what they saw as their responsibility. After the war, the boy was helped by a Jewish charitable organisation to resettle in France, to where some of his relatives had escaped. To Miroslav's knowledge, he was never reunited with his parents.

Miroslav himself had very little contact with Jews during his childhood. And later, at Umprum, there were no Jews in any of his classes. Indeed, he remembers meeting only one non-Czech of any kind in Umprum, a young man from Slovakia. Franta, on the other hand, worked extensively with the Jewish businessmen who dominated all aspects of the costume jewellery trade, and there was one Jewish home in Jablonec where he often went for dinner after work. The Jews whom he knew were rich, but Franta never displayed any animosity toward their high position in commercial society. He wanted only to emulate their success. If anything, Miroslav recalls, Franta's view was that the Jews were 'better people'.

Throughout the years of occupation of Czechoslovakia, there was a kind of underground partisan opposition to the German regime. The partisans chose to act through sabotage and assassination, rather than the full-scale warfare being pursued by Tito in Yugoslavia. For that reason, the acts of these partisans could be just as intimidating to civilians as those of the Germans, and included terrifying bomb attacks on railway installations.

One evening in the middle of June 1942, Miroslav was travelling home to Bismarckstrasse from Umprum on what was known as Tram Number 6. The tram, which ran along the edge of the Vltava, suddenly stopped about a hundred metres away from the river and close to the onion-domed Russian Orthodox Church. There was a tremendous commotion. Fire-fighters were furiously pumping water. And then a series of gunshots rang out from deep inside the church.

Miroslav did not suspect until he read the newspaper the following day that he had been only a short distance from one of the most notorious historical dramas of the war. Nazi troops were attempting to kill the three Czechoslovak partisans who had returned to Prague from their exile in England to assassinate the

Nazi commander, Reinhard Heydrich. Two were Czechs and the third was a Slovak. They were members of a resistance group of expatriate Czechoslovaks who had fled to England before the German occupation.

The Heydrich murder inflamed the Nazi leadership. He had been killed in Prague by a hand grenade thrown at his car as he returned from his summer villa to his headquarters at Prague Castle. Actually, three hand grenades were thrown but only one went off, and so the partisans finished the job by machine-gunning the occupants at close range. Amazingly, Heydrich survived for two days after the attack. The Nazis gave him a huge funeral in Prague and then launched a reprisal campaign in which they killed hundreds of suspected partisan sympathisers.

As Miroslav sat in Tram Number 6, Heydrich's assassins had been cornered in the Russian Church. The priest had concealed them in some catacombs beneath the main altar, and had been sending them food through a tube that was passed beneath the altar. They were betrayed for a cash reward. The Judas was a 22-year-old Czech man working with the butcher who provided strained beef stew for the hidden men.

Later, the pumped water and the gunshots were explained. The German soldiers had been unable to make a direct shooting attack on the partisans, since the only access to their hiding-place had been sealed and there were only three small sloping windows located high above the outer wall of the catacombs. Instead, they forced the fire brigade to pump hundreds of gallons of water down the feeding tube into the catacombs, and when the water burst out through the tiny windows, three loud gunshots were heard – the stricken men had used their own revolvers to commit suicide.

Around the same time, the horrible massacre in the coal-mining village of Lidice took place. There, only twenty kilometres outside Prague, the Germans thought that a number of Allied parachutists were being protected by the villagers. They combed the village but found nothing. Then they surrounded and sealed off the village and executed every single person there. The only survivors were two men who by chance had been working a late shift at the coal mine, but they too were later killed.

After the massacre, the Germans sent planes to bombard the village, and forced conscripted Jewish workers to level the rubble. Even the little river was diverted and run in a different direction. The Jewish workers were also executed after the operation was completed. Lidice simply disappeared from the face of the earth. Nobody today can indicate exactly where Lidice was located, but Miroslav points out that, to Czechs, the word 'Lidice' is as well-known as a watchword for terror as the town of Guernica that is immortalised in Picasso's painting.

The German occupation also affected Miroslav's family more directly. Two of Anna's nieces were married and living on the outskirts of Prague, and he had visited them on several occasions during his earlier life. In fact, he stayed with one of his cousins, Helenka, during his first month at Umprum but then decided that he would prefer to live closer to the city centre. Helenka's husband committed suicide in the Vltava River in 1942 when he was about to be arrested by the Gestapo. He was a bank official and it appears that he had been funnelling some money through the bank to the account of one of the partisan groups. He was never actually arrested, but he had a feeling that he had been betrayed by someone at the bank.

The strangest part of the story is that Helenka assumed after her husband's disappearance that he had already been arrested and was being held in one of the city prisons. Every day for two months she visited as many of the prisons as she could manage, asking for news of her husband. It was a brutal and impossible task, given the chaos of a justice system that was obsessed with the arbitrary incarceration and execution of so many people. Every evening, she read the newspapers to check whether her husband was among the twenty or thirty people executed at the prisons during that day.

Finally there was a press report that an unidentified body had been recovered from the Vltava. It was a unique enough event to trigger the family's suspicion. They decided that Franta should go to the city mortuary to check the identity. He went, and indeed was able to confirm that it was Helenka's husband. But he was sickened by the experience of identifying a body that had been in the cold waters of the Vltava for nearly three months.

Franta's noble side, however, was still losing out to his demons. Forgetting the lessons of his earlier prison experience, he was still prepared to take risks in the name of making a little money, even during wartime. The following episode testifies to this lack of discretion.

Horses were very much part of village life at the time. They were used for hauling coal from the mines, but also for food. Franta knew that, with petrol in such short supply, the Germans were busy rounding up good horses to assist in the war effort. These horses, subjected to horrible tasks such as pulling heavy artillery, were treated very badly by soldiers who were concerned most with their own safety. A horse-breeding farmer in the mountains came to Franta, his drinking buddy, with the ludicrous idea that they could buy some of these horses used by the Germans, recondition them, and sell them back to the Germans as fresh. These deceptions would happen at the Tanvald horse show, the place where the German officers gathered to buy new horses for the army. Franta liked the scheme immediately.

Working with a couple of butchers from the town of Velké Hamry, Franta and the farmer brought some of the German military buyers to the breeding farm to show them a fine stock of healthy horses. Franta told the Germans that he would be bringing these horses for sale at the Tanvald show. In another part of the farm, the conspirators were feeding the eight or ten worn-out horses they had acquired cheaply at auction from the German Army. These were the animals they were actually planning to bring to the market. Franta, who was no saint, stuck little needles in these horses' necks to keep their heads up during the show. Even more astonishingly, the four conspirators brushed the horses' coats and spray-painted them with a brownish colour to give them (as they thought) a fresher look.

At the show in Tanvald, a middle-ranking German officer who had just joined the Army horse-buying team suddenly recognised one of the nags as a horse that he had formerly ridden. 'This is my horse,' he said to a startled Franta, with the same emotion as if he had just laid eyes on his faithful old sheepdog. The luckless Franta, the horse-farmer and the two butchers were immediately taken to the Tanvald prison. Anna was able to bail Franta out after a few days, but it took thousands of scarce crowns to do it. She moved quickly to assemble the money, borrowing much of it from family friends, because she knew very well the potential consequences of Franta's fraud. He could easily have been sent for trial to one of the ruthless Nazi *Sondergerichten*. The tribunals routinely handed down the death penalty with nothing in the way of due process, no witnesses and no right of appeal.

Franta arrived back in Držkov, Miroslav recalls, looking grey not only in his hair but also in his face. According to Miroslav, searching for an explanation of his father's behaviour, the war was still just distant enough from life in Bohemia that Franta and his fellow conspirators never properly took into consideration the huge risks of their daring scheme. And, of course, they were a like-minded little team of what Miroslav calls, using an Irish term, 'chancers'.

It is not clear what kind of investigation the Germans conducted into the whole bizarre episode, or why Franta was set free (as was the horse farmer who concocted the original idea). But Miroslav suspects that the horse-painting fraud could not have been the main focus of the arrests. The Nazis must have had other charges against the Hamry butchers. One of them was executed soon after and the other had his business taken away and was sent to unload coal from the freight trains stopping at Železny Brod. One day, he got into some kind of argument with one of the Nazi guards and waved his shovel at him in a vaguely threatening way. The guard, who knew that the butcher was unarmed, executed the poor man on the spot. 'He was trying to escape, so I had to kill him,' the guard told his superiors. This, at any rate, was how Franta later heard the story. He was not in the least surprised.

# Nazis, Partisans and Communists

Despite the upheaval of the world around him, Miroslav was now entering his third year at Umprum. Looking back at his experiences at the school, Miroslav still thinks he should have earned better marks. However, he can recall that he had increasing trouble hearing in the larger auditoriums, and he found his hearing problems very off-putting. Maybe he had undetected childhood auditory problems, a common experience in an era without school medical officers. But there was another, more immediate reason why his hearing began to malfunction while he was at Umprum.

Not long after his third year started, Miroslav found himself snatched away from lectures on art and aesthetics to become part of Germany's wartime labour conscription policy. The Germans insisted that every graduate school in Prague, including Umprum, must dispatch its students to spend one or two months working in support of the war effort, whether in the armaments factories that ringed the city or further afield in the coal mines. Miroslav's particular assignment must have struck both him and Franta as ironic. He was conscripted to work four months in the huge coal mines at Duchcov, about a hundred kilometres north-west of Prague and very close to the original border with Germany.

Miroslav's task at Duchcov was to sort coal from pieces of stone on a long conveyor belt, quite a contrast to his evolving artistic formation in Prague. Sometimes he was assigned to what was considered a more desirable job down in the shaft, wielding a hammer to break up some of the larger coal pieces.

Conditions were not comfortable, standing naked in communal cold showers before leaving the mineshaft and sleeping fitfully in hard bunk beds in the local hostel. As the workday began and ended in total darkness, he never knew what the weather was like on any given day. He remembers that he had a nice pair of shoes, which he insisted on holding in his hand as he stood beside the belt, rather than exposing them to the filthy ground inside the shafts. That may have looked a little precious to the tougher types – most of them not Umprum students – labouring down there in the gloomy pits.

The atmosphere in the mines was gritty, smoky and humid, and Miroslav sweated profusely while he did his sorting and breaking. He claims that the constant wiping of his coal-powdered hand against his wet brow wore away the curly hair on either side of his forehead, leaving him with a swept-back Hercule Poirot look, an island of resistant follicles between two desolate peaks, that he has kept into his eighties. Much more serious, however, was the consequence of an explosion one day somewhere deeper within the mineshaft. The shock effects of the explosion struck him in his right ear. Miroslav knew that something awful had happened, and when he came up from the shaft he went in search of medical help. But there was no doctor on-site, not even a nurse's aide, since all the medical types were working with war casualties. He cleaned the blood from his ear and stuffed cotton wool into it. The bleeding eventually stopped, but the hearing in his right ear worsened.

The first serious medical attention Miroslav received for his ear was from an Irish doctor in Dublin in 1948. By then, his hearing had severely diminished, and in fact the doctor felt that, because of the extent of decomposition, he had no choice but to remove all of Miroslav's right inner ear. It took him a long time to adjust to the complete absence of any sound on his right side.

As it turned out, his left ear was also weakened, maybe by the explosion and maybe by heredity. Hearing aids were simply unavailable in the aftermath of the war, and it was not until later in 1948, after his operation, that he was fitted for a hearing aid in Dublin. Poor hearing is one reason why Miroslav, after nearly sixty years in Ireland, still keeps the vocal intonations of the late Polish Pope.

By the spring of 1945, as Miroslav approached the end of his disrupted third year at Umprum, the coming defeat of Germany was being deeply sensed in Prague. Wireless broadcasts from the Allied forces promised liberation. Miroslav remembers the anticipation of something 'big' about to happen, and the expectation, cruelly denied by history and the machinations of the Allied leaders under General Patton, that the Americans would reach Prague first. This was a reasonable expectation. The Americans had reached Plzeň (Pilsen), only one hour by tank from the capital. Miroslav remembers how the Big Power leaders (Roosevelt, Stalin and Churchill) repeated the insult by the French and British at Munich and handed Prague over to the Russians at the Yalta Conference.

The Czechs felt tremendous bitterness toward the Germans. The Nazi SS atrocities continued to the very end. Miroslav knew two young men, office workers at the factory where he had just started an internship, who were executed in 1945 by German soldiers after alighting from a train at the President Thomas Masaryk central railway station in Prague. Miroslav had played volleyball with them only the week before. They boarded the Brno–Prague mainline train at Světlá nad Sázavou, where the factory was located, and were engaged in the innocent task of carrying books to an antiquarian book dealer in Prague. Even at that stage of the war, travelling by rail carried the risk of a partisan attack or a German air assault, but the passengers arrived safely in Prague. However, a squadron of German soldiers was waiting on the platform as they left the train. Every single passenger was put up against a wall and executed. There is a huge plaque at the Masaryk station which lists the names of all the men, women, and children who died on that day, only weeks before the city was liberated on 9 May 1945. For Miroslav, it was one of the worst things that ever took place in his beloved Prague.

After the German defeat, Miroslav joined the many young and excited Czechoslovak volunteers assisting in units set up to supervise the ethnic German population. These units essentially ran what was left of the war in Bohemia, and were set up to prevent the very real possibility, while the Czechoslovak Army was stationed at the battlefront, that the local populations would start to massacre ethnic Germans in an explosion of retaliation.

Miroslav wore one of the special uniforms which the US forces dropped by parachute to waiting unit commanders. The units were supplied with very heavy rifles which had been manufactured in Japan. Meanwhile, German soldiers were scurrying like crazed animals around the countryside, terrified of being caught and slaughtered by the advancing Russian Army.

On one occasion, Russian partisans captured about sixty German soldiers just outside Držkov. The Russian Army itself was still far away, and the partisans instructed Miroslav's unit to march the soldiers down to the soccer pitch at Železny Brod where a big round-up and encampment of captured military was being coordinated. Miroslav's unit leader, or captain (who was formerly the chief of the local Sokol), put Miroslav and one other young man in charge of marching the soldiers cross-country for ten kilometres to the Brod camp. Miroslav remembers the incident with some bewilderment. Neither he nor his comrade had any idea how to fire the Japanese rifles they had been given. If the soldiers had decided to attack their two guards, what would he and his fellow volunteer have done? At the soccer ground, the local unit commander told Miroslav that he didn't want custody of the soldiers because the makeshift camp was now full. Miroslav kept the commander in negotiations for almost four hours and finally the commander had the soldiers moved under guard to a different venue.

Miroslav's motorcycle – that remarkable gift from Franta – also played a role in these events. The unit captain called Miroslav with what he said was a crucial assignment. Some of the Russian partisans were trapped near Velké Hamry, about ten kilometres north of

Držkov. They had guns and rifles but were running out of ammunition. 'Mirek,' said the captain, 'I want you to take your motorcycle and go up to Hamry and somehow get the ammunition to the partisans.' The road from Držkov through Plavy to Hamry had many German patrols. At the entrance to Hamry, where the road passes by the river, was a textile factory with a flat roof on which the Germans had placed a series of big machine guns. The captain didn't instruct Miroslav about any of these traps and he had no idea he was in any danger as he rode his motorbike to the Russian camp. He handed over the ammunition with little ceremony and headed straight back along the same route. Only later did he discover how many people had been killed on that route, especially along the most treacherous stretch between the river and the textile factory.

His survival was a miracle, some of his fellow unit members told him. He thinks that the Germans must have assumed that Miroslav was himself German, because so few Czechs at the time had motorcycles or fathers who gave them motorcycles. Miroslav complained to the unit captain, who replied in his characteristic clipped fashion that danger is always a feature of wartime.

That wasn't Miroslav's only brush with danger because of a motorcycle. Around the same time as the Hamry incident, many remnants of the battalions of the German Army were on the run westward towards Germany. Indeed, Miroslav and his unit comrades regularly watched them from rocky outcrops high in the local forests. As these soldiers were arrested, Miroslav's unit, like so many others, took custody of their armoured vehicles, their guns and ammunition and their motorcycles. The booty was stored in basements all over the region. Miroslav's unit captain, remembering the young man's expertise with his own motorcycle, asked him to deliver a captured German motorcycle, one of the really big ones with a sidecar and machine guns attached, to a partisan camp in the nearby mountain village of Lastibos. He would have to return in the dark on foot.

Miroslav allowed his enthusiasm for motorbikes to colour his decision to agree, and he became accustomed to the big machine in just a few minutes of testing. The light was already fading as

Miroslav took off for Lastibos, and within a few minutes the batteries had run down and his headlights were blinking on and off. But he knew the roads by heart and got to the camp before he lost all electrical power. As he arrived at the entrance to the camp, he was immediately stopped and surrounded by five armed and angry Russians, who were shining bright torches on his motorcycle and pointing in obvious anger at the swastikas painted everywhere on his machine. Miroslav knew instantly what they were thinking, and he was petrified. He held onto the handlebars of the bike with a frozen grip. Suddenly one of the partisans said something loudly in Russian and a big man came out of the darkness in response. Miroslav immediately recognised the man as a friend of Franta's, a local architect from Hamry. The man spoke passable Russian and gave Miroslav the benefit of an instantaneous translation to the agitated Russians: 'Oh boys, stop – this is Havel from Držkov. They must have given him a motorcycle to bring to you.' The architect then gave a relieved Miroslav a lift back to his home village. 'Next time, take the damn swastikas off the bike,' Miroslav later advised his unit commander in strong Czech.

With the Third Reich in ruins, Czechoslovakia was swept by Communism. Before the war, according to Miroslav, the Communists were a presence in the Republic but were absolutely 'non-influential'. Communist partisans had fought bravely against the Nazis, but what made them powerful as the war ended, Miroslav says, was the arrival of the Red Army. Russian soldiers fanned out across the country to support Communist fellow travellers among the Czechoslovak population. The immediate trigger for the Red Army's supremacy was the Yalta carve-up and Roosevelt's agreement to allow the Soviets to enter Prague first. The Russians, as mentioned previously, were 250 kilometres from the city when the Americans had reached Pilsen, and, even without meeting any opposition, they could not have beaten the Americans to Wenceslas Square. But Stalin outfoxed both Churchill and Roosevelt, and Czechoslovakia paid the price of being sucked into his nightmarish 'revolution'.

The Communists put on a huge show in Prague, Miroslav

remembers, with red flags and the hammer and sickle appearing everywhere. General Patton got a decent reception when he arrived in Prague, but it was already obvious that the political order was changing profoundly. President Beneš returned from exile in London and immediately agreed to give the Communists the key posts in his government. In Miroslav's own class at Umprum, almost all of his fellow students declared themselves Communist.

The rapid spread of Communism started nearest to the Russian border, in Slovakia. That part of the Republic had been led during the last year of the war by an eccentric priest-turned-Communist, Dr Jozef Tiso, who tried to appease Hitler in return for a promise of Slovak autonomy from the Czechs. But Tiso had a streak of independence, too, which always antagonised the Nazi leader. Miroslav recalls the oft-told story of Hitler's phone call to Tiso seeking back-up as the Germans retreated from Russia. 'Yes, Adolf, I will send you one tank,' said Tiso. Hitler reacted angrily, so Tiso continued: 'Okay, I will send you both of them.' But Tiso's appeasement was not forgiven by the Russians, and after the war he was tried and hanged. According to Miroslav, Tiso's execution was the beginning of the slow drifting apart of the Czechs and Slovaks that led to the division of the Republic into two independent states in 1993. The Slovaks were always inclined toward independence, Miroslav feels, and would probably have embraced Communism even if the Czechs had joined the West.

There were no elections as such as the war ended. As soon as the Red Army soldiers liberated a city, town or village, they dismissed the mayor and council and appointed a so-called 'national committee' of Communist sympathisers instead. On 4 December 1945, President Beneš bowed to the inevitable and issued a decree accepting the legality of all of these committees. The Communists, Miroslav says, went 'berserk'. They were determined to take the whole country under their control and to make it appear that they were the Republic's only saviours. Other parties simply gave up. The popular socialist mayor of Prague and ally of President Beneš, Dr Petr Zenkl, was quickly ousted by a Communist, Jozef Vaček.

Miroslav remembers how quickly all of this happened at his

own local level. Suddenly, even as early as 1944 and 1945, the whole village of Držkov became Communist. Sensing the new dispensation, people were everywhere 'self-declaring' themselves as Communists, as Miroslav puts it. There was a meeting in the village to choose the new leaders for the 'national committee'. A 'group of five' set themselves up as the new village bosses. They met in the very restaurant where Franta used to hold court, and drank merrily while they drew up five-year plans, and the rest of the village watched in fear and silence. They quite simply 'took the village by the throat', Miroslav recalls.

The chairman of the group was a Communist self-declarer who, according to Miroslav, had spent the entire war hiding in the attic of a village farm building. The results of the so-called election were announced the next day, although in fact the vote was by a public show of hands and everyone at the meeting made sure to raise a hand in favour of the five bosses.

Franta, as it happened, was not allowed to attend the organising meeting. As noted earlier, his money-making ventures before the war had given him the reputation of being rich and a 'bourgeois'. Miroslav, as his son, was guilty by association. He, too, was told in advance of the meeting that he should not try to attend. Indeed, the whole family suffered a loss of recognition as the new bosses took control. Miroslav's cousin, Ludiška, on the basis that she was Franta's niece, was denied admission to a higher school and spent the next year cleaning up at the local piggery.

Franta could have tried to fake support of Communism like so many other former opponents did, and he had the bravado to get away with it. The Communists were well aware of how many sudden conversions were swelling the ranks of the party from 600,000 members throughout Czechoslovakia in June 1945 to over a million nine months later. But, even at the personal cost of staying at Most at the coal mines, Franta had a visceral hatred for the new system and refused to have anything to do with it.

# The Světlá Factory and a Fateful Invitation

Meanwhile, Miroslav was completing his fourth year at Umprum. He was fortunate, despite the issues affecting his family in the Communist era, still to have his place there, and he was determined to graduate. Of course, the war had prevented him from getting a continuous education, not only because of his service at the coal mine, but also because the professors at various times were prohibited from teaching. Another year would make him fully qualified, and a sixth would have taken him to the rank of university professor.

It was, however, a chaotic time at Umprum. Classes were only slowly returning to a normal schedule, and many of the students were still absent because of wartime disruptions such as forced labour service or because, like Miroslav, they were volunteering with some of the partisan units.

However, even though economic conditions were uncertain and the aftermath of the war even more so, Miroslav did have some options because of his association with Umprum and with Professor Štipl. For one thing, he was toying with putting his name down for an art teaching job that would be opening up in Semily, a large provincial town about twenty kilometres east of Držkov. Many Umprum graduates became art teachers once they had completed four years at the school, and Miroslav thought that this would be a good use of his knowledge and qualifications. Again, it would have been possible to realise Anna's dream for him.

But again, it never happened. As noted earlier, Umprum liked to place its students in real-life factory and studio experiences, and Štipl had a strong recommendation for his star student. The professor undoubtedly wanted Miroslav to pursue higher studies and to concentrate on glass sculpture, but he was also a firm believer in practical training. Štipl's friend, Karel (Charles) Bačik, had an internship available at his fairly large cutting and engraving factory – known as the 'Karlov' factory – in Světlá nad Sázavou, a town located conveniently about mid-way between Prague and Brno on the main railway line. The internship was almost certain to lead eventually to full-time employment, and Štipl offered to support Miroslav if he applied for the opportunity. 'Spend as much time as you can with Bačik,' the professor advised, 'and then make sure that you finish your sixth year with Umprum.'

One of Miroslav's classmates, Frank Zemek, was already working at the Karlov factory. Zemek was a pretty persuasive individual. He convinced Miroslav that Semily and art teaching were bad ideas and that he should go to the Bačik factory: 'He will be glad to have you there, Mirek. He has nobody to design for him and he's relying too much on old-fashioned pieces.'

In fact, not only did the Karlov factory not have any designer, it had no engravers. The entire output of the factory came from 250 cutters who did fancy cutting on glass blanks that were blown in another Bačik plant. The factory was just getting ramped up again for commercial production after nearly two years during which the Germans had forced Bačik to produce only periscope glass for military use. Miroslav was intrigued by the idea of getting some design experience, as well as becoming the only engraver on the Bačik staff. He decided to try this new opportunity. He had just started work at the factory in Světlá when the terrible news broke of the loss of two of the factory's employees in the Masaryk station massacre.

As things would turn out, Miroslav's attachment to Charles Bačik, and to Bačik's glass factory, became the fateful connection of his life. In 1945 and 1946, however, he was a young craftsman, undecided in his mind about an academic or an industrial career, and the internship at Světlá was a way not just to indulge his creative interests but also to postpone any final career decision. Although Miroslav and his new boss were to spend a lifetime together, most of it in another country, and indeed were to become personal friends, they never changed the formal mode of address that they used in those first days in the Karlov factory. It was always 'Mr Havel' and 'Mr Bačik', their formality a product of the times, and also related to the formality of the classical Czech language and culture. Mr Bačik was a factory owner, and Czech business etiquette in those days required that he be addressed as 'Pán Tovární Bačik', literally, 'Mr Factory Owner Bačik'. 'Pán Tovární' later became a term of abuse and contempt under the Communists. Miroslav, however, a lowly student intern in the Karlov factory, followed that traditional style as soon as he arrived at Světlá, and carried it over to his relationship with 'Mr Bačik' in Ireland as well.

As the only engraver at the Karlov plant, and still an intern, Miroslav found himself working very hard and at a relatively slow pace, but what he most remembers was the total freedom he enjoyed. Bačik did not hold him to any particular hours, and often he came in late in the morning and worked until late at night. His sleeping arrangements were reminiscent of his days as a Duchcov miner, sharing a big room with several Karlov employees in a local youth hostel. But at least this time the furnishings were of a better grade and, as an added bonus, Bačik paid the rent for the five or six employees who were using the room at any given time.

Miroslav became quite friendly with a number of his room-mates who had backgrounds in mechanical engineering and whom Bačik hired to develop an acid-polishing system for the Světlá plant. Czech glass was not typically polished, so Miroslav got an unusual insight into acid-polishing techniques which he would later find useful in Ireland.

Hiring Miroslav and then taking on these engineers were signs that Bačik had plans to modernise his production at the Karlov plant. Although he owned three other glass factories, he always thought of the Karlov location as his jewel and he had high ambitions for its future. In the meantime, however, Miroslav's increasing practical experience seemed to justify Professor Štipl's recommendation. He continued to enhance his engraving skills, and did some designing of glass shapes. Still hoping that he could emulate Štipl, he also took time to sharpen his skills in the theory of glass sculpting, mostly by making shapes in sand and clay. Finally, he deepened his training as a cutter beyond his experience in Železny Brod. He was becoming expert in what he calls 'typical Czech cutting', where the full shape of the glass is cut ornately and delicately from top to bottom and not a single piece of the surface is left blank. These full cuts were applied to every kind of crystal-glass product coming out of the Karlov factory.

After a few months at Světlá, Miroslav began to feel that things finally were settling down in a disordered universe. Now his studies at Umprum would include regular stints at the Bačik factory, and the work he was doing there was also earning credits at Umprum. Just after he arrived at Bačik's factory, also, he started to date a woman about five years his junior. Her name was Růžena Štolfová, and she worked at a nearby printing factory. Miroslav does not recall where he first met Růžena, or Rosa, as he always referred to her while he was in Ireland – perhaps at a works party at the Karlov plant – but they went for a drink together, liked each other, and started to date. The 'drink' in question was alcoholic drink, which was notable because Miroslav, who so often shied away from the model set by his father, had hardly ever indulged in alcohol by the time he went to work for Bačik.

Not long after that first meeting, Miroslav took Rosa to meet Franta and Anna in Držkov. Anna was enchanted by the young woman, and immediately gave her a gift of one of her two enormous but highly fashionable fur coats, and an elaborate fur hand muffler. Miroslav still has a photograph of Rosa wearing that bulky but eminently practical coat, her hands invisible inside the huge muffler.

Franta and Anna, as they studied the picture of the young lady in the fur coat, may well have imagined that they were looking at a snapshot of their future daughter-in-law. Rosa had something of the same idea, according to Miroslav, which is clear also from her letters to him during his early years in Ireland. She certainly could not have expected that her new boyfriend would soon be leaving Czechoslovakia forever. She continued to see Miroslav's parents from time to time, because she and Miroslav had made a point every so often of showing up together in Držkov for Sunday dinner.

Miroslav's wages at the Karlov factory were not stellar, but he knew that they were at least as much as Bačik's cutters were earning. In fact, even though Miroslav was the only specialist engraver and the only employee with a professional training in glass-making, the union organisers at the plant would not have tolerated paying Miroslav a wage that was greater than that of the cutters. They certainly would not have conceded that engraving was in any way a 'superior' craft activity to cutting, and they probably would have called a strike if Bačik had taken a different view (which he did privately). In the new Communist era, Miroslav could see, the unions were acquiring much more control over the hiring and firing policies of their nominally independent employers.

In any event, he prized the experience he was getting much more than the income. The Karlov factory was beginning to seem like it had a very interesting future. Mr Factory Owner Bačik was continuing to diversify his hiring beyond the usual teams of new cutters. Miroslav was joined by some new engravers and etchers (the latter could be described as 'painters' of glass), and Bačik appeared to have the resources and connections to overcome Frank Zemek's stinging criticism that the production at the Karlov factory was hopelessly old-fashioned.

By now, Miroslav was thoroughly fed up with Czechoslovak politics, which were becoming increasingly bitter and polarised as the Communist takeover continued to gain momentum. He had an unpleasant personal experience of the changing political environment while he was at Světlá. It was a Monday morning in late October 1945, and he had just arrived off the train from Prague. There had recently been some parliamentary elections, although it was still over two years before the final Communist takeover by coup d'état. Miroslav came to the factory wearing the white laboratory coat that Bačik required for all his cutters and engravers. On the front pocket of the coat, he had pinned a badge bearing the logo of what was then called the Czech Socialist Party.

As he entered the front door of the factory, Miroslav was stopped by two men he recognised as union officials. 'Mr Havel,' one of them said officiously, 'you cannot go in.'

'Why not?' Miroslav asked. 'I work here.'

'Well, if you go in, you have to put that badge away,' came the quick reply.

Miroslav knew what was happening – the only kind of public support that was tolerated, even at Bačik's own factory, was for the Communist Party. Rosa wrote to him in February 1948 that the party had finally taken over the Karlov factory after the national coup. The employees elected one of Bačik's former partners, a convert to the party, as the new 'manager'. As Rosa put it, he had 'jumped the fence'.

The Communist trend in the factories had been visible for some time. Miroslav recalls how, as the war ended, employees at the Světlá factory, in common with thousands at many other factories outside Prague, had been ferried by bus to the capital and issued voting cards to support the Communist challenger to Mayor Zenkl. Because of the Communist control of factory unions, business owners not only had to accept the absurdity of half-empty factories, but they were forced also to provide written statements that the employees were genuinely working in Prague and were unable to return to vote in their home districts. Such was the fantasy world of the new Communist order.

At Světlá, Miroslav increasingly saw Charles Bačik in the role of a mentor, although he could never have predicted how powerful this role was about to become in his life. Sometimes he reflects on the mystery of who Bačik really was. To the end of his life, the man seemed to cultivate this sense of mystery about himself. He was physically dominating, six-foot-four inches in height (even taller than the imposing Franta), with a large head crowned by a high wall of jet-black hair and facial features etched so deeply he could have been a glass sculpture himself. Bačik was rumoured to be of German origin, and he was avowedly not a Communist. He was rich, clever and multilingual. He had an engineering degree which people in Ireland later inaccurately assumed to reflect a training in civil or mechanical engineering but which was actually a degree as an 'engineer of languages', a qualification that was offered in Eastern European universities.

Bačik's 'bourgeois' credentials were impeccable. His father was a medical doctor, and he had met his wife, Edith, at the University of Vienna. She was the daughter of the Yugoslav ambassador to Austria and was learning Czech at the university. They were well-matched, Miroslav recalls, since they both were extremely tall and both maintained a lifelong fascination with the many languages they spoke. In the Bačik household, even when it operated in Bohemia, certain days were designated as 'French days', or 'German days', or 'Italian days', when only those languages would be spoken. This seemingly eccentric arrangement nevertheless produced children who enjoyed extraordinary linguistic skills.

However, the mystery persisted. Above all else, Bačik was a businessman, with a very strict attitude to all of his business affairs. He was well known in Bohemia, and he knew a lot of people well. He may have had just too much visibility in those tense days after the war, and he was certainly a target of resentment as the new Communist orthodoxy continued to splinter the nation into supporters and bourgeois opponents. Miroslav describes him as having been a 'big bourgeois', much more in that league than Franta could ever have been.

Yet Bačik seemed to have survived what Miroslav remembers as the first wave of 'cleaning'. He managed to avoid becoming a Communist and, although Communists were all around him, to keep control of his factory and even to be elected chief representative of the entire glass industry in Bohemia. Many people supported him for that position. And he continued to live well. He travelled in a big car, and lived in a beautiful Japanese-style villa, the kind of accommodation rarely seen in those frugal post-war days. When Miroslav last saw the villa, in 1973, it had been converted into a dowdy block of flats, with ugly metal chimneys poking out of every other window.

Despite all of this surface security, Miroslav thinks that Bačik was aware for some time that 'it was all over for him'. Towards the middle of 1946, he was rarely seen at the factory in Světlá. Certainly, there were perfectly plausible reasons for his prolonged absences. One of the great advantages of his role as chief of the Bohemian glass industry was that he could travel outside the country with little hindrance. He was able to get a passport, and used it to move extensively around the European mainland. And he was often in Prague on business connected with a consortium of ten Bohemian glass factories with which he was involved. When he took these frequent journeys outside Světlá, his wife would take over the running of the factory. Miroslav remembers Edith as gracious, although her deep gravelly voice sometimes gave people the opposite impression.

In November 1946, when Miroslav had been working on and off at the Karlov factory for over a year, it was suddenly announced that Edith Bačik was taking over as the director of the factory. She had previously been listed as the assistant director, but until that point ownership had always been solely in her husband's hands.

Shortly after that strange announcement, Miroslav was back at Umprum and perusing a cork notice-board located at the entrance to the school near the usual gallery of distinguished portraits. The board was covered with an assortment of small ads, and he was hunting for a new flat. Suddenly he spotted an envelope pinned to the board, addressed to him and bearing stamps from a country, Éire, that he could not immediately identify. But he knew the handwriting. He could never mistake the wild up-and-down strokes of the penmanship of Charles Bačik. He showed the envelope to some of his student friends, but nobody had a clue about the origin of the stamps. Miroslav ran to Umprum's library and consulted the Czechoslovak national encyclopaedia. He discovered that Éire was the Gaelic name given to Ireland by the new constitution of the Republic of Ireland, adopted in 1937. Only then did this lifelong stamp collector finally open the actual letter.

The letter was Miroslav's first realisation that his boss had actually escaped from Czechoslovakia. Bačik, in a word, was already gone. Miroslav had not been at the Světlá plant for several months and did not know that Edith Bačik and her four small children had joined her husband on a holiday in Switzerland, and that, from there, the whole family had made its way westward to Ireland. In Miroslav's opinion, the letter, which explained all of this, was cleverly constructed. Bačik wrote that he had indeed left Czechoslovakia for good, along with his family, and that he had resettled in the city of Waterford, Ireland. He said that he had a good memory of Miroslav and of his work at the Karlov factory.

Then the letter switched to the history of what he called the 'Waterford Glass' company, and of how well known it was in the world at that time. Finally, Bačik invited Miroslav to work with him at Waterford Glass for a while, and asked him to request Professor Štipl to grant Miroslav a three-month leave of absence from Umprum in order to do so. The letter quite clearly tried to convey the impression that Bačik was already engaged in making glass at Waterford. And, in closing, Bačik offered a promise of good things in Ireland, which he knew would tempt his intern: 'I have to tell you, Mr Havel, this is a very fine country and we have plenty of bananas and oranges here.' He asked Miroslav to send a note in reply if he had any interest in the proposition.

Miroslav has always wondered why Bačik wrote specifically to him. Even though he had solid engraving and designing experience, he always had the impression that Frank Zemek was closer to the Karlov boss. In fact, he has a suspicion, which was never confirmed, that Bačik might first have invited Zemek to join him. This was the same Zemek, a specialist in glass etching, who was Miroslav's co-worker and classmate and who had encouraged Miroslav to join the

Karlov factory rather than teach art. Zemek, unlike Miroslav, was a full-time employee at Světlá, and his family was deeply entrenched in the Bohemian glass industry. His older brother was an executive in one of the consortium factories and had a good working relationship with Bačik.

However, Zemek, even if he had wanted to go, was an unlikely candidate for an internship in a distant country. For a start, he was a bit older than Miroslav, thirty to Miroslav's twenty-five. This narrow gulf in years seemed relatively vast to his classmates and caused the poor man to be mocked as the 'father of the class' at Umprum, although the school had no required maximum age of admission, and passing the entrance exams guaranteed admission irrespective of age. Moreover, Zemek, as well as being seen as virtually a geriatric, was also married.

Furthermore, Zemek's wife was a Prague prosecutor, and she was, according to Miroslav, 'one hundred and five per cent Communist'. He thinks that she probably would have turned Bačik over to the Czechoslovak police sooner than allow her husband to join him in a mysterious adventure in Ireland. Zemek himself also 'played a Communist', according to Miroslav, because his wife's career demanded it. So, Miroslav suspects that Zemek must have turned Bačik down, perhaps even before the boss left for Ireland, and that he may have recommended Miroslav in his place. Frank Zemek would eventually come to a sticky end. When he was only forty-five, he was murdered by being pushed under a train in Prague, allegedly by some anti-Communists unhappy with one of his wife's political prosecutions.

Why did Bačik suddenly leave a country where he had so successfully established himself and when he seemed so adept at surviving the political changes? Were there, as the glass industry rumour mills had it, too many financial tricks? He had a high position, and a high family background, and his sudden von Trapp family departure through Switzerland seemed unnecessary even in the changed post-war circumstances.

Miroslav remembers being told by Zemek that Bačik carried

some sort of black book that detailed past financial shenanigans, but nobody ever saw such a book and someone in Bačik's position is unlikely to have been so reckless. That kind of rumour could just as easily have been started by the always vengeful Communists. And the unexplained suicide of his cousin, another glass entrepreneur who ran a factory just a dozen or so kilometres from Světlá, added even more grist to the rumour mill.

The most likely explanation remains the simplest one: Bačik probably knew, as Miroslav suggests, that his bourgeois history would eventually prove too unpalatable for the new leadership, and he wanted to spare the Communists the bother of ruining him. He might even have expected to be arrested by the new regime, Miroslav thinks, on some trumped-up charges. Once again, it testifies to the old-world formality of their relationship that Miroslav and Bačik never discussed the subject of the great escape, even though it must have crossed Bačik's mind that Miroslav wondered about it in nearly five decades of close proximity.

Whatever their motivation may have been for leaving Czechoslovakia, fleeing to Ireland seemed to make business sense to Charles and Edith Bačik. Bačik had been doing business with the Fitzpatrick family in Dublin, owners of a company that put corporate mottoes, insignia and stickers on unfinished plain glasses imported from the Bačik factory in Světlá. That relationship had existed for several years, and there were some fiscal advantages to the Fitzpatricks in adding value in their domestic factory, since the imported glass came in at lower duties than if it had been a finished product.

The Fitzpatricks, led by family patriarch Bernard J., were jewellers and silversmiths in Dublin. They were part of what was then considered Irish high society. Bernard's eldest son, J.J., was well-regarded in the elite sport of showjumping. Bernard himself was, Miroslav recalls, a 'very tiny little man, but very pleasant'. Miroslav is sure that it was Bernard Fitzpatrick's idea that Bačik should relocate to Ireland. The intriguing thing about the Fitzpatrick/Bačik relationship at this point is that somehow they figured out together that a revival of high-quality cut crystal glass could be a popular export to the United States. Fitzpatrick was obsessed with the fact that he had personally seen many old Waterford glass crystal chandeliers in public buildings in Philadelphia. He must have had numerous conversations with his Czech counterpart on the subject. But, in this respect, exactly whose initiative was uppermost remains unknown.

One thing is certain, however. The Fitzpatricks themselves were not producing the kind of fine-cut crystal that Bačik was turning out at Světlá. And if Miroslav had more of a suspicious mind, he might have figured out much earlier the nature of Bačik's plan. Some months after he arrived in Ireland, Miroslav remembered that he had seen a crate at Světlá, labelled for delivery to an address in Ireland, into which he helped to load a full-sized German-manufactured engraving machine. Why would the boss of the Karlov factory send such an expensive item to Ireland? Bačik, of course, was well aware that there was no glass factory in Ireland that resembled the Karlov plant in Světlá. In retrospect, Miroslav realised that Bačik was making preparations to have technical equipment in place for the premium crystal-making that he hoped to launch in his adopted country.

Bačik's letter to Miroslav said very little about his new country or its glass industry. The trusty encyclopaedia correctly stated the official Gaelic name of this fabulous destination, but was wildly misinformed (and apparently so was Bačik) about the country's climatic characteristics. The encyclopaedia did correctly state the political fact that Ireland had been under British sovereignty for much of its history. But then it proceeded to assure Miroslav of the accuracy of Bačik's grand promise of bananas and oranges – the entry on Ireland described the climate of this windswept location at the edge of the cold Atlantic as 'largely tropical'!

As to the glass factory, Bačik wrote a few remarks about the terrific history and high reputation of Waterford glass. Miroslav and his Umprum friends did a little background research on this famous product, which, they were convinced, must have escaped their attention during lectures at the school. Neither the encyclopaedia nor their various glass-history textbooks made reference to any glass industry in Waterford. Eventually Miroslav tracked down a brief passing reference to something called 'Waterford glass', but the reference appeared in the encyclopaedia under 'Great Britain: Industrial History', rather than under 'Waterford' or 'Ireland'.

However, he was glad to notice that, in the mid-nineteenth century, English glass merchants had employed many young Bohemian glass engravers under short contracts. He remembers thinking that Bačik must have had something like that in mind for him. But he was puzzled that the entry in his encyclopaedia also revealed that crystal-glass production in Waterford, which it complimented for high quality, had ceased 'in the last century'.

Not suspecting that the authors of his encyclopaedia might be confusing Ireland with the Bahamas or Bermuda, and trusting his old boss more than he should have on the subject, Miroslav wrote back to Bačik and declared himself ready to join him for a three-month period in Waterford. 'I am very interested in extending my knowledge of other glass factories,' he stated in perfect innocence, writing back without much hesitation. He felt that he was only in his mid-twenties, after all, and that a little adventure would be interesting. In any case, there were very few opportunities at that time to arrange a legitimate departure from increasingly Communist Czechoslovakia. Even rarer was the chance to be allowed to take a real job (even a temporary one) outside the country.

However, although his belief in Bačik as a mentor was unshaken by Charles and Edith's hasty exit, Miroslav was more than a little sceptical that he could get to Ireland without becoming ensnared in official resistance. 'I must also tell you, Mr Bačik,' he wrote, 'that I will be unable to leave Czechoslovakia without a valid passport and the necessary transit visas for the journey to Waterford.' Miroslav knew perfectly well that passports and visas were the most exotic of flowers in Czechoslovakia's Communist hothouse.

But Bačik's mastery of intrigue had not deserted him. Just a few weeks after Miroslav posted his reply, a second letter from Éire appeared on the Umprum notice-board. Bačik wrote on this occasion that he was well aware that Miroslav would need a passport and visas. While he didn't believe that Ireland would require an entry visa, transfer visas would be needed for the train journey through Germany and Belgium, and a British transfer visa to get from Dover to the Irish ferry boat at Fishguard. Miroslav knew already that his journey would be by land and by sea. In those early post-war days, nobody except the military and an elite class of government and business leaders and aristocrats was able to get regular access to air travel. 'I was just a miserable student so I would not get into that circle,' Miroslav recalls. The British visa, according to Bačik, would be the most difficult to secure.

The letter concluded with a mysterious flourish. It advised Miroslav that Bačik had certain well-placed 'friends' in Prague ('but I can't tell you the names or anything else about them'). If one of these 'friends' should contact Miroslav, he was told, he should 'keep it to yourself'.

And so it was that, a few days later, another episode of the little notice-board drama took place. One morning, as he conducted his daily routine of checking the board, Miroslav picked up a small envelope with a note-card inside. 'Mr Havel, I would like to meet you at the porter's desk in Umprum next Monday at twelve noon. I will be wearing a grey chalk-striped suit and blue tie.' There was no signature, and no indication of who the sender might be.

Miroslav met the man in the grey suit as requested, and provided him with all his personal details and a photograph. 'I am just the go-between,' the man told him in best Graham Greene style. A few days later, a thick envelope addressed to Miroslav was pinned to the notice-board. It contained a valid Czechoslovak passport with transit visas through Britain, Germany and Belgium, all freshly stamped inside. The passport had actually passed through Charles Bačik's hands at some point, because it had an Irish visitor visa that had been visibly stamped in Dublin. Of the four countries involved in Miroslav's coming journey, only Ireland did not have a diplomatic office in Prague which could issue visas.

Many years later, Bačik confided to Miroslav that the man in the grey suit was acting on behalf of a senior official in the Czechoslovak Ministry of External Affairs. The official had obviously taken some serious risks on Bačik's behalf, because the period after 1946 and before the final Communist coup in 1948 was a period of extreme neuroticism in the Czechoslovak government. The 'cleaning' process of purging bourgeois retainers from the old Republic was in high gear, and the prisons were packed with unreliables. Fast-tracking travel papers for a lowly student who was heading to Ireland to join a rich deserter was bound to arouse suspicion. Miroslav was amazed at his former boss's ability to use connections in the government of a country from which he had so recently plotted an 'escape'.

Once he had possession of his passport, Miroslav went immediately to Professor Štipl to inform him that he had a passport and the visas to get to Ireland and would need a period of extended leave from Umprum. Štipl, always keen for Miroslav to have practical experience, was completely in favour of the unusual trip. Miroslav suspects, in fact, that Bačik had already alerted Štipl to the plot. Štipl, in turn, persuaded the quite sceptical director of the school to grant written permission for a three-month sojourn in banana-rich Ireland. Under currency regulations, Miroslav was able to get four British pounds sterling from his bank in Prague. (The official Irish currency at the time was the Irish pound, but sterling was still accepted as legal tender in the country.) Finally, he made whatever train and boat reservations were possible from Prague. He remembers doing all of this at the notorious Masaryk station, and how complicated it was to make all the necessary connections to Ireland.

While all of this unusual activity was going on, back in Držkov Franta was facing the final demise of the remnants of his costume jewellery business. The currency freezes had damaged him considerably, and the Communists were making sure that able-bodied comrades like his bead-assemblers no longer worked in their homes but in the factories, where their work could be monitored and tabulated for its contribution to the national economic miracle. Franta became a target of police and official harassment. Several times, he was taken to Železny Brod for police questioning about his 'bourgeois' past, and he was warned by Communist civic officials not to try to revive his business covertly. There was no such thing as unemployment assistance, and Franta would have been 'high and dry', as Miroslav puts it, had he not possessed the sheer determination and the guts to continue doing the wartime jobs for which he had volunteered at the Most uranium and coal mines.

By now, Franta was in his fifties, and Miroslav has no doubt that the hard work of the years in the mines diminished his father physically. Even though he had become a union organiser at the coal mine, after the war the shortage of experienced labour meant that he was forced back down to the coalface on many occasions. It was not the way Franta had expected things to turn out for himself, and one can imagine his rages when he took to the taverns in the evenings and considered his lot. But he never stopped working or gave in to depression. And he certainly never gave anyone the pleasure of hearing him admit that he wasn't proceeding in accordance with some grand self-determined plan.

Miroslav knew that he had to break his own startling plan to Franta and Anna. He went home to Držkov for two days to tell Anna what he had decided to do. She was not pleased, but she did not interfere and accepted her son's apparently fixed intention. Franta, as usual, was away in Most, and Miroslav asked her to convey the news to him about the Bačik invitation. It is hard to imagine what the image of Ireland conjured up for Franta and Anna – it must have seemed as remote for them as Tibet or Mongolia might today.

When Miroslav finally took possession of his tickets, he returned to the village for a weekend to say his farewells. His father was still away and so he didn't get a chance to say goodbye to him. On Monday morning, 28 July 1947, he was ready to go. He left the house at about ten o'clock to catch the train back to Prague. Anna was crying and did not feel able to accompany him down to the train station. 'She had some feeling that something would go wrong,' he remembers.

The last person he saw was his grandmother. From his earliest days, she had been like a second mother to him. She hobbled with him on her bad leg out of the house and stood crying outside the big front gates as he began his walk down to the railway station. She was well over eighty at the time, hair as white as Bohemian snow, and Miroslav remembers her also as a 'pretty hefty little woman'. 'Mirko, have a good time,' she said as they finally parted, using the Czech diminutive of his name as she always did, not really sure where he was going. He kissed her, they embraced, and as he walked down the little road away from the house, he could still see her waving gently, a tiny stooped figure receding into the distance. He never saw her again.

# A Journey to a Far Country

After this last sojourn in Držkov, and little suspecting that he would not visit his little village again for a quarter of a century, Miroslav took the train back to Prague. He was about to embark on a complicated expedition, transiting through Germany, Belgium, and then England, before heading on to what was then one of the poorest and most religiously conservative countries in Western Europe. For someone who had never been out of the Czechoslovak Republic, it was a daunting prospect.

Miroslav had kept the day of his intended departure a secret even from his classmates at Umprum. 'I didn't want to make a parade of it,' he recalls. True enough, but he also admits that he was reluctant to advertise his plans too openly because of the constant risk of Communist meddling. It was, after all, a 'miracle' that he had obtained permission to leave the country in the first place. But he did write to Rosa ('my girl in Světlá') and asked her to come up to Prague to see him off at the railway station. And he told Frank Zemek that he would like him to be there (deciding to overlook the fact that Zemek's wife had the highest Communist credentials).

On 29 July 1947, a Tuesday, Miroslav stood once again at the Masaryk railway station in Prague, ready to board the afternoon international train to Germany which was leaving the capital at three o'clock. He expected to be away for three months, not a

1. Miroslav's home in Držkov.

2. Miroslav on skis, winter 1938. For him, skiing was a sport of beauty, out on his own, surrounded only by snow.

3.  Miroslav with his parents, Anna and František, July 1938.

4.  Miroslav with Charles Bačik, 1949.

5.    Miroslav on Gladstone Street, Waterford in the early 1950s.

6.   Miroslav with his first team of engravers, circa 1949. *Clockwise l-r:*
     Tommy Caulfield, Danny Byrne, Tommy Wall and Miroslav Havel.

7.  Managing director Noel Griffin (front centre) hosted the first ten-year dinner for Waterford Glass employees in 1961 and these ten-year dinners became a company institution. The picture, taken at the '30 Years Dinner' on 3 October 1980, shows many of the first Waterford Glass cutters, blowers, batch mixers, checkers, furnace operators and foremen. Charles Bačik, Miroslav Havel and Con Dooley are visible in the second row (fourth, fifth and seventh from the right respectively). Tom Kennedy, the company's first employee after Havel and Bačik, is pictured in the second row, fifth from the left. Mary Prendergast, the first woman foreman, appears in the front row, fourth from the left. Also in the front row, third from the right, is Miroslav Havel's design assistant throughout his career, Frances Cahill.

8.   The Lismore suite.

9.    Sketches of Miroslav's unproduced vase designs.

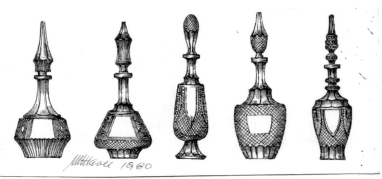

10. Sketches of Miroslav's unproduced presentation decanters from 1979 and 1980.

11.   The Colleen suite.

12.   The Sheila suite.

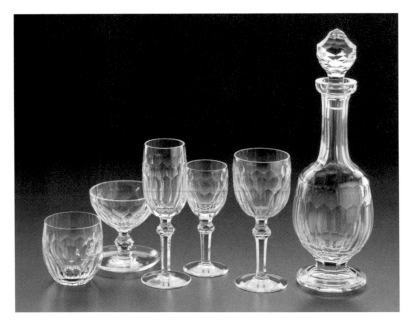

13. The Curraghmore suite.

14. The Hibernia suite.

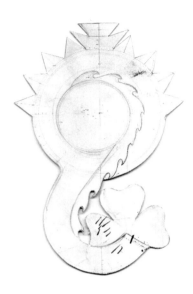

15. The original sketch of the Waterford Glass trademark.

REGD.

16. The Waterford Crystal trademark designed by Miroslav Havel.

17. The registered trademark of Waterford Crystal plc.

18. The Bing Crosby Pro-Am Golf Trophy. The tournament was held in Pebble Beach, California, and at its height was the second-biggest US sporting event after the football Super Bowl.

19. The Chief Designer of Waterford Crystal meets Muhammad Ali in autumn 1984.

20. Miroslav's original concept for the Westminster chandeliers.

21. The chandeliers in the central nave of Westminster Abbey. The commission came in 1965 from the Guinness family, to coincide with the 900th anniversary of the cathedral.

22. The chandelier in the President's Lounge of the John F. Kennedy Centre for the Performing Arts in Washington, DC. The chandelier was specially ordered by Jacqueline Kennedy Onassis. The Kennedy chandelier is 3 metres in diameter and weighs approximately 500 kilos. It is supported by three massive metal rims from which are suspended over 4,000 separate pieces of crystal, lighted with 116 bulbs.

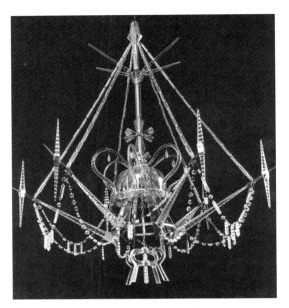

23. The Romanov replica chandelier.

24. The Shelbourne Hotel chandelier.

lifetime, and so his small case was packed accordingly. He had an extra pair of trousers and a shirt, some socks and a few apples to snack on while he travelled.

He still felt a terrible indecision about whether to stay or go. Something in his heart was warning him that his decision could turn out to be very different from what he imagined. Why did he trust Mr Bačik so much? Why didn't he just take that job at Semily and make his mother happy? He suddenly felt that he was being stupid and impetuous. He felt that he had no clue what lay in front of him, and he could clearly see what he was leaving behind. He and Rosa cried together on the platform. Zemek also showed up. Out of earshot of Rosa, he said starkly to his departing friend: 'Mirek, don't tell me lies – you are not coming back.'

'Why do you think that?' Miroslav demanded, upset by the candour of Zemek's daring remark.

'Because I know Bačik,' came the reply.

Suddenly the adventure was under way, and Miroslav was facing a new and uncharted future. In an interview with *The Irish Times* newspaper, published on 10 May 1990, Miroslav is quoted as saying that he headed west to Ireland in July 1947, 'walking across much of Europe'. That was a rather absurd exaggeration, probably the result of a misunderstanding of his English, but his journeys by train and boat were certainly not pleasant ones.

The train from Prague moved across desolate post-war territory, a 'broken continent', as he remembers it, passing by collapsed bridges and the burnt-out shells of houses and factories. Many times, the train had to stop and wait because only a single track would be available for both directions. He had his permission letter from Umprum, as well as his passport and stamped visas, and it was obvious from his papers that his final destination was Ireland. The German border check was straightforward, since Germany and Czechoslovakia were still practically the same territory in the messy aftermath of the war. The Belgians, however, gave him and his fellow passengers a much tougher time, holding the train at the border for over three hours while they meticulously examined each passport.

At the time, the authorities were obsessed with catching ex-SS soldiers trying to escape war-torn Europe.

Having travelled through the night, he eventually cleared the Belgian border check in the early morning, and arrived at the port of Ostend on the Belgian coast. For this land-bound Czech, it was his first sight of the sea. It was also his first opportunity in seven years to buy bananas and oranges – a great joy to someone who has always loved eating fresh fruit. He used what little Belgian money he had to pick up a big bag of fruit. The bananas were so tasty that he wolfed down the entire bunch as he sat waiting for his boat to be announced.

Around midday, Miroslav took the ferry across the English Channel to the historic port of Dover, and, in the mid-afternoon, he arrived in England. As soon as he had set foot on the boat, for him a truly novel experience, he sensed that it was moving beneath him even while anchored in the harbour. Not long after the journey began, he felt immensely sea-sick, and the bananas and oranges returned to fertilise the waters of the Channel. As a first-time sailor, he was feeling so constantly nauseous that he practically lost consciousness, but was fortunate that a fellow sufferer was watching out for him. 'My stomach was like mad,' he remembers. It was a very different nautical experience from the flat, waveless waters of the lakes back in Czechoslovakia.

From Dover, Miroslav resumed the train journey to London's Paddington Station. By now, he was acutely aware that his language skills, especially in English, were sorely lacking. In fact, on his arrival in London, Miroslav had scarcely a single word of English, except his destination, Ireland. Paddington was a popular arrival point for Irish emigrants to Britain (of whom there were many at that time), and somehow he made himself understood by wild gesticulations to sympathetic Irish listeners who helped him figure out that to get to 'Vaterford', as he was calling it, he needed to catch the train to Fishguard in Wales, from where he could catch the ferry to Ireland.

He reached Fishguard late in the day, after a miserable train journey across the rainy south of England and into an equally sodden

Welsh countryside. His vision of a tropical paradise at the edge of the Atlantic was already being shattered, and he began to wonder at Bačik's sanity. He had eaten very little and was exhausted. 'I was a dead man by the time we got to Fishguard,' he recalls. Not only was he physically wrecked, but on his arrival he found the port of Fishguard totally deserted. Now he really needed someone to give him some information.

On his journey, he had constructed a small label from a stiff piece of cardboard buried at the bottom of his suitcase. In his painstakingly neat script, he had written the words 'Waterford Glass' in bold capitals on the front of the label. At Fishguard, he decided that it was finally time to pin this home-made sign to his lapel as a cry for help. Eventually he found his way to the station-master's office.

The station-master seemed to recognise the name 'Waterford', but not the reference to 'Glass'. Somehow, this friendly Welshman made clear to his foreign guest, by a lot of pointing and picture-making, that he needed to get the 'boat' to Rosslare in County Wexford, and he told Miroslav that he could sleep in the station office and someone would wake him when the 'boat' came in. Neither of them could figure out whether or not Miroslav had a ticket for the onward crossing to Ireland, but the station-master apparently told him not to worry about it.

So, Miroslav slept on the couch in the station-master's office. Very early in the morning, the station-master woke him and brought him down to the dock and pointed to the waiting vessel. It was not a stately craft. In fact, it wasn't a passenger ship at all, but a kind of rough-and-ready transport for ferrying workers going to and from Britain. The only seats were hard wooden benches.

Despite the horrible fittings and his fear of being sick again, Miroslav had no trouble sleeping on one of the benches as the boat sailed back to Ireland on that chilly wet July night in 1947. As he slept, he dreamed of eating carp and maybe even goose at home in Držkov at Christmas, only a few months away.

# Part Two

# IRELAND

# The Factory That Wasn't There

The Rosslare ferry docked in Ireland on a wet and drizzly morning. Miroslav's fellow travellers, workers all, disappeared quickly. Miroslav wondered what he should do next. His first realisation was that he was not, in fact, in Rosslare. The name of the port, a strange agglomeration of unfamiliar letters, was Dun Laoghaire (Dunleary). 'This was not mentioned in my travel instructions,' he recalls. For someone raised in a language where every word is pronounced exactly as it is written, the Gaelic name of this Irish port just south of Dublin was especially puzzling. He immediately suspected that he and his station-master friend must have had some kind of misunderstanding about how to get to Waterford, but it was too late to worry about that.

He had no idea where he was. He stood on the quayside for a long time and watched trains coming from and going to various destinations. Finally, with more frantic gesticulations and pointing to his home-made label, he was somehow directed to a train going south to Rosslare. He scrambled aboard as the little three-carriage steam train was leaving, and was never asked to produce a ticket. He felt that his weight had dropped so much on his three-day odyssey that even the railway officials must be afraid to approach him. He describes himself as having resembled 'a skeleton on the run'.

When Miroslav got to Rosslare, having slept most of the way, he saw that there were only two rail lines at the station. He assumed that the other line ran to Waterford and he got on the first train to depart on that line. He was so tired by now that he was operating by intuition rather than the exhausting process of asking for help.

The last leg of the journey did indeed take this bewildered young Czech man from Rosslare to the city of Waterford. The steam train was ramshackle (diesel locomotives would not arrive in Ireland for another four years), and his first waking impressions of Ireland were disheartening. As the train took a long rest in the shabby village of Campile, Miroslav wondered what kind of country he'd arrived in. When the train moved on, stone walls and small cottages passed him by, and the rain seemed relentless. Where were the bananas and the oranges and the peaches? The train stopped on a couple of occasions to load cattle onto some of the rail wagons, or sometimes to allow a herd of farm animals to cross the tracks. The pace of life as he watched it through the dirty train windows seemed to make Držkov resemble Paris.

Finally he stepped off the train at what seemed to Miroslav to be the end of the world – Waterford. Again, he was at a place where there was hardly a soul to be seen. Nobody was there to greet him. The railway station stood in the same place it stands today, except that it was an earlier, uglier version. Waterford, at that time, was an important departure city for emigrants, especially via the Rosslare train line, but on that afternoon it was as if everyone who could leave had already left.

The weather was misty and drizzly, not a trace of sunshine in the sky, as Miroslav emerged, hungry and exhausted, from the station. There were no taxis or any other visible means of public transport. Directly in front of the station, he saw the city's creaking Redmond Bridge across the River Suir (a river said to be as wide as the Thames at London and the Seine at Paris). The bridge had been declared obsolete in 1943 but would only be replaced forty years later. 'Okay, Miroslav,' he said to himself. 'Go over that bridge and see what it is all about here.' The bridge took him to what looked like the main part of the town, snaking along the broad quays on the other side. He remembers catching a glimpse as he crossed the bridge of the nearby historic Clock Tower.

The streets were whispery quiet, apart from the occasional clip-clop of a horse and cart or, much more rarely, the sight of a car. It was 1947 – Ireland had been left out of the Americans' grand plan for post-war aid, and the country was still poor, agricultural and dominated by the spectre of emigration. Almost at the corner where the bridge opened onto the first of the quays, Miroslav came upon an establishment called 'Breen's Hotel', a decrepit building but a welcome sight to the weary traveller.

Today, the same hotel stands in glory over the refurbished quay district, but that is not how Miroslav first viewed it nearly sixty years ago. 'They saw that I was nearly gone,' he says of the hotel staff, and they told him to go upstairs and rest in one of the rooms. He did so, not entirely certain how he would pay for this pleasure, and slept restlessly for the remainder of the day and through the night, wondering all the time about Franta and Anna, about Rosa, about Umprum, about all the things that he had so recently taken for granted.

In the morning, breakfast was served in the little dining room. It was late July, but a coal fire burned merrily in the fireplace. He was offered a bowl of porridge, but couldn't even look at this mysterious gruel. Sausages and rashers came next, another novelty. But he tucked in ravenously, even though the piece of bacon was (he still recalls) too tiny for the human eye. The eager waitress poured him his first Irish 'cup of tea', but ruined it by then putting milk into the cup, an idea that offended him. For Franta, a cup of tea was always an excuse for a liberal dose of rum, and even for the more restrained Anna and her only son, tea was accompanied only by a small slice of lemon. He sipped the tea nervously, put it aside as a horrendous mistake, and his first cup of tea was never finished. When he later wrote to Anna about his maiden Irish breakfast, she replied that she was happy that he was getting to eat some foreign 'delicacies'.

After breakfast, the manager of the hotel asked Miroslav if he would be staying. Exactly how this exchange occurred is impossible to figure out, but once again Miroslav resorted to his home-made label. There was much chatter among the staff, but eventually Miroslav figured out that nobody at the hotel had ever heard of any thing or place called 'Waterford Glass'. Waterford in 1947 was a much smaller, more compact place then it is today, and certainly the presence of a glass factory would not have escaped the notice of the staff of the largest hotel on the city's main street.

Miroslav Havel must have cut a strange and exotic figure as he walked the streets of Waterford in search of Charles Bačik and his glass-making facility. As he stopped people and pointed to his trusty label, he was greeted with no information but plenty of amazement. Men, women, and children were fascinated by his unusual garb, which indeed had probably caused a trail of bewilderment from the time he arrived in Dover. Miroslav was decked out in plus-fours – shortened trousers worn with very high and colourful knee socks. His socks were a kind of burnt yellow and his plus-fours sported a garish plaid pattern. His gleaming black shoes had fancy buckles and bright silver buttons along the side. On his head, he wore a floppy plaid hat, more like a beret than an Irish farmer's cap. All of this was proper attire in the spa towns of western Bohemia, but in Ireland he had managed to acquire the look of a leprechaun come to life.

The children danced around him and pointed gleefully at his trousers and shoes. Miroslav, always a man with a keen sense of the absurd, laughed along. But he was getting no closer to his destination. Nobody had heard of Mr Bačik or of 'Waterford Glass'. He began to think that it was time to head back across the bridge.

Miroslav was surprised by how poor the inner city seemed to be. There was a general air of shabbiness and deprivation everywhere he walked. He saw many little low terraced houses in narrow streets. Many of the children went barefoot because leather was in such great shortage. No new public housing had been built by the Waterford City Corporation since 1941. Moreover, at the time Miroslav arrived in the city, there was a tuberculosis epidemic in the urban slums – an epidemic that would take most of the next decade to eradicate.

However, he found the people he met to be co-operative and friendly, and he persisted in his quest, always pointing to his home-made label and stumbling through some of the basic English he was now starting to pick up. He spoke decent German, but was afraid to use it in those difficult post-war times.

On his second day, he decided to explore some of the areas beyond the inner city. He walked west toward Ballytruckle, the location of the Ursuline Convent (a big local landmark at the time) and then turned south across empty fields where today lie the built-up residential districts of Newtown and Johnstown and St John's Park. Finally, he spotted, standing on a hill across some wet ground, a large and elegant red-brick building with a turret and an arched glass roof, and, lo and behold, a chimney rising at one side. There was no paved street leading to this grand and beautiful building, and so he endured his sparkling shoes being splattered with mud as he walked across the soggy field. There was a large paved square in front of the building, lined with benches. A few older men and women were sitting on the benches, some expressionless like mummies, some gesticulating wildly with their hands. When he approached them, they moved away. What an odd glass factory, Miroslav thought, and no sound of any machinery.

Suddenly a man in a white coat appeared before the gazing stranger, asking the inevitable question, 'Who are you looking for?'

Miroslav gathered what the man had said, and pointed once again to his label: 'I look for that,' he said, ungrammatically but accurately.

'Well, it's not here,' came the sharp retort. Obviously, the white-coated man caught some of Miroslav's heavy accent, and asked him if he were German. Miroslav nodded affirmatively, not wanting to enter into a discourse on the great distinctions between Germans and Czechs.

The man ran off and came back with another white-coated official. This second man spoke reasonably good German, and revealed to Miroslav that he and his colleague were doctors and that the beautiful structure behind them was a psychiatric hospital, St Otteran's, one of the largest institutions of its kind in Ireland. Miroslav was taken aback, but also secretly and desperately hoping as he asked his vital question, '*Kennen Sie Herr Bačik?*' ('Do you know

Mr Bačik?'), that his former boss was not in fact a patient at this asylum.

To Miroslav's great relief, the doctor had indeed heard of Charles Bačik, and certainly not as a patient. 'I know this man fairly well,' said the doctor in his earnest German. 'We sometimes go for lunch together to the Savoy restaurant and I practise my German with him.'

'I know what he is doing here,' the doctor added helpfully. 'Look, you go back the way you just came here, to Ballytruckle. Go to the soccer pitch there, and next to that pitch you will find a little green shed, and that's where the glass factory will be built.'

Miroslav was puzzled by this emphatic use of the future tense. 'You mean there is no glass factory?' he asked.

Without remotely appreciating the effect of this information on the young foreigner, the doctor informed him that a glass factory would be built there and that he had seen 'about ten people' doing something there in the previous few months.

So, Miroslav left the grounds of St Otteran's and trudged back to Ballytruckle, mystified by the doctor's words. Along the way, he spotted what indeed looked like a soccer pitch, and at its edge, as the prophet had predicted, a small green shed. Walking towards the shed, which looked like the kind of simple wooden structure builders put up on a new site, he noticed a home-made sign that bore the stark and unforgettable words, 'Glass factory to be built here'. He was exhausted now, his legs were weak, and he could hardly remember when he had last eaten a decent meal – he discounted the porridge and the sausages and bacon and the vile tea. He saw some men gathered around a pile of concrete blocks, no doubt contemplating the mysteries of how to build a glass factory, and pointed one more time to his label. Pointing in response, they directed him to the shed, located just a few metres away.

As Miroslav approached the little green shed, he saw through a small window the unmistakable profile of his once and future collaborator, Charles Bačik. Miroslav was twenty-five then and Bačik was about forty, and Miroslav remembers what a handsome and striking figure the older man was, although his tall frame looked ridiculously cramped inside the shed. In these fateful few moments, with Miroslav peering in through the window and Bačik sitting inside his builder's shed in deep concentration, the future 'Waterford Crystal' was truly born.

Bačik looked up from the table where he was studying a document, and found himself staring back through the small window at his former intern from Světlá. As Miroslav recalls it, Bačik looked as if he had been struck by lightning. 'It took some time before he realised that it was me, Havel from Czechoslovakia, tired, unshaved, and many pounds lighter,' Miroslav remembers.

The older man rushed out, shook hands vigorously, and pronounced that the starving Czech student looked like a corpse. 'Mr Havel, we have been looking for you everywhere,' Bačik exclaimed. 'We were checking the airport and the harbour and the trains for two days and there was no sign of you. We even called the police. I knew that you were on the way, and I was worried that you had disappeared somewhere.'

But then Bačik moved quickly to a more pressing matter. 'We must eat,' he pronounced, scanning the skinny frame of his guest. The two men, speaking in animated Czech, got into Bačik's small Ford car and drove back down to the town centre for a meal at Bačik's favourite haunt, the Savoy Restaurant on Barronstrand Street in the middle of the city. The meal, Miroslav remembers, was a godsend. And the sun came out, revealing 'a brighter side of Waterford'.

Miroslav hardly had time to bring up the subject now occupying his thoughts – where was the much-heralded glass factory? – before Bačik launched into a discussion of his activities since coming to Waterford. They talked and talked all afternoon, and Miroslav got his first pieces of information about what would be happening during his own three-month stay in what was then Ireland's fourth-largest city.

Through contacts in Waterford Corporation, Bačik had managed to get a lease for three acres of land at Ballytruckle. For about a month, he had been supervising the construction of a small cutting factory on that property. He had hired a solicitor to obtain trademarks for the names 'Waterford Glass', 'Waterford Crystal', and even 'Waterford Technical Factory'. Miroslav was quietly amused that Bačik, still almost a total newcomer in Ireland, was already busy making and using contacts.

Bačik told Miroslav that when he had first arrived in Ireland, in late 1946, he had noticed that there was a town called 'Carlow' about eighty kilometres south-west of Dublin. 'Carlow' struck him as not dissimilar to 'Karlov', the name he had given to his factory in Světlá, and indeed also somewhat resembled his Czech first name, 'Karel'. The connection between Karlov and Karel and Carlow was so intuitively appealing that he proposed to Bernard Fitzpatrick that he open his new factory in that midlands town. But Fitzpatrick rejected the idea out of hand. 'You can't go into the middle of the country – it's all farming,' he told his future business partner. 'You have to go to Waterford – that's where the glass was made.' Thus died the possibility of a great worldwide brand name called Carlow Crystal.

Bačik assured Miroslav that he was also in the process of contacting some of his past customers in Europe, and hoped to open for business very soon. He had plans to install six cutting machines and one engraving machine, and to run a fairly tight but efficient operation.

'How many people are working with you now?' Miroslav asked naively.

'There's just you,' Bačik replied, without a trace of humour.

# 'A Man in the Air'

Being philosophical about it, Miroslav was relieved to discover that Mr Bačik was not in the asylum, and that he did have his own builder's shed and a plan for some kind of new factory. Three months of this might actually be somewhat interesting and amusing, and he would have a good story to tell his parents – although he felt sure that Franta would be wearing his smuggest 'of course I could have told you' expression.

Bačik paid to put him up at Breen's Hotel for another few days, and then he took his little suitcase to Portree House, a guesthouse on Mary Street where he expected to stay (despite the expense) for the remainder of this three-month visit to Waterford. Compared to what he found at the glass factory site, or in the city at large, the little guesthouse was luxurious. The lodgers were almost all working in local banks, and the place had an air of quiet prosperity. Here, at mealtimes, he immediately began his training in English, learning important phrases such as 'pass the salt' and 'pass the pepper'. He attributes the slow progress he made in English to his terrible hearing.

Meanwhile, Miroslav gradually began to figure out the pieces of the strange puzzle. As mentioned earlier, Bačik had made contact with the Fitzpatrick family – in particular with Bernard Fitzpatrick and his brother Hugh, a prominent solicitor, who turned out to be the legal agent who had secured the trademarks requested by Bačik.

The Fitzpatricks were successful entrepreneurs in a bleak economy, and had widely dispersed business interests. But their main income came from a high-profile jewellery shop in Dublin. The Fitzpatricks had good business connections, too, including a beer and lemonade wholesaler in Limerick who was prepared to put some money into a new glass-making operation.

Bačik told Miroslav in August 1947 that Bernard Fitzpatrick and his associates had invested £5,000, but that he himself had matched that figure through sales of some crates of glass he had smuggled out of Czechoslovakia. But Bačik had also managed to get a loan of £10,000, based on a life insurance policy. A loan like that, for a speculative industrial enterprise, was highly unusual.

Putting all of these sources of funding together, the share capital of the new Waterford Glass at its inception was in the region of £20,000. As Edith Bačik herself often said to Miroslav, her husband was a proud, stubborn and determined man, and many times in those early months he confessed to Miroslav how much he wanted to keep the kind of independence and control in Ireland that he had enjoyed at Světlá. Bačik was well aware that the Fitzpatricks had capital to invest in his new glass venture, and already he was afraid that they might seize too much control. But, from what Miroslav could tell from his first months in Ireland, Bačik seemed to have enough working capital to run his Waterford factory with little outside interference.

The Bačik plan was to develop the 'little spot', as he called it, on which sat the builder's shed that had been his office since his arrival in Waterford. But a plan to construct an entire glass-making factory in a poor Irish city, and to produce sellable products in that factory, was intimidating not only to the Fitzpatricks, but even to Bačik himself. What kind of glass could be produced? Where were the craftsmen who would produce it? Where would this product be sold?

Even Bernard Fitzpatrick, who was well-acquainted with the luxury goods market through his jewellery business, and who also had strong connections to the Irish manufacturing sector, was hard-pressed to provide answers to these tricky questions. One thing seemed certain to everybody – production of heavily-cut lead crystal, the signature product of the old Waterford industry, was impossible for the foreseeable future.

Bačik's immediate plan to get the operation up and running involved importing pre-made glass and then doing some simple cutting. He was definitely not thinking of anything as elaborate as molten glass in furnaces and craftsman blowers. In September 1947, he started to import cheap uncut soda glass which was manufactured by a company he had encountered while travelling in Belgium during his term as chief of the Bohemian glass industry.

Miroslav, meanwhile, started to work on some designs that might be used to decorate the imported soda glass. This kind of glass is produced by fusing sand, sodium carbonate and limestone. It is primarily used in making bottles, electric light bulbs, and window glass. Soda glass is truly at the other end of the quality scale from heavy crystal, being both thin-walled and without lustre. The brilliancy and hardness of crystal glass is produced from a much higher grade of sand, as well as potash and red lead in place of soda and limestone.

Before Miroslav's arrival, Bačik had originally expected that a good part of the new factory's production could be sourced in continental Europe. But only two years after the war, Europe's economies were still lethargic, very few factories were operating at full speed, and those that were wanted cash in advance before making a single piece.

With Miroslav now in Ireland, however, Bačik expected to be able to use his young Czech expert to train some local apprentices with the skills to apply simple cuts (crosses and zigzags) to the imported glass. Miroslav persuaded Bačik that some of the designs he was working on for the soda glass, including shapes he thought might be distinctive for Waterford Glass, should be produced in the Belgian factory. Although Bačik wanted only to import pre-made standard blank glass pieces and to have them cut and possibly also engraved in Waterford, he did agree to send some of Miroslav's designs to Belgium. But none of them was ever produced.

Miroslav, in fact, had plenty to do as the factory emerged. During construction, he pitched in and helped the builders to lift concrete blocks. He even sometimes applied mortar, a probable violation of union rules. Meanwhile, his room in the Mary Street guesthouse was festooned with Belgian-made decanters and jugs and salad bowls for which he was trying to think up basic easy-to-execute designs. He knew that it would be impossible to put fancy cuts on this kind of cheap glass, which is brittle and impure compared to the fine lead crystal that would later be produced at Waterford. He was also continuing to sketch much more ambitious designs for future production, although not without some sense of frustration. He was already thinking in a rather abstract way about the idea of reviving some of the exquisite old Waterford patterns that Bačik was always talking about, but he knew that none of that would be possible without a specialised team of master cutters.

By the middle of August 1947, Bačik had somehow managed to smuggle a single cutting machine from Czechoslovakia, supplementing the single engraving machine he had shipped to Ireland before his escape. Miroslav was actually starting to do some work on both machines, but of course the two men realised that the production process required more than just Miroslav doing everything from designing to packing the finished glasses, with Bačik supervising imperially from his little office. Moreover, while they might be able to get by with just one engraving machine, they needed more cutting machines. Bačik made contact with an iron foundry in Cork which he knew did some impressive casting work, and he sent the cutting machine down to Cork to see if the foundry could make six replicas.

The Cork company was delighted with the order, and executed it with such perfection that the cast machines even had the original Czechoslovak manufacturer's name and the phrase 'Made in Czechoslovakia' emblazoned along the sides (ignoring all the laws of intellectual property). Miroslav was at the site when the foundry's lorry arrived with the six machines. Always ready to volunteer, he picked up a crate containing one of the machines and tried to carry it on his back to the nearby cutting floor. Within seconds he had collapsed under the unexpected weight, and barely avoided dropping the crate and smashing the machine. As he sat, bent over on the ground in pain, an unsympathetic Bačik arrived and asked him what was wrong.

'I cannot straighten up,' Miroslav shouted in Czech.

The older man then grabbed him by the back of the neck and yanked him to his feet. 'That's the best way to recover,' Bačik said to his wounded soldier. Mr Bačik's management style, Miroslav realised, was not for the faint of heart.

Bačik rewarded Mr Havel, his sole employee, with a princely £3. 8s. a week in wages, which Miroslav thought was quite decent money from a company that was producing absolutely nothing. 'I was straight away given enough money to sweeten my life,' he recalls.

Miroslav spent this income lavishly. In his very first week, he purchased a crisply tailored navy-blue blazer at the local haberdashery for £2, thinking that he would need to show Franta and Anna at Christmas that his trip had produced at least one tangible result. He also wrote to Rosa that he planned to fly back to Prague from London, despite the added expense, because he just didn't want to face all those ferries and trains. He probably could just about have managed the cost of the flight. The general cost of living at the time was very low, and Miroslav indulged himself in an occasional beer at two pennies (2d) a pint, or a ticket for the Regal Cinema, Waterford's finest, for about 3d.

Miroslav continued to come to the factory construction site every day. Even as work progressed on building the little factory, he was already counting the days until his three-month stay would be over and he would head to Rosslare and the journey home. Life had turned out to be fairly easy for him at Bačik's factory. Most of his time was spent helping out in construction, doodling new designs, and playing with the engraving and cutting machines.

However, at the beginning of September 1947, Bačik suffered a ruptured appendix and was forced to spend an extended period of over a month recuperating at the County and City Infirmary hospital, the old Waterford fever hospital. It was a debilitating and dangerous condition, especially given medical knowledge at the time. Edith Bačik, no doubt acting on the strict instructions of her ever-vigilant husband, begged Miroslav to extend his visit to Waterford until Charles could get back on his feet. She told Miroslav that she had four children to look after and pleaded with him to stay at least another month. And she had one more enticement to seal the deal. She informed Miroslav that her husband was already making preparations to build a real melting and blowing room. 'I cannot tell you any details,' she said. 'It's all just on paper right now, but I promise you he is going to do it.'

So, not only was Miroslav's conscience pricked by Edith's heartfelt appeal as a mother with babes-in-arms, but he was also encouraged by the real possibility that Bačik was going to do something more with the factory than simple cuts on cheap Belgian soda blanks. He also knew that the factory operation needed immediate attention, including recruitment of some apprentices and the ongoing work on the actual construction.

Miroslav agreed to stay and became the effective boss of the little Ballytruckle operation for the next two months or so, running up to November 1947. Every day, after work, he cycled the eleven kilometres to Tramore, the nearby seaside town where the Bačik family lived, to give Edith a report of the day's events. Then he cycled all the way back again to Waterford. He admired Edith immensely. She was a strong woman, he recalls, absolutely determined that 'Charlie's business' would not fail just as it was coming to life.

A few days after he started his exhausting regime of daytime boss and evening reporter, he put a classified ad in a local newspaper, the venerable *Munster Express*, offering £1 a week for someone to help with the administrative work of running the new factory. Edith drafted the text of the ad in perfect English. Only one person, a man named Tom Kennedy, answered the call. He showed up at the famous builder's shed on 29 September 1947, and found Miroslav, now sitting in the place of Mr Bačik. 'Give me one pound a week and I will do anything around here,' was how he stated his qualifications. Miroslav, struck by the man's sincerity, hired him to take over the administrative work that he and Bačik had been doing on their own. Tom Kennedy was Waterford Glass's first employee (other than Miroslav himself), and later rose to become a cutter and then a senior foreman.

By the time Bačik returned to work in November, Miroslav had hired six Irish apprentices and had set about giving them some basic training in cutting on the machines from Cork. Despite Bačik's continued fretting about the absence of high-skilled employees other than Miroslav, using master cutters to work on cheap soda blanks would have been absurd. And so, to find these new apprentices, Miroslav had not used any newspaper advertisements. Rather, with Edith's backing, he had gone to the Central Technical Institute on Parnell Street and recruited four young men (aged about sixteen or older) to work in the new factory. He also hired two other youngsters from a technical school in Wexford that Bačik had recommended. Edith had coached him in making his appeal at both schools, and everything he said was written out for him in bold capitals on a large piece of paper.

In the climate of the times, with jobs so scarce, the youngsters were willing to overlook Miroslav's halting knowledge of English and to focus on the intriguing opportunity he was offering. The Waterford city boys also had to overlook the objections of one of the local priests, who warned their parents against putting the sons of Éireann into the hands of these 'foreigners' at the new factory. Miroslav heard about this later from the apprentices themselves. It would not be the last time he picked up a current of anti-foreigner bias, particularly among the Roman Catholic clergy. But, at least at that very early stage in the factory's history, he could understand the thinking behind what the priest was saying. 'Nobody in Waterford knew who we were,' he recollects. 'Except the people at the Savoy restaurant where Mr Bačik and I went for our meals almost every day.'

To try to sustain his small pool of local Irish talent, Miroslav took a part-time appointment to teach glass design at the Technical Institute. Many students from his class would go on to become apprentices at the growing factory. Occasionally Bačik would come to the class to lecture in glass technology. To publicise his new course, Miroslav held a small exhibition of his work at the Municipal Art Gallery in early December 1947. Here is how the event was announced in a local newspaper, the *Waterford News*:

> Announcing an Art Exhibition at the Municipal Art Gallery, December 1st, 1947, of three engraved vases by M. Havel, who is the technician in charge of the new Waterford Glass factory and who also gives instruction in glass cutting in the Central Technical Institute.

Miroslav had no illusions about how much work his early apprentices could do, but he thought that these young Irish lads proved themselves to be 'quite acceptable, showing really good talent for cutting'. And at least they had plenty of glass blanks on which to experiment. In the last few months of 1947, hundreds of boxes containing Belgian glass blanks had arrived at the Ballytruckle site. There were lots of conical tumblers and tulip vases. Miroslav had the unpleasant job of opening all of the boxes and stacking the glasses in neat rows along shelves built on the upper floor of the new factory building.

Bačik's use of uncut glass blanks had the distinct advantage (learned from the Fitzpatricks before him) that he never had to pay duties on the imported glass. For customs purposes, the glass was classified as unfinished and therefore duty-exempt. Miroslav was not entirely sure that the glass was being properly classified as 'unfinished', as he found many pieces where a fancy pattern had already been cut onto part of the glass. Was more cutting to be added in Ireland? Unlikely, Miroslav thought, because the Waterford company lacked the experienced cutters who could do it. In any event, he never approached Bačik with these concerns. It was not his role to enforce the Irish customs and excise laws.

In those infant days of the factory, Bačik was 'full of troubles', Miroslav recalls. But he still held on to his long-term vision, which

Miroslav always encouraged. The older man wanted to recreate his earlier success in building the Světlá business. He wanted a real glass-production operation at Waterford, with the in-house melting and blowing capability that Edith had promised Miroslav. Relying for his output on glass blanks imported from somewhere else, which would then be 'cut over' in Waterford, was not going to satisfy him for very long.

Bačik and Miroslav were busily collecting catalogues from other factories in continental Europe, but their ambition in Ireland was that ultimately Waterford-made crystal would not be anything like the highly coloured French, German or Czech glass. They were looking for a niche in a market heavily dominated by existing German, French, Czech and even English glass-makers. By the mid-twentieth century, the world glass-making industry was quite mature, and 'a lot of things had already been done', according to Miroslav. The huge emigration of Continental craftsmen to the United States, for one thing, meant that America, Bernard Fitzpatrick's big target market, already had a tremendous indigenous crystal glass industry and strong traditions in elaborate blowing, cutting and engraving.

The two men had an obvious place to turn to for inspiration – their common background in Bohemian crystal. But Miroslav's years of training in Železny Brod and Prague had convinced him of the aesthetic limitations of his native product. He disliked its preference for very tiny cuts, its mixture of highly polished and unpolished designs on the same piece, and, most of all, its obsession with cutting intricate patterns onto every part of the glass surface, leaving little or no empty space to provide a visual contrast to the decorative design. Nor did the Czechs pay enough attention, in Miroslav's opinion, to the shape of the glass as a design feature in itself. Still, from a business perspective, the idea of sticking to what they knew made some sense. Bačik had his eye on former customers in Germany and Czechoslovakia, and he wondered whether Irish-made 'Bohemian' crystal might have an unusual marketing appeal. So he thought long and hard about contacting his old customers, and about re-starting his Světlá business – including all of his old designs – from scratch in Ireland.

Miroslav seems to have won the argument, in part because Bačik was still quite weak after his recent illness and therefore not quite as dogmatic as he might usually have been. Miroslav felt that anything that imitated the mainstream production of European glass would be dismissed as derivative. He pressed Bačik to take advantage of the existing traditions in the British Isles, and to try to base the new factory's production on the patterns produced by the old Irish factories, including Waterford, throughout the eighteenth century and into the nineteenth century. Bačik and Bernard Fitzpatrick again discussed this idea, which of course Fitzpatrick had always thought would give 'new' Waterford a distinctive marketing edge among the American Irish.

Fitzpatrick liked the concept of reaching out to the huge multi-generational market in the United States with a luxury product that would have the resonance of the homeland. Some of those glasses were still circulating in antique shops and fetching high prices at auctions. Auctions attract affluent people, and clearly old Waterford had managed to retain a good deal of luxury cachet.

The two men agreed that a little research needed to be done. Someone would have to find out everything that was available about the old Waterford production. Other than some chandeliers in the local chamber of commerce building (and chandeliers were very far from the minds of these would-be glass-makers in 1947), there were no easily available old Waterford specimens in the city of Waterford itself. In fact, it was no longer possible to determine, without pure guesswork, even where the old Penrose glass factory had been located in the city.

Two questions presented themselves, therefore, to the entrepreneurial team of Fitzpatrick and Bačik. How would this research be done? And who would be their researcher? As to the latter, inevitably they looked once more to their only skilled employee. The research that Miroslav would do, they decided, would be possible only at the National Museum of Ireland in

Dublin, where some of the old Waterford glasses were on display in the Museum's permanent collection. The only other option – sending Miroslav by ocean liner to inspect the old Waterford collections that Fitzpatrick knew were in the private homes of rich Philadelphians – was financially and logistically unthinkable.

The Museum's collection was by no means the most comprehensive, Miroslav recalls, but it was certainly representative of the old Waterford tradition. Fitzpatrick, like Bačik, was a man with interesting connections. He used these connections to arrange that the actual crystal exhibits would be taken out of their display cabinets at the National Museum and placed in front of the visiting Czech artist in a small windowless room in the bowels of the building.

Miroslav was always a master counterfeiter when he needed to be, and he carefully measured each piece and created perfect full-scale drawings of every one of the dozens of items of antique crystal that he inspected. The process was painstaking, not only because of Miroslav's excruciatingly accurate work, but also because each piece had to be brought separately from its display or storage case, and then returned, before the next piece would be brought to Miroslav's underground lair. As far as Miroslav could tell the Museum itself did not have a single sketch in its records.

Miroslav's scholarly sojourn at the Museum is one of his favourite reminiscences from those early days. He spent three weeks there from mid-January to early February 1948, and came several times for shorter periods after that for a total of nearly three months. When he was at the Museum, he felt very much like the dusty academic researcher he had sometimes imagined he would one day become. He arrived at opening time and stayed until closing, never leaving his sketching room, and eating only in the evenings. He not only sketched the glasses, but he also held them in his hands to scrutinise the depth and dexterity of each type of cut and how particular types of cutting were combined to execute old Waterford's exquisitely detailed patterns.

When Miroslav first saw the collection at the Museum, he told the curator that he assumed that the pieces must be of Continental origin. However, he was informed that most of the pieces were surviving relics of a Waterford factory that had shut down a century before. The cutting certainly resembled Continental cutting, he thought, but the shine from the glass seemed to him to be much brighter than the Bohemian glass with which he was most familiar, and the complex patterning of the precise and very deep cuts was also quite distinctive.

The young designer was so amazed and thrilled to discover the Waterford glass heritage that he delved into the company's history, reading some of the Museum's books on the subject of the early Waterford glass business. He learned of how two English Quaker brothers, George and William Penrose, had opened the glass factory that put Waterford city's name on the map of world commerce from 1783 to 1851.

The Penroses were rich glass-making merchants who decided to move their business to Ireland to avoid excise taxes on the export of English-made glass imposed under war legislation passed in 1777. They came to Waterford because of its excellent port facilities. Other English businessmen later established centres of glass-making in Dublin, Cork and Belfast.

The Penroses had no knowledge of glass themselves, but they brought with them their own glass-making expert, Worcestershireman John Hill. Hill recruited as many as seventy of his fellow English craftsmen to come to Waterford, then developed the glass compounds and designs, and directed the whole manufacturing process. The Penrose factory kept going under their successors until 1851, but the extension of the war taxes to Ireland eventually destroyed the Irish crystal industry. As he reflected on all of this rich history, Miroslav could be forgiven for imagining the parallels to his own situation as the resident non-Irish expert for the twentieth-century Penroses – Messrs Bačik and Fitzpatrick.

While Miroslav sketched and read, he contemplated how the flamboyantly ornate designs and closely interlaced cuts of his eighteenth-century predecessors could be adapted, as he says, 'for normal cutting'. And he felt just a twinge of excitement that he was joining Bačik and Fitzpatrick in a bold attempt to reclaim a wonderful heritage that had been dormant or, more accurately, dead for a long century – even though he was determined that he himself would be heading back to Czechoslovakia within a very few months.

Before Christmas, Miroslav had arranged with Umprum to get a three-month extension of his academic leave of absence. Professor Štipl, agreeable as always to practical experience for his best students, imposed only one condition on the extension – he instructed Miroslav to bring back samples of his work at the new Bačik factory so that he could be given academic credit for it.

This suggestion alarmed Miroslav rather than comforted him. Some simple cuts on cheap Belgian soda glass would be unlikely to impress Maestro Štipl. So Miroslav called to a number of the local primary schools to find an art teacher who might have some good ideas about indigenous Irish art and design which might impress his teachers in Prague. Through this almost desperate effort, he came into contact with a local Waterford painter and sculptor, Robert Burke. Together, the two men set off on various field trips to make tracings of Celtic Revival designs that Burke had discovered through many years of patient investigation in some of the old cemeteries around County Waterford and south County Kilkenny. 'This will give you a good sense of the disks and circles of our Celtic tradition,' Burke told his eager new student.

That was fine in theory, but in practice it subjected Miroslav once again to Ireland's native muddiness, as he traipsed through overgrown damp graveyards and crouched down on his knees, making tracings of moss-encrusted old stones. Determined to stay on Professor Štipl's good side, Miroslav also took some sculpture classes at the Technical Institute, and later wrote a long paper describing the history of old Waterford Glass and his reconnaissance mission to the National Museum of Ireland.

However, Umprum's benevolence was not all that Miroslav needed in terms of official permission to remain in Ireland. His exit visa from Czechoslovakia was also set to expire, and he needed his passport endorsed with the terms of his academic extension. He was also getting ready to go back permanently to Czechoslovakia at the end of the next Umprum extension, and he wanted all his papers in order. At the end of January 1948, he travelled again to Dublin with his passport to get the endorsement from the Czechoslovak resident consul-general, a gruff and bureaucratic ex-army general who styled himself 'chief of the consular office'. Miroslav, feeling good about how he had organised his affairs, showed the consular chief the Umprum extension, accompanied by letters from Professor Štipl and the school director. He asked for a permit to validate the extra months he was spending in Ireland. The chief, however, was not willing to take responsibility for this apparently unprecedented request. 'We are not in a position to do anything here,' he told Miroslav. 'You must send your passport to London.'

Miroslav was much displeased by this lack of service from one of the few other Czechs then present in Ireland, but he did as the chief told him and sent his passport to the Czechoslovak Embassy in London. In early February, the Embassy returned the passport to him, without the requested endorsement and without even a letter of explanation for its absence. He sensed that he was in a 'spot of trouble', as he puts it, and went back to the consulate in Dublin. 'Leave it with me,' declared the chief, demonstrating just a little more sympathy. 'I will see what we can do about it.'

Miroslav was naturally reluctant to surrender his only proof of identity or citizenship, particularly with news coming from Czechoslovakia of an increasingly aggressive Communist infiltration of the government. But he felt that he had no choice. That was the last time he laid eyes on his passport. The middle of February rolled around, and Miroslav was growing anxious as the days and weeks kept ticking by with no word from Dublin, London, or even (something he half-expected) from the Ministry of External Affairs in Prague. He did receive a letter from Rosa, though, in which she reminded him of his assurance to her in December that he would be on the 9.30 a.m. train from Prague to Světlá on 28 February – a promise he had written in a mad moment of optimism and which he now regretted.

Then, 'boom!' – as he puts it – the Communists seized control of the central government and national assembly of Czechoslovakia in a long-threatened peaceful coup d'état that was all but completed by the end of that month of February 1948. President Beneš departed, and Communist leader Klement Gottwald began the process of taking over every aspect of state life through a network of purge committees. A new constitution in May 1948 gave legal recognition to the pre-eminence of the Communist Party, all industry was nationalised, and party membership doubled by May 1949.

When the takeover occurred, all passports of the old Czechoslovak Republic were voided, and the one-man consulate in Dublin was immediately closed. The consul-general simply abandoned his post and fled with his wife to the United States. Like many of his counterparts from the old order, he recognised that going home would expose his family to the unpredictable risks of a new elite bent on purging its predecessors.

Shortly afterwards, the building that housed the Dublin consulate mysteriously burned down. The only thing saved was a grand piano. Miroslav knows that the piano survived because he later saw it, to his astonishment, immaculately installed in Bačik's living-room. Apparently, the Bačiks were quite friendly with the consul-general's wife, and somehow had managed to get custody of the consulate's only showpiece before she and her husband decamped to America.

Nevertheless, Miroslav was left in the exact position he had feared – stateless and without a provable identity. The Communists had taken over the whole country. He was, as he now recalls, 'high and dry', without anything except the navy-blue blazer he had bought for going home at Christmas. The whole process of getting his passport back was now 'dead as a stone', he recalls. He didn't know where his passport was, much less how to get it back.

Whether it would have made any difference if he had held on to his old passport is hard to say. The point was that he now had no papers whatsoever. He knew, like the consul-general himself knew in his own situation, that if he tried to go home in these new circumstances he would be treated badly in the turmoil of the Revolution. Very likely, as the son of an accused bourgeois, he would have been thrown in jail on some trumped-up desertion charge.

Even Rosa, who so much wanted him back, warned him in letters immediately after the coup that if he were to come home now, 'they won't ever let you go out again'. A lawyer friend of Rosa's told her that 'If I were in Mirek's shoes, I would not come back.' On 15 March, according to Rosa's letter of the following day, the Communist government announced that all Czechoslovak students outside the country should return home regardless of when their permits expired, or risk being imprisoned for treason if they ever did try to return. Rosa expressed herself plainly: 'If you do not return now, you will never come back ... think about it carefully ... if you think this will change quickly you are mistaken.'

In 1950, Rosa reported to Miroslav that her own brother, who had been assigned to a mining labour camp to break stones, had been jailed for trying to flee across the border to West Germany. Under Communism, nobody could be considered 'unemployed' and these labour camps were rapidly becoming the official method of disguising unemployment.

Miroslav was well aware from newspaper reports of how the new Czechoslovak government treated its enemies – those who stayed, and those who wanted to come back. Nevertheless, he began what would become a decades-long campaign of writing letters to Czechoslovak government leaders, always asking for a passport or at least permission to go home. He wrote letters directly to Czechoslovakia's new Communist president, Klement Gottwald, and to Gottwald's successor, Antonin Zapotocky. He wrote these letters in his flawless classical Czech, and then he re-wrote them and re-wrote them again, always trying to get their tone and substance exactly right. But in all those years – twenty-five more years – he did not receive a single word in reply.

During this time, Miroslav thought a great deal about Franta and Anna, and also of Rosa, and of how soon he would get to see them all again. In his letters to home, he never mentioned that his passport had disappeared into a bureaucratic black hole. Already in late 1947, Rosa's letters had been filled with frustration and confusion that his plans had become so uncertain:

> Miroslav, you write that you have a contract until the fifteenth of December, so shall I understand that you will come for Christmas or did you change your mind? ... I don't really understand what you are doing, but then I also think that they wouldn't allow you to stay there any longer since you only have a permit for a half year.

His parents and Rosa accepted that he would not be coming home for Christmas, but they were sure that he would come back sometime early in the New Year of 1948.

In an age dominated by instant correspondence through internet and email, it is difficult to imagine the slow and painful process of writing and receiving letters that sometimes took months to make their journey between Ireland and the far-off country of Czechoslovakia. But Miroslav patiently wrote to his parents every week, and just as patiently he wrote to Rosa. As the months went by, he started to understand that he might never be able to tell the whole story in his letters. The new Czechoslovak government had adopted a policy of censoring incoming international mail. He sent a few pictures of his early days in Waterford but they were confiscated without any explanation. His letters to home (and also letters from his parents and Rosa to him) were very obviously cut open and re-sealed. So he kept to very general topics about his work life, and never mentioned the political situation or the difficulties he now faced after the Revolution.

Month would follow month, and year would follow year, but it never occurred to Miroslav that he would not return again to Czechoslovakia for twenty-five years. He finds it hard to explain how he felt in those early years, but he remembers how tightly he clung to a dream of getting some word of being allowed to return. He felt, he says, 'like a man in the air'. In almost every month of every one of those years, as well as writing to the Czechoslovak President, he also sent letters to the Ministry of External Affairs in Prague, and to the very important Czechoslovak Embassy in London. For ten years or more, he begged for a passport, and later (after he had finally won Irish citizenship) for a visa to allow him to visit. Always the replies were short and disappointing: 'Your request is refused.'

The joyful event of a visa did not occur until 1972. Within a few days of getting it, he did something that very few people in Ireland would have contemplated in those isolated and self-conscious years just before entry into what was then popularly referred to as the European common market. He took his wife and children by car, in effect re-tracing the steps of his first journey in 1947, across Belgium and Germany and through the Communist frontier, the Iron Curtain, into his former homeland. But that was much, much later than this present moment in Miroslav's story.

His hopeful message to Rosa was particularly difficult to maintain. He certainly did not want to waste her time with forlorn promises of future marriage, but he never allowed himself to think that he would not be back in Prague sometime in the near future. Rosa was loyal in her way. She visited Miroslav's parents in Držkov every few months and they shared their mutual hopes for his early return.

In April 1948, Anna and Rosa's parents wrote a joint letter to Miroslav from Světlá, telling him that the renovation Anna had been doing in his old home in Držkov was now complete. She had partitioned a separate set of rooms downstairs 'and everything is ready for you and Rosa to live there.' Miroslav was startled when he read this. He knew about the renovation from an earlier letter, but had no idea until then that it was being done for Rosa and himself to live there. Probably Anna and Rosa's family knew that these hopes were becoming a fantasy, especially as the new glass factory rolled out its first production, but they continued to believe in them anyway.

Three years after Miroslav left, Rosa told him that she was occasionally dating a local boy in Světlá, a forester. 'Nothing too serious,' she wrote affably. 'But we go to some dances together.' That information did upset him more than a little, but he did not raise any objection and continued to assure her that he was doing everything he could to get back. He just couldn't tell when or how.

When four years had passed, Miroslav told Rosa in his last letter to her that they should agree 'to forget our future together'. He remembers what a sad letter it was, coming seven years after their relationship had begun. It explained his long series of difficulties with the Communists and how he had reached the end of the road. It recounted Anna's unsuccessful efforts in Držkov to do something to allow him to come home, humiliating herself in the local Communist offices to plead her son's cause. His mother wrote often to tell him that she hoped that someone among the village officials would act on his behalf, but it never happened. He was blacklisted, she was told over and over again – the son of a bourgeois who had vanished before the Revolution, in cahoots with another notorious bourgeois, Charles Bačik.

Miroslav expressed his deep sadness to Rosa that his last effort to save his relationship with her, which involved asking the Czechoslovak Minister for Foreign Affairs to permit Rosa to begin a new life in Ireland, had been rejected. Franta himself had even stepped in to help Rosa with the process. He asked Miroslav to provide a letter, witnessed by a notary public, affirming his intention to marry Rosa. On 3 February 1950, Miroslav swore an affidavit to this effect, which was witnessed by a Waterford solicitor, Peter O'Connor. The affidavit was entitled, 'In the Matter of A Proposed Marriage Between Růžena Štolfová and Miroslav Havel'. The title was a little disingenuous because Rosa and Miroslav had never become formally engaged, but O'Connor told Miroslav that the affidavit must refer to his 'fiancée' or it would look suspicious. The English original, with a Czech copy prepared by Miroslav, was sent to Rosa, who then filed both versions with her other papers. Here is the English text of the affidavit, with the same capitalisation used in the original:

I, Miroslav Havel of Riverview Ferrybank in the City of Waterford, Ireland (Éire), Make Oath and say as follows:

1. I was born on the 26th May 1922 in Czechoslovakia and up to the time I left for Ireland resided at Držkov 183

Czechoslovakia, and during the past two years I have resided at the above address in Waterford, Ireland, and have been employed as a glass technician in a Company known as the Waterford Glass Ltd. and have been paid a good salary out of which I have been steadily saving money with the object in view of getting married.

2. My fiancée, Růžená Štolfová, who for many years has been a dear friend of mine, and with whom I have been corresponding since I arrived in Ireland, has expressed her willingness to travel to Ireland for the purpose of marrying me, and I am equally anxious and willing to marry her as soon as possible after her arrival. She is of full age and resides at Světlá Nad Sázavou Nádražní Ulice Czechoslovakia. I have asked her to apply for a passport, and if a passport is granted to her, I shall send her sufficient money to defray all her expenses from Czechoslovakia to Ireland. I attach hereto a letter I signed in the presence of Reverend William Hallinan, Catholic Priest, Waterford, who has promised that when my fiancée arrives he will see that she boards in a good Catholic home until our marriage is celebrated.

Miroslav carefully added the diacritics (accents) to the Czech version with a black pen. One can assume that the final reference to boarding Rosa in a 'good Catholic home' was inserted to satisfy Miroslav's Irish clerical and legal advisers, and not because the godless Communists would deny Rosa a visa unless they knew she would be under the moral supervision of the Church.

Miroslav was pleased with how O'Connor constructed that affidavit, but it met the same fate as his own official correspondence with the Communists. Rosa was refused a passport, even the special kind of exit passport the Communists sometimes gave to people (such as Jews) whom they wanted to leave the country permanently.

There was one more twist at the end of the Miroslav–Rosa romance. Franta wrote to Rosa after her passport was denied and boldly asked her if she would 'wait for Mirek'. She responded in a letter to Anna, dated 27 July 1951, reporting that she had not heard from Miroslav for many months and that she now assumed their relationship was at an end. But she asked Anna to urge Miroslav to write a letter confirming her assumption. And she told Anna that the Communists at her factory were taunting her with rumours that Miroslav had married 'one of Mr Bačik's daughters'. In closing, she wished for Anna that she and Franta would soon see Miroslav again 'in your full health'. When Miroslav wrote back to Rosa in his final letter, he solemnly assured her that he was not already married, except, maybe, to the ever-increasing demands of Waterford Glass.

Miroslav never asked Bačik to intervene in his situation, even though Bačik, at least when he had first invited Miroslav to join him in Waterford, seemed to have had contacts at the highest levels of the Czechoslovak government: 'I did not ask him that, because he had problems of his own, and he never got permission to go back himself.' Indeed, Miroslav faced the ironic situation, different from that of almost all of his countrymen, of trying to get into a country from which many of its citizens were trying to escape. He was essentially an illegal alien in Ireland, bereft of a passport or citizenship, and only an official permit to go back to Czechoslovakia would allow him even to contemplate surrendering himself to a very uncertain fate.

Rosa wrote back fondly in a final letter, much different in tone from her letter to Franta and Anna, and agreed that it would be best to put aside their plans for the future. A year later, she married her forester.

Miroslav kept every one of Rosa's letters, held together in little bundles that he managed to hold onto even after he married his Irish girlfriend, Betty, some years later. The letters are a melancholy account of their slow drifting apart, although also a source of some curious bits of information. Miroslav's elegant Prince Rainier moustache, for example, arrived in June 1949, much to Rosa's dismay: 'I hate facial hair, and if I ever get a passport I will tell you to get rid of it ... I wouldn't kiss you.'

Betty, who entered Miroslav's life three years after the Rosa chapter had ended, found the bundles of letters in a box under the stairs when she married Miroslav. To her annoyance, although she knew perfectly well who had written the letters, she had no idea what intimacies the correspondents had shared with each other in their classical Czech. To her credit, however, she never disposed of the bundles of Rosa's letters.

Rosa left the printing company after it was liquidated in 1950 under the first Communist five-year plan. She had spent nine years working there and lost all of her seniority and experience. Instead, she was offered a choice of socialist assignments, to be a train conductor in Brno or to work in a factory near Světlá that assembled hand-mills for meat and flour. She chose the factory so that she could stay near her ill grandfather.

After the intensity of their four years of correspondence between 1947 and 1951, Miroslav and Rosa now exchange only Christmas cards and a few lines each year. Rosa had two sons, and her husband succumbed to cancer in 2002. Now aged 79, she still lives just two train stops from Světlá, not far from the old Bačik factory where she first met Miroslav. He remembers that they did not part in some 'dreadful' way (reserving that particular word to describe his first few days in Ireland), but that the sadness in their letters was 'very pronounced'. His mother sent him some pictures of Rosa's wedding about a year after their parting, and she also sent Rosa the pictures of Miroslav's wedding in Waterford some years later.

When Miroslav and Rosa stood together crying on the train platform at Masaryk station on that late July day in 1947, they could not possibly have imagined that they would never see one another again. Frank Zemek's words ('Mirek, don't tell me lies – you are not coming back') were destined to come true.

# A Bohemian's Life in Waterford

As Miroslav approached the end of his first year in Waterford, with no prospect of regularising his status, he decided that his Mary Street guesthouse, Portree House, was no longer a viable option. It was, after all, intended to have been a three-month stay in this costly accommodation. Around this time, he was contacted by Fr William Hallinan, a sympathetic priest from the city's Dominican Church, who had just returned to Waterford after several years in Scotland.

Fr Hallinan was well aware that many of his clerical colleagues were sceptical of the strangers in their midst, but he was determined to reach out a friendly hand and, Miroslav thinks, maybe to win a few converts in the process. 'Somehow we hit it very well,' Miroslav says. And, indeed, Fr Hallinan was totally successful in converting Miroslav.

As Miroslav searched for new lodgings, the priest tipped him off about a room that was available at Mrs Catherine Cronin's house in a little side street just off 'The Glen', one of the wide streets around Ballybricken, the hill-top square that overlooks Waterford's city quays. For many Waterford people, Ballybricken was and remains the centre of the authentic city, the place from which the seven tribes of Waterford are supposed to have originated. It was also the scene of the city's last public hanging in 1862. Now Miroslav Havel would be living there – one of the new 'foreigners'.

Catherine Cronin's house was in a terraced row of about twenty houses. Waterford in the 1940s had many similar terraces of small and narrow houses. The house was 'joined together' with its neighbours, as Miroslav puts it. This was quite a change from his home in Držkov, an imposing detached fortress that kept its distance from all the other imposing detached fortresses that were scattered in and around the village.

He stood with Fr Hallinan outside Mrs Cronin's house and did not like it at all. Then he listened as the good father chatted with Mrs Cronin and her husband, and even though he understood almost nothing of what they were saying, he had the sudden sensation that the Cronins would be the perfect landlords. They would not interfere with him at all, and he would have a perfectly quiet life under their roof. After all, he thought, lodgers are always getting into trouble with things – being subjected to all kinds of absurd rules and boundaries – and he felt that the Cronins would spare him that fate.

Standing at Mrs Cronin's door at eight o'clock at night on a cold evening, he was prepared to agree even to her rather steep demand for ten shillings a week in rent to cover room, breakfast and an evening meal. Hers was 'not the cheapest' place he could have found, Miroslav remembers, but he was acting on his intuition.

At Mrs Cronin's invitation, he took a look around the house. There was not a great deal to see. Downstairs there were two rooms – a cosy sitting room with a small piano where occasionally Mr Cronin would sit and warble some old Irish tunes, and a dining room which Miroslav always called the 'eatery'. By now, Miroslav needed to use the bathroom and so he signalled to Fr Hallinan and the Cronins that he was heading upstairs. There, he noticed two rooms. The first, which he correctly guessed would be his, was very compact indeed – barely more than six-foot square. It had a chair, an iron bed, a wardrobe and a little table on which stood two impressive items of pottery – a capacious bowl and a large jug filled with water. This was the water that Miroslav would use for daily ablutions, as there was no piped water in the house. Miroslav found the absence of taps and sinks to be a little disconcerting.

Across from Miroslav's room was the family bedroom. He looked around for the door to the bathroom. There was a door that opened into a closet, but no other door. *Jesusmaria*, he thought in Czech – first Bačik is running a glass factory out of a builder's shed and now I'm going to be a lodger in a house with no bathroom. He stayed upstairs long enough to arouse Mrs Cronin's suspicion. "What is he doing up there?' he thought he heard her say to her husband and the priest waiting at the bottom of the stairs. He was in distress. Not only was he looking in vain for the bathroom, but he actually urgently needed to use it. He couldn't remember the word for 'toilet', which he had perhaps never had to use before, so he shouted down the Czech equivalent: *záchod*.

Mrs Cronin had no idea what he was talking about, of course. They met halfway up (or down) the stairs, and Miroslav realised that he needed a better word or a gesture. Unfailingly polite, he couldn't bring himself to make the obvious gesture, which might have caused his prospective landlady to topple back down the stairs. So, he joined his hands together at the fingertips in a gesture of prayer, and simply spoke the English word 'please'.

Amazingly, Mrs Cronin seemed to twig what he meant. She shoved him back up the stairs, opened the door to her bedroom and pushed him in. He was wondering what possible reason she could have for bringing him into her bedroom. Then, as the door closed menacingly behind them, she pointed triumphantly to a huge statue of the Virgin Mary which towered over the far side of the room. 'The poor woman was thinking I am looking for a place to say my evening prayers,' he remembers. Miroslav decided that he would have no choice but to relieve himself in the back garden. He ran past a puzzled Mrs Cronin, who now thought that he was a pagan after all, raced down the stairs, and out into the garden, which extended about twenty metres behind the house. At the end of the garden, he found a little hut, in which there was not a toilet as such, but a plank and a hole, a rope and a bucket. He had evidently found his *záchod*. Later it would transpire that, in the absence of a bathroom, Mrs

Cronin would arrange for her lodger to go down once a week to the Granville Hotel on the main quay, for a proper bath. The price for this indulgence was one shilling.

At Mrs Cronin's, Miroslav actually learned how to cook, something he had never done in Czechoslovakia but which he continues to do with gusto many decades later. His new landlady tried to get him to enjoy her Irish stew, but he was put off by the 'large pieces of turnip and potato'. In fact, Miroslav was using these very vegetables at the glass factory to dissolve bubbles in melting glass and he just didn't fancy having them swimming in his dinner bowl as well.

There was, it is true, a certain unconventionality to the cooking facilities at Mrs Cronin's. The gas cooker was just outside the back door, at the edge of the garden, under a narrow tin roof about two metres long. It seems as though no pipes of any kind ever penetrated that terraced house. He had a happy time preparing his meals, though, and Mrs Cronin kept encouraging him to save money by doing so.

Her husband was on the sales staff in the men's apparel department at Shaw's department store on the main quay, Waterford's only big department store. He was an old IRA man, according to Miroslav, who had the bad fortune to have a son who emigrated and joined the British police force. No picture of the son in uniform was ever on display in the Cronin household. As Miroslav continued to learn English at Mrs Cronin's, he got a steady diet of Irish Republican propaganda from old Mr Cronin.

Back at the factory, Bačik was by now having some success in attracting a few 'foreigners' or 'Continentals' from Germany to join his new enterprise and bolster the small group of Miroslav-trained Irish apprentice cutters. Bačik travelled extensively in that first year, mainly to Germany, in search of skilled craftsmen. Some good cutters and blowers were available – ethnic Germans who had escaped or been expelled from Czechoslovakia and other Eastern European countries immediately after the war, and many of whom were still living in State refugee camps inside the German border. 'Displaced craftsmen were only available to us because of the war,' Miroslav recalls.

These men were embittered by their circumstances, and were not interested in coming to the Waterford Glass factory just to achieve Charles Bačik's grand educational purpose of training Irish apprentice blowers and cutters. They wanted only to make money. 'Give me glasses and I will cut,' one of them told Bačik abruptly. So he hired three skilled German cutters – one of them quite exceptional – but they were unwilling for a long time to teach the younger Irish apprentices. Miroslav had to do that on his own, and to make the factory work more efficiently, he even created designs that could be half-finished by the masters and then completed by the younger apprentices.

The best of those early foreign recruits, according to Miroslav, was Oskar Ilg, a highly educated man who by then was already in his fifties. Ilg was a taciturn, bristly character, very proud of his German heritage even in the poisoned atmosphere after the war. Only much later did Miroslav discover that Ilg was actually a fellow Czech. He was one of the ethnic Germans whom the Czechoslovak government had expelled from his home near Liberec under a mass transfer of Sudeten Germans approved by the Allies at Potsdam in 1945. Despite the shared geographical background of the two men, Ilg's resentment of how Czechoslovakia had treated him and his fellow ethnics ran too deep to allow him to be anything other than coldly formal with Miroslav – even more coldly formal than Czech tradition required. Ilg, indeed, considered himself a true German, and never liked any of the 'real' Germans Bačik brought to Waterford.

However, all of the new immigrants to Ireland had one thing in common. They were treated with some reserve, if not suspicion, in Waterford. Soon after the German cutters arrived, Miroslav heard of another incident involving a Catholic priest warning his flock, this time from the pulpit, to be wary of the 'foreigners' now moving in their midst. This was not a trivial matter in the 1940s and 1950s when the Roman Catholic Church in Ireland wielded considerable power and influence.

With master cutters arriving on the premises, and a vision of old Waterford glass still dancing in his eyes, Bačik recognised that the early days of working with imported soda glass blanks would eventually have to end. To do that, he would need to ensure a consistent production of quality glassware and the only way to do that was to create an in-house glass melting and blowing facility – as Edith had once promised Miroslav.

Melting of glass is conducted in beehive-shaped fire-clay containers called glasshouse pots, which are typically about four feet high and three feet in diameter. The pots sit on a platform and are heated from a furnace underneath. After several hours of boiling the ingredients (usually the night hours are preferred for melting), the pots contain a brilliant, molten mass. This melted glass is then collected on the blower's iron, when it is soft enough to be manipulated like potter's clay or even cut with a scissors. It is a skill that was not easily taught – not to mention the challenge of teaching the skills of decorating the hardened glass with fine cutting and engraving. Given that Waterford's last glass-makers had left in 1851, Miroslav and Bačik faced a daunting prospect.

Money still being terribly scarce, Bačik had to scale back his ambition to a two-pot furnace that was designed and built by a French company with which he had been negotiating for some time. Bačik was always keen on technical innovation, and he allowed himself to be persuaded by the French experts that the traditional solid clay pots from Scotland were too old-fashioned for Ireland's bold new glassworks. The traditional pots also had the cost disadvantage of frequent replacement as they deteriorated under the sustained high heat of the fusing and melting process, when temperatures routinely exceeded 1,500° centigrade. Some pots lasted as short a time as ten days before they cracked. When they were hauled outside to the yard, they were so red hot that it would be three days before anyone could touch them.

'We have a new system,' the French engineers assured Bačik brightly, and he went along with it. Their system replaced the conventional solid pots with permanent pots assembled from large concrete blocks, which slotted together like oversized Lego bricks. According to the French technical experts, the melting glass would seep into the spaces between the blocks and hermetically seal the entire structure. Miroslav found out accidentally what Bačik was planning, and he was immediately suspicious. 'It was looking beautiful,' he remembers. 'But it just did not ring the bell.' He could not recall the 'block theory' from any of his training in glass technology. It seemed counterintuitive to him that melting glass could act as a kind of mortar. But he did not consider himself an architect or a process technician, and he stayed quiet as the elegant new brick pots were installed at Ballytruckle.

The French proposed a date for the first test of the new pots, and Bačik excitedly decided that he would invite Bernard Fitzpatrick, as well as some of the new company's other financial backers, and maybe a local dignitary or two, to witness the historic moment of the first batch of melted glass being blown – the first in over a century to be blown in Ireland. In anticipation of the great day, Bačik and Miroslav had recruited two master blowers – one from England who was of Polish origin and served in the British Army in the Second World War, and the other a recently arrived Estonian. It might have been wiser to wait for a private test of the pots before inviting outsiders, but Bačik was too anxious about his financial support to wait any longer to impress people like Bernard Fitzpatrick with his French-inspired new glass technology.

The melting process began promptly at five in the morning. The process created, and still today creates, an extremely noisy environment. Bačik was expecting his visitors to arrive in the afternoon, and was busy in his office working on the welcome speech – which he would have to give outside the plant because of the uncomfortably high decibel level of the furnace. The molten glass had been bubbling for three hours and was visibly starting to melt inside the pots, so the timing of the blowing demonstration for the middle of the afternoon looked highly favourable.

Suddenly, at about ten o'clock, the two brand-new pots simply exploded. The concrete Lego bricks separated and disintegrated with violent pops, and the molten glass poured out through the seams onto the surrounding wooden platform where the company's two blowers were supposed to stand. The platform itself was consumed by fire – the temperature of the liquid glass, flowing like lava out of the broken pots, exceeded 1,600° centigrade. It was a spectacular moment of total technical failure. In those days, the blowing room was usually pitch-black except for the intense glistening of the molten glass in the pots. Against that gloomy background, the escaping melted glass and the licking flames were a vision of Hell. It would take two days before the ruins cooled down.

Miroslav remains convinced that, at that very moment, as he and Bačik ran to the blowing room to see what had happened, Bačik's crown of black hair turned to the frost-white it would remain for the rest of his life. The older man was devastated. He was also mortified that, as the three cars containing his guests pulled up in front of the factory at the appointed hour, all they would see was a mass of white smoke billowing into the sky, and a small group of firemen running outside and inside with their water hoses.

Bačik's speech of welcome was replaced by a hasty explanation that the blowing demonstration would have to be rescheduled because of technical problems. The visitors were unceremoniously ushered away in their cars, and Bačik invited them to assemble later at the Savoy restaurant for a more coherent explanation. He later confessed to Miroslav that the day of the disintegration of the pots was one of the hardest days of his life.

However, Bačik was nothing if not resilient, and he was very persuasive with his various backers. When he had said a temporary farewell to his well-heeled guests, he brought Miroslav for a drive. They sat in the car looking out at the wide beach at Tramore and had another of their long talks. They smoked many cigarettes that afternoon. Bačik mentioned that both of the blowers had come to Waterford with their families, and that he intended to pay them even though there was no glass for them to blow. He told Miroslav that he had insurance coverage that might provide at least some funds for replacement pots.

Bačik later contacted Bernard Fitzpatrick about building a replacement blowing facility. Fitzpatrick, despite his puzzlement at the whole pot-explosion fiasco, was a 'very solid man', Miroslav remembers, who 'kept his head'. He was content to act once again as Bačik's financial angel of mercy.

Not long afterwards, Fitzpatrick and Bačik contracted with an engineering company in Edinburgh, which agreed to design a melting furnace that would be oil-based rather than using less-efficient coal or wood. Scotland had continued its own glass-making tradition, and the new company later recruited one of the owners of Edinburgh Crystal, John Barraclough, to become a director of the Waterford Glass company. Barraclough was a trained glass chemist, and played a major role in improving the recipe compounds for what would become Waterford's signature heavy lead crystal. It was Barraclough, in fact, who built the house that Miroslav would buy in 1967.

Meanwhile, everyone at the Waterford factory, including Miroslav, joined in the urgent task of building a temporary and much cheaper furnace to bridge the gap until the new furnace and pots came on stream. The makeshift furnace was put together in a corner of what was supposed to have been the new blowing room.

As he had at the beginning, Miroslav found himself once again carrying blocks and mixing cement in a cause greater than himself. Some of the German master cutters were not at all pleased to be working as common labourers, but they understood that their future depended on a quick and successful re-launch of the furnace.

A small square ashtray that was created from the melted glass brewed in that little furnace is still in existence today. On its surface Miroslav engraved the image of a leprechaun repairing brogues, and the words 'From Ireland'. The piece betrays the dull, greenish hue of the cheap soda glass produced by the factory in those early years. The new furnace and pots, however, would still produce greenish soda glass. For financial reasons, Bačik had made the decision not to import the much more expensive ingredients that could produce the kind of luxury 'old Waterford' heavy lead crystal that he had already decided he wanted to market in the future.

It was not, Miroslav thinks, an especially wise strategy. The factory was recruiting men with advanced skills in cutting, but Bačik was gearing up to produce more soda glass. Admittedly, the home-produced glass would be of superior quality to the Belgian glass blanks which Waterford Glass had been importing, but it was still well below the quality needed for a breakthrough product.

Even with the new furnace and pots running, the glass blown at Ballytruckle was at first visibly flawed. Miroslav remembers, diplomatically, that the glass was 'not one hundred per cent clear', meaning that it was pock-marked with little bubbles. The little ashtray shows those blemishes vividly. The blemish problem improved as each group of pots became seasoned, but it was never entirely eliminated. One positive development was that Bačik had successfully imposed the specification that his replacement pots should be completely leak-proof and built from solid material. He did not want any more risky experiments to derail his business plan.

The business plan at this point was looking a little murky. For all the hopeful talk of selling luxury crystal to the Americans, the actual output in the early years of the Waterford Glass factory was primarily targeted at the Irish pub and hotel market. With no stem-makers to make the kinds of wine, sherry and port glasses for which Waterford was later to be renowned, most of the early production comprised beer glasses in pint and half-pint sizes for ordinary bar use. Bačik had also used his stay in the infirmary hospital to good effect – he cajoled the registrar into giving him a contract to supply all of the hospital's jugs and tumblers. Given this limited marketplace, even Miroslav could agree that Bačik's reluctance to buy more expensive glass-melting ingredients was perfectly understandable.

There were also many technical headaches in those early days. The new oil-based furnace was showing some early signs of a bad temperament. A small fraction of the oil was not burning off. Instead, it was spraying out of the furnace and falling into the pots. There it burned itself into the molten glass, distorting the temperatures and spoiling some of the production.

Cooling the blown glass was also a significant problem that needed to be addressed quickly. The laws of physics dictate that when the glass is blown at the end of the glass blower's hollow iron pipe, it is already in the process of cooling down, even though it is still three times hotter than boiling water. If the newly blown glass is simply left lying down, it cools too quickly from the outside and not from the inside. If it continues to cool in this distorted condition, the contrast in temperatures will cause the glass spontaneously to fracture and even to explode.

It was not a very efficient way to maintain production, and Miroslav warned Bačik that the factory (just like the factory in Světlá) needed to come up with some kind of cooling or 'annealing' room for all of its blown glass. The trick, Miroslav told his boss, would be to ensure that every glass blown would remain initially at the same temperature as the molten glass inside the furnace, and the glass would then be cooled down overnight at a regulated rate.

Bačik often showed mild irritation when he was reminded of some of the more vexing properties of the product he was always so keen to produce. He told Miroslav brusquely to 'go ahead and do something'. Miroslav, who never considered himself a glass-making technologist, was nevertheless always willing to conduct experiments on the factory floor. He came up with the idea of putting two large static cooling kilns into an empty room at the rear of the furnace area. The room was already quite hot because of the ambient radiation of the oil-fired furnace, and additional heat could be carried to the kilns through pipes from the oil burners.

The new cooling room was accessed from the furnace area by an up-and-down sliding door, made of a heavy metal alloy. Miroslav organised a team of assistants to carry the blown glasses one-by-one through the metal door to the kilns, and to stack them on their sides inside the kilns. Then the kilns would be locked, and overnight the temperature inside them would be raised close to the melting point and then gradually cooled down to room temperature. The uniform temperature in the kilns was supposed to eliminate any initial stress in the blown glasses.

Modern annealing ovens allow the glasses to move individually on customised conveyor belts, but at that time Miroslav had to live with the risk that glasses in the lowest stacks or layers, where the temperature was the least regulated, would bond together before they had cooled properly. Sometimes six or seven of these unstable glasses would fuse into a single piece. It was an infuriating problem, but it was unavoidable given the extremely cramped conditions of the cooling room and the kilns.

Miroslav had one really bad experience with his cooling-room idea. When the glasses were ready to be taken out of the room in the morning, the temperature in the room would still be as high as 180° centigrade. That kind of demanding temperature is important for the glass, but not at all sustainable for a human being. Miroslav went into the cooling room one morning and was busily cleaning the inside of the kiln in preparation for the day's production. Suddenly, the metal sliding door came crashing down and locked him in.

The door was sealed fast and he couldn't get any purchase on it to push it back up. A long five minutes of panic ensued before one of his assistants heard his muffled yells and dull pounding. As the door was lifted, he emerged totally dehydrated from his unwanted sauna, and looked even more skeletal than his usual gaunt appearance. He never found out why the door had suddenly malfunctioned, although his great love for Agatha Christie mysteries might have given him pause for thought as he walked around the factory in the following weeks. In any case, after the sliding-door incident he decided that he would no longer be involved with cooling-room work.

The story illustrates Miroslav's pioneer's tendency to get involved in every aspect of the factory's production. However, he was also keen to impress on the local Waterford apprentices that all of them, from the blowers to the kiln stackers, were engaged in a craft enterprise. There was no recent glass-making tradition to draw upon, and so for most of the new Irish employees who came to the factory in the late 1940s and early 1950s, the factory offered a job, but not (in their thinking) a 'special' job. And, to be entirely fair, and despite Miroslav's almost religious obsession with his craft, the new workers could hardly be impressed by an operation that, for all of its insistence on recruiting foreign-trained blowers and cutters, was basically churning out beer glasses for the bar trade.

In time, Bačik felt the need to fire up sales for the new company, which until this point employed only himself, Miroslav, a small coterie of foreign blowers and cutters, and the Irish apprentices whom Miroslav was dutifully training. In January 1950, Bačik put an advertisement in several of the Irish national newspapers, looking for an experienced salesman to represent the new Waterford Glass product. Like Miroslav's early classified ad a few years earlier, the response was almost zero.

Just as in early 1948, however, someone did show up eventually. Remarkably he was a German living in Galway, and he came down to Waterford to ask Bačik directly and in person for the job. Bačik was impressed that this man, Fritz Marckwald, had made such a personal mission to offer his services to the company. 'Okay, Fritz, you can do this job,' Bačik told him.

Marckwald, as it turned out, had worked before the war as a salesman with Dresden China. He made no claim to any artistic ability or insight, although his wife, who had accompanied him to Galway just before the Nazis seized power, was an accomplished hat-maker. Still, he did not look like someone who could easily push sales to grumpy Irish publicans. He was exceedingly lanky, and his face was dominated by a pair of oversized black-framed glasses, with lenses as thick as the bottom of a Coke bottle to combat his chronic short-sightedness. He claimed that he could drive a car, a distinctly rare ability in early 1950s Waterford. Bačik gave him a car – a second-hand Hillman Hunter – and told Fritz that he wanted him to become one of those classic travelling salesmen.

Marckwald's very first sales trip, to Cork city, about a hundred and forty kilometres west of Waterford, made Bačik queasy, not about Fritz's sales ability, but about his driving skills and the financial consequences of those skills. After nearly six hours of driving, Marckwald called Bačik on one of the new telephone trunk lines. 'How is Cork, Fritz – how are things going?' Bačik asked his new sales representative to the nation.

In response, Marckwald sheepishly disclosed that he had only reached Dungarvan, a town about a third of the way to Cork. His horribly poor eyesight apparently forced him to drive at a snail's pace, which he could get away with because the roads at the time were practically empty. For Bačik, the really disturbing consequence of Marckwald's painfully slow driving speed was that he would be claiming expenses for overnight stays.

As Miroslav remembers it, Marckwald was in fact the first employee who worked outside the factory: 'He was our traveller.' In any event, Fritz Marckwald (who was one of Miroslav's favourites) puttered around in his little Hillman, visiting pubs and gift-shops and persuading the owners in his profoundly accented English that 'Vaterford Glass' should be their source for barware or gift items. It was only a modestly promising activity, not terribly rewarding financially, but enough to keep the furnaces burning at the small factory in Ballytruckle.

Meanwhile, the rebuilt furnace and pots were definitely producing better quality, although still only 'very ordinary glass', according to Miroslav – much like the soda glass that can be found on bar counters all over the world. Miroslav kept encouraging Bačik to lift the company's sights toward production of the kinds of high-quality glass and elaborate cut and engraved designs that had so impressed both of them at the National Museum just a few years before. Bačik certainly listened, and wanted to listen. Even while he held his focus on soda glass, he kept up the momentum of trying to hire more trained Continentals who could help him achieve his ambition for a more sophisticated product. Miroslav recalls that Bačik was even placing advertisements in the British and German newspapers.

The rising number of foreigners helped their collective reputation in Waterford. The Irish employees were spreading the word, in Miroslav's recollection, that 'these foreigners were not thieves and murderers'. And, in fact, Canon Michael Barron, the local parish priest in Ballytruckle, accepted an invitation from Bačik to tour the factory. With the clergy on board, what could stop him now?

# The Irish Take Over

What caused Waterford Glass to ramp up to the high-quality product for which it later won global acclaim? Bačik and Miroslav had put together a competent team of craftsmen, and the factory in its early years was at least breaking even. But the transition to a great product, which also meant a considerable upgrading of the manufacturing process used in the factory, had still not taken place.

Restless as always, and anxious to break through the quality barrier, Bačik dispatched Miroslav to Sweden to visit the famous Orrefors glass factory near Stockholm, and to make notes about the production process there. Miroslav, of course, had no passport, either Czechoslovak or Irish. He accomplished his mission through Bačik's connections with the International Red Cross and the United Nations Refugee Agency (UNRA). Miroslav never knew exactly what these 'connections' were, but Bačik was able to secure a Red Cross/UNRA certificate for Miroslav. Although far from being a passport, the certificate would at least allow Miroslav to pass across several Western European borders and to avoid getting himself arrested as a kind of international vagrant. Looking back at the situation, it seems clear that Bačik had somehow managed to have Miroslav classified as a refugee under international legal protection, even though Miroslav was actually travelling from his apparent country of refuge to another country.

Orrefors was established in 1898 and has always specialised in abstract glass shapes and the application of light colour. Miroslav spent a week at the plant, engaged in blatant but unhindered industrial espionage. He watched the manufacturing process, counted the numbers of blowers and cutters and engravers, and in fact did the kind of consulting work that nowadays seems to require teams of graduates from big business schools. Miroslav's final report to Bačik could not have been more direct. He was impressed by the 'clearness' of the Orrefors glass, and he had his eye on other technical aspects of production. Here is an extract from Miroslav's report, as translated later by Bačik:

They are able to produce articles of large size with minimum apparent blemish. Certainly the rejects on account of bad melting are far lower than we have at the moment. I was very much impressed by the care taken in making a batch. The cullet [broken glass used to speed up melting of new batches] is broken up in a special drum which uses non-metal hammers. Great care is made to ensure that the cullet powder does not come into the batch. The system of weighing parts of the batch is automatic. Delivery of the batch is done in covered wheelbarrows. The batch itself looks to me much damper and I did not notice any dust rising when it was loaded.

He emphasised also that the factory had a separate design department which masterminded its entire glass-making enterprise. All the blowers and cutters, as well as the engravers, were steered by the blueprints that emerged from the design department. At the Waterford factory, on the other hand, Miroslav was generating his designs 'on the fly', while working in the cutting room, training the cutters, and while holed up in a little engraving shop he had set up in a former storage room.

And these were not the elaborate designs that would represent a generational shift beyond those he had seen and sketched in the National Museum of Ireland. They were the same kind of simple patterns that the factory had been putting on soda glass, imported and home-blown, since its inception. Miroslav's true design work, to the extent that he saw himself emerging as a creative artist, was being done in his rooms at Portree House and Mrs Cronin's, but was not yet emerging from the production line.

So the Waterford factory was at a turning point in its history. What happened next would see Bačik losing his grip on the little company. Indeed, he would never again enjoy the sovereignty he had in those early days. The company would suddenly become less 'foreign' and more conspicuously Irish, and that, too, would remain the case for the decades to come. Yet it need not have turned out that way. Bačik, after all, was hardly a naive businessman. He understood very well what needed to be done to take his company to the next level. His report from Miroslav could not have been more explicit. And he had never found himself unable to raise cash when he needed it. As 1950 dawned, he had financial and operational control of Waterford Glass.

However, there was another interested watcher of events. The Fitzpatricks were also associated with an enterprise established in 1932, the Irish Glass Bottle Company (IGB). Under the control of managing director Joseph Griffin, a crusty old-school Irish businessman, IGB quickly became the largest supplier of glass jars and milk bottles in Ireland. In those days, the notion of a cardboard carton of milk would have seemed like science fiction. IGB's chairman, Joseph McGrath, was a businessman with diverse family investment interests, including the controversial Irish Hospital Sweepstakes. He was also a successful politician, having served in two Irish cabinets as Minister for Labour and Minister for Industry and Commerce.

Griffin and McGrath were members of the 'Lemass generation', a group of men (including future Taoiseach Seán Lemass) who came of age in Irish business and political life in the twenty years after the Second World War. They set the standard for the rise of an indigenous industrial base that would expand beyond the only major Irish brand of the time, Guinness. In January 1950, Griffin and Bernard Fitzpatrick joined Joe McGrath and his son, Patrick (Paddy), on a fact-finding trip to observe the Waterford Glass operation. According to Miroslav, Griffin and McGrath senior offered to 'co-operate' with Bačik's plans for expansion, and they talked with him also about Miroslav's reconnaissance missions to the National Museum and to Orrefors.

Bačik refused any offers of co-operation. When the visitors got back to Dublin, however, they proved to be interested less in co-operation than in outright ownership and control. As the next month passed, the financial condition of the company began to deteriorate badly. In February 1950, IGB and Joe McGrath made an offer to buy out Bačik and to take a 51 per cent controlling interest of Waterford Glass. In a truly ironic footnote to all of this, IGB itself went out of business in 2002, destroyed by cut-price competition from Eastern Europe.

The eventual deal seems to have occurred precisely because Bačik was hunting for money to expand. He had already secured a bank loan and a government trade loan, adding about £25,000 to the company's capital, but he knew that he needed much more. He admitted later to Miroslav that he had himself re-opened contacts with IGB in 1949. Many meetings followed in the spring of 1950, and before the final deal was done, Bačik certainly extracted value for his ownership of the various Waterford Glass trademarks that he had registered several years before. But ultimately, it seems, the nature of the final deal was worked out between Joe and Paddy McGrath and the Fitzpatricks in Dublin, at meetings which Bačik did not attend and to which, in all probability, he was not invited.

It is interesting to speculate on what might have motivated the McGraths to make this offer to Bačik, and what in turn might have motivated Bačik to accept it. One could reasonably imagine that Griffin and the elder McGrath envisaged folding Waterford into IGB, turning it into a division that still produced the beer glasses that Ballytruckle had been churning out virtually since its inception. That alone would have made a good deal of strategic sense. But something else must also have been at the back of their minds. Surely they would have had long conversations with Bernard Fitzpatrick about the development of the little company up to that point. Only a few years previously, after all, Fitzpatrick had been bewitched by Bačik's evocation of the history of old Waterford glass, and indeed he had supported and facilitated Miroslav's expedition to inspect and copy the antique glassware at the National Museum. And maybe, too, they had had a glimpse of Miroslav's report from Sweden about the importance of a proper design department.

Thus, even if Fitzpatrick harboured doubts about the viability of a luxury crystal product coming out of a factory geared up to produce beer glasses, he was still keenly aware, as he had been from the beginning, of Waterford's potential American market. He obviously persuaded the McGraths that it was worth taking the risk to upgrade the Ballytruckle operation. Miroslav thinks, too, that there was some tension between Bačik and Fitzpatrick about the idea of such a potentially prominent national industry being in foreign hands. At that time, Ireland still had a *sinn féin* ('ourselves alone') attitude to ownership of its economy. It was obvious to Miroslav from what Bačik was saying around this time that Bačik's Irish backers (and probably now also the McGraths) were rather annoyed that they had not come up with the idea of a Waterford Glass revival all by themselves.

And Bačik's own motivation for selling? Maybe he hesitated too long in his ambition to raise Waterford's profile. He knew that he needed to invest more money, and he knew that a new factory probably needed to be built. A serious crystal-glass factory would have a more sophisticated manufacturing process, and also a suite of offices and a showroom. He knew the potential, but he also knew how poorly equipped the pilot factory was to achieve his and its ambition. In his office, he probably looked wistfully at Miroslav's beautiful copies made at the National Museum, and at the hundreds of design ideas that Miroslav had derived from those copies in his rooms at Mary Street and The Glen. But how could he make these things happen if all the factory could do was to break even based on sales of pub glasses? And breaking even by early 1950 had become an optimistic scenario. Although Bačik never confirmed it, Miroslav heard some years later that even in 1949, despite an investment of over £45,000, the glass factory was almost insolvent.

Charles, Edith and Miroslav were chatting one evening in the Bačik family living-room in Tramore not long before the sale happened. 'My husband is so stubborn,' Miroslav recalls Edith saying. 'He will do anything to keep control of this damn factory.' She told Miroslav that she was sure that he and Charles were already 'well-established' with the new owners, and, more importantly, that the company would make much faster progress once new investment arrived. There was even talk, which Bačik himself seemed reluctant to confirm, that the McGraths were thinking about building an entirely new factory in the Johnstown area of the city, not far from where Miroslav had once wandered into St Otteran's psychiatric hospital in his quest for his lost leader. Then she turned to her husband and addressed him with her characteristic directness: 'Charlie, sell it!' Edith was right – her husband was stubborn, and he held out as long as he could.

Bačik probably regretted his decision, and the resulting loss of his influence, for the rest of his life. That was what Miroslav perceived more and more as the years went by. Miroslav was very involved in the family's life in those years and continued to visit the Bačik household in Tramore several times a week. Every year, on 5 December, he would dress up in a long white beard and long velvet cloak, put a mitre on his head and a golden crosier in his hand, and play Saint Nicholas, the Czech Santa Claus, for the Bačik children. Bačik, always seen as a rather austere figure, surprised the Irish factory employees when he wrote a touching report of these escapades in the first issue of the Waterford Glass factory magazine in December 1956:

'And do you know, Mr. Havel,' said little Henry, 'that Saint Nicholas had the same shoes you have?' 'How is that?' replied Mr. Havel. 'Look, you have the same hole in your shoe that Saint Nicholas had!' Next year, and every other year while we lived at Tramore, Saint Nicholas came, and every time he wore black slippers. Mr. Havel always came a little later, and so he missed him, but every time Mr. Havel wore shining brown shoes.'

From his many visits to Tramore, Miroslav formed the impression that his old comrade was 'heartbroken' about the loss of his factory. Bačik, when he let himself talk a little, sometimes reflected on how things might have gone differently and on his suspicion that, in some respects, he had been railroaded by the IGB people. In the six months or so before the sale, for example, IGB had purchased thousands of pub glasses on the Continent and sold them at a steep discount throughout Ireland. These glasses were all of the cheaper soda variety, but they had a distinct cost advantage over Waterford Glass because they were made mechanically, by the process known as 'pressing', rather than being mouth-blown like the Ballytruckle production. And there were other rumours of subtle industrial sabotage being practised against Waterford Glass. One prominent Limerick publican and beer franchisee, for example, had invested some money in the Bačik operation and was reportedly warned by IGB that if he continued doing business with Waterford Glass he would be cut off as an IGB customer. It was certainly suspicious that this publican suddenly told Bačik just before the IGB takeover that he wanted immediate full repayment of his Waterford Glass investment.

For Miroslav, still only in his late twenties, the transfer to new ownership was nonetheless a positive development. He was tired of the banal production at the pilot factory. He might as well have been back at Umprum, since his creative energies were mostly occupied by designs that never went into actual production. His greatest solace during those early years was when he could escape into his little engraving area, spin the copper wheels, take an item of that infernal soda glass in his hands, and start to perform the magic of being an artist in glass.

His repertoire in those years was limited by the quality of the glass, of course, but also by the production needs of the factory. Beer glasses did not need to be ornately engraved, although occasionally a pub-owner would want to individualise an order using a set of initials or a pub name. Other than that, and other than the times he spent just practising his skills, Miroslav engraved popular Irish motifs – things like harps and shamrocks, leprechauns and donkeys – on small souvenir gift items such as ashtrays and Christmas decorations. Bačik liked to give these little items as Christmas gifts to customers, instead of sending cards.

Bačik also dreamed up the idea, which would later develop into one of Waterford's biggest marketing coups, of donating large pieces of crystal as sports-event trophies. His factory didn't actually make any of these early trophies, but every so often (and it didn't happen more than a half-dozen times), Bačik would arrive in Miroslav's engraving cubby-hole with a large item of heavy crystal that he had obviously acquired on the Continent. Miroslav so loved those rare opportunities to spend long hours with real lead crystal that he sometimes scolded his boss for not being more generous with his trophy awards.

In any event, the old order changed over the winter of 1950 to 1951. Early in 1951, Joe McGrath and Joe Griffin put Griffin's son, Noel, a young Dublin accountant, into the position of general manager of Waterford Glass. Mr Bačik made way for Mr Griffin, and stepped back into the shadows as a kind of director without portfolio.

Miroslav never knew what kind of relationship Griffin had with Bačik, if indeed he had any. Bačik would always be accorded a nice office suite, but he was never again in a position to make decisions about production or marketing, and he very seldom appeared on any part of the factory floor at Waterford Glass. From his conversations with Bačik, Miroslav got the sense that the older man spent much of his time after the IGB takeover using his language skills to translate the factory's correspondence with European suppliers and customers.

Noel Griffin, on the other hand, was part of a new generation of Irish businessmen, a younger wave of Lemass acolytes in their thirties and forties who were ready to peer beyond the borders of their little agricultural island and to engage with the international industrial economy. Had he lived to see it (he died in a drowning accident in 1982), Griffin would have savoured Ireland's transformation into the Celtic Tiger and entry onto the list of the world's wealthiest economies.

Griffin was not in any sense an artist, and on taking over Waterford Glass, he concentrated like a laser on production issues. He immediately set about acquiring better technology, including the company's first customised machines for flat-cutting and new diamond-based machines for slicing the glass residue, known as the blower's 'cap', off the top of each newly blown glass. But his signature achievement in those first years of Irish ownership was to bring to fruition Bačik's plan for a new factory, moving from the cramped pilot operation in Ballytruckle to a new facility a few kilometres north at Johnstown.

The new site was closer to the middle of the city but, more importantly, it was adjacent to the city's gasworks and therefore to a steady supply of furnace gas without the need for a lengthy and expensive new piping infrastructure. It would be, as Miroslav recalls, 'a proper factory', with a large blowing section built around a line of eight to ten pots, and a series of cutting shops that would employ up to 300 craftsmen and apprentices.

Griffin's idea, building on Bačik's, was to ensure that Johnstown could eventually produce the kind of quality crystal that was simply undoable at Ballytruckle. The new factory would benefit from the extraordinary powerhouse of foreign talents in blowing, cutting, and now even stem-making – Czech, German, Italian, Austrian – that Bačik and Miroslav had been putting in place at Ballytruckle, even though they had never been able to gear up to take the best advantage of those talents.

However, the establishment of a design department was still not in Griffin's early planning. Miroslav remembers that he found himself, even after the move to Johnstown, occupying what he rather disparagingly remembers as 'a little hole in the corner', but which was actually a table he set up at one end of the new and still small engraving section. These disappointing physical conditions were not much different from the tiny space he had carved out for himself at Ballytruckle. Even when the engraving shop was extended the following year to accommodate five engravers, there was still no independent design department, and he continued to use his corner table as the nerve-centre of his design work.

It was not that Griffin failed to understand the importance of innovative design to the company's future success. Almost as soon as he took over, he had pored over the design and manufacturing blueprints remaining from the Bačik era. As he dusted off and leafed through Miroslav's National Museum portfolio, he talked again with Bernard Fitzpatrick and the McGraths about the excitement of recapturing the history and reputation of old Waterford. He also discovered Miroslav's Czech-language report from Orrefors, recognised the name of the Swedish company and Miroslav's name on the cover, and quickly asked Bačik to provide a translation. He told Miroslav that he agreed that Waterford Glass needed a real design department, but first he wanted to figure out the potential markets and the competition. He was particularly interested in whether, even before attacking the American market, Waterford Glass could 'Europeanise' itself as a direct competitor to the traditional Continental glass-makers, and even to its old suppliers in Belgium.

Thus it was that Miroslav departed in the spring of 1951, this time at Griffin's request but still armed with a refugee certificate courtesy of Mr Bačik, on another fact-finding espionage mission to the Continent. He went first to Norway, then to Germany and Austria, and finally back to Belgium, where he visited some of the factories that had supplied the early production for the revived Waterford company. In Belgium, too, he attended a world exhibition of commercial glass, and his stomach both rose and sank as he contemplated, in turn, the sheer beauty of the crystal pieces in the exhibition and how difficult it would be to break through against such formidable competitors.

On a personal level, Miroslav had painful feelings as he travelled in Germany and Austria, countries that border his native land. But it never occurred to him to make a crazy dash across the Czechoslovak border, abandoning Waterford Glass and Griffin, in the hopes of making it home undetected to Držkov. And it would have been a mad adventure. At that time, Eastern Europe was so closed to the

West that the Irish travel agents who organised Miroslav's trip to the Continent didn't even book travel to any points behind the Iron Curtain. At some psychological level, too, he was getting used to conducting his life outside Czechoslovakia, while still determined that one day in the near future he would go back there – maybe even as a citizen of another country.

While Miroslav was away in Europe, the official ground-breaking ceremony for the new Johnstown factory took place. When he looked later at the press photograph of the event, he noticed that Bačik was far off on the right-hand side of the official group, while Canon Barron, who had preached warnings against the infiltration of foreigners into Waterford, was smiling happily in the dead centre.

Oddly, Miroslav had as yet no official position with the glass factory. He had not held one even while Bačik was the commanding officer. His affidavit for Rosa described him as the company's 'glass technician', but that was really just his solicitor's language. Certainly, he had always been one of the best-known presences at Ballytruckle and at Johnstown, and so in a real sense his title seemed to be his name. 'Mr Havel will do this, Mr Havel will do that,' he remembers people saying if a technical problem needed to be addressed, and there were always technical problems needing to be addressed. In effect, therefore, he was serving as the company's 'Mr Havel'.

He did, however, keep one unusual sign of special status that Mr Bačik had given him in Světlá and which he never abandoned – a white laboratory coat, variations of which he wore over his street clothes every day at the factory from the beginning to the end of his career. From time to time, brown and green coats were issued to workers in other departments, but nobody else was ever daring enough to appropriate the white coat that became Miroslav's personal career trademark at Waterford Glass.

# Mr Havel Takes a Holiday

As 1952 rolled around, and as he approached his thirtieth birthday, Miroslav decided that he needed to take some kind of a break after nearly five years of psychologically testing life changes and his unexpected transition from innocent artist in Czechoslovakia into innocent artist immersed in the harsh realities of business and commerce in Ireland. As the old Ballytruckle factory began its slow shutdown, Miroslav had Bačik update his Red Cross/UNRA refugee certificate so that he could take a fourteen-day holiday to attend the second post-war Summer Olympic Games in Helsinki, Finland, in July 1952. UNRA, with financing arranged by the Marshall Plan, was about to finish its activities in Western Europe, and so this would be his last foreseeable chance to leave Ireland.

Throughout his life, Miroslav has retained a great interest in every kind of competitive sports activity, no matter how obscure. He was excited that the legendary Czech athlete, Emil Zatopek, would be competing in the 5,000 and 10,000 metres, as well as the marathon, at Helsinki. Bačik, for whom sports ranked somewhere below the Communist Party in the degree of his contempt, indulged Miroslav's desire to travel to Finland, despite his expectation that even Red Cross and UN protection would not avoid border-crossing complications.

Bačik's concerns were borne out when the actual journey took place. On arrival at Turku, the Finnish town across the Gulf of

Bothnia from Sweden, Miroslav's papers were rejected, and he was whisked off to jail. Despite fearing that he was about to emulate Franta's long incarceration, Miroslav encountered leniency at the hands of the Finns, who released him after only seven hours. (Had Bačik miraculously intervened?) When the police returned to unlock his cell, they handed him back his transit papers and his packet of Olympic event tickets, and told him to stay on the train to Helsinki and not to make any detours in Finnish territory, either going to Helsinki or on the way back. Finland at that time was still essentially a province of the Soviet Union and Cold War tensions were high.

Next, he boarded the train at Turku for the 160-kilometre journey to Helsinki. After about twenty minutes, the train came to a screeching stop somewhere in the countryside. A whole platoon of what appeared to be Soviet soldiers scrambled on board, running up and down the carriages, and shouted orders that all the blinds in all the compartments must be closed immediately. The passengers were told to remain still. For over an hour, Miroslav sweated. As an expatriate Czech with no passport, and therefore an escapee from Communism, he sensed himself as vulnerable to whatever might be the object of this unannounced search.

Then, with no further warning, the train started to chug again, slowly. As Miroslav peeked out under his blind, he could see that the train was moving through a stretch of Finnish territory that seemed totally devoid of inhabitants. Later, he heard from one of his fellow passengers that the soldiers had placed a big cardboard hammer and sickle on the front of the train. After leaving the zone of high security, wherever it was, the blinds were raised and the train picked up speed and made its way without any further interruptions to the main railway terminal in Helsinki. Given that Finland was technically independent, it had shocked Miroslav to see Soviet military personnel so far inside the Finnish homeland.

After such an eventful passage, it was good that Zatopek, at least, did not disappoint. Not only did he take gold medals in all of his three events, but, in a highly unusual Olympic marital triumph, his wife also captured gold in the women's javelin competition. Miroslav remembers being in the stadium, 'sitting nicely in the third row', for the final moments of the marathon. Unlike today's media-savvy spectators, the stadium crowds at Helsinki were relatively quiet until Zatopek had almost completed his final circuit of the track. The loud cheering one normally expects to hear started only as he hit his stride for the final hundred metres or so. Another world-renowned athlete, Englishman Jim Peters, dropped out at mile nineteen despite holding the world record. A statue of Zatopek was later erected just outside the Helsinki Olympic Stadium.

Miroslav had a wonderful time wandering around Helsinki, almost totally broke, bunking in school dormitories, and subsisting on bread, cheese and milk, his favourite food choices even today. He met a young man in the same financial straits as himself who worked at the Morris motor car factory in England. The two of them spent time together at the stadium and pooled their little bit of cash to ensure a steady supply of Finnish dairy products. They each had a book of tickets for Olympic events which included not only athletics but also, because of an effort by the Finnish organisers to promote less popular sports, a couple of other competitions, including boxing and gymnastics. Miroslav and his English friend were able to sell their boxing tickets to a group of Americans.

Between them, also, they managed to collect the entire series of Olympic programmes for every sport and every event. Miroslav later made a grand collage of his programmes, surrounded by an unconventional picture frame which he made out of Finnish newspapers published during the Games, cut up and pasted together in a strange but striking example of papier-mâché. This very personalised piece of memorabilia hung for years in the front hallway of Miroslav's first house in Waterford, until he took up oil painting for a brief but productive period in the early 1970s and replaced the Helsinki collage with one of his new abstracts.

He remembers thinking, as he strolled in the cool evenings through this compact city, how strange it was that Helsinki, a 'sad-looking' place and not at all prominent in the immediate post-war world, had been able to snag such a huge international event. The stadium, in fact, seemed almost absurdly outsized compared with the small scale of everything around it. Sometimes, his professional antennae would be triggered by the sight of some especially rich display of Finnish crystal in a shop window, and he would wander in the next day to make some mental notes of what he saw.

One night, as he took his usual evening walk through Helsinki's quiet city centre, he spotted a large Irish flag, the tricolour, hanging outside a small bar about two kilometres from the stadium. The raucous singing going on inside was audible even to Miroslav's challenged hearing. Curious, and violating his usual practice of avoiding pubs, he went inside and distinctly heard a tuneless but extremely boisterous rendition of 'It's a Long Way to Tipperary'. Peering closer in the smoky semi-darkness, he soon identified the well-known Waterford figures of Paddy Keating, owner of the city's biggest electrical appliance store, and the redoubtable J.J. Walsh, editor and proprietor of the leading local newspaper, the *Munster Express*.

Walsh, in fact, held a record for having personally attended every Olympic Games for some decades past, a record of continuous attendance that he and his successor, his son Kieran, have yet to yield. The electrician and the journalist were happy to stand free drinks for the gaunt Czechoslovak man who told them some crazy story about coming to Ireland and working as the designer for Waterford Glass.

Miroslav took the long way home to Ireland, ignoring his earlier police orders by diverting through Lapland, where he marvelled at the sight of the midnight sun and the pyrotechnics of the aurora borealis. The coach trip north to Finnish Lapland was organised by the country's Ministry of Tourism, and was offered free to under-funded Olympic visitors like Miroslav.

From there, he made his way by train down through Sweden, meeting up along this journey with the members of the American wrestling team on their way back from the Helsinki Games. He got the gold medal winner of the group to sign one of his Swedish kroner notes, but the demands of bodily sustenance meant that he eventually had to spend this precious currency. After taking the short sea-ferry crossing from Malmö to Copenhagen, he walked off the ship and directly onto a transcontinental train which was standing at exactly the same level as the ship, thanks to a remarkable system of sea and river locks.

His next ferry crossing, from Ostend in Belgium to Dover, was not quite so pleasant. Miroslav recalled how his first journey to Ireland, in that grim time just two years after the war, had been travelled in almost total silence. Now people were starting to relax and the cheap drinks on board the ferry made it a night of drunken hell for those who did not, or could not, partake.

When he arrived at London's Victoria Station, he was greeted by Sheila Power from Waterford, whom he knew from the factory. Sheila was in London visiting her mother, and all three of them took a taxi together to Paddington, where Miroslav would begin his journey back to Ireland. Miroslav by now had absolutely no money left, and he was hugely relieved when Sheila's mother brushed aside his fraudulent offer to pay the taxi fare and took care of the charges herself.

And it wasn't just the taxi fare that made him nervous. He had no ticket for the Paddington–Fishguard train, but he did manage to disappear inside the absolutely jam-packed carriages and to avoid the ticket collector. It was the first time he had seen England and Wales in good weather, and he rather enjoyed the parts of the journey when he wasn't locking himself in the toilets as the rail officials passed through the corridors.

The train pulled into Fishguard well after dark, and much too late for that day's boat crossing, so once again, as in 1947, Miroslav prevailed on the station-master to let him stay the night in his office. He was detained briefly the next morning by the local police, suspected of being an illegal alien because he was not carrying a passport, but eventually his Red Cross papers did the trick, although he admits that he was getting tired of these border-crossing headaches.

Boarding a much flashier boat than the one he remembered from his first journey, he made the bumpy crossing directly to Rosslare. As he settled into his seat on the train to Waterford, luck was with him one more time when he ran into Joseph Kretzen, one of the German blowers who had recently arrived at the new Johnstown factory. Kretzen kindly paid Miroslav's train fare. However, as the two men chatted amiably about the Olympics, they began to notice how their scheduled departure time had come and gone. They counted the passing minutes – twenty, thirty, then sixty – and still no sign of the engine kicking into life. By now they should already have been close to Waterford.

It turned out that the men had boarded the carriage closest to the station, but that the carriage was not connected to the rest of the train. The train had literally left them standing at the station. Miroslav jumped off the carriage and betrayed a little of that fiery artist's temper that would become one of his well-known characteristics in future years. He demanded that Kretzen's money for both tickets be refunded and that the two men be permitted to travel without charge on the next train to Waterford.

Perhaps taken aback by the unfamiliar experience of an angry man yelling at them in a very pronounced foreign accent, the red-faced railway officials conceded that it would have been a good idea to put a sign on the carriage that was staying behind in Rosslare. And so they agreed to Miroslav's audacious demand. The last part of his long journey back to Ireland, therefore, was legally and genuinely free.

# A Troubleshooter's Life at
# Waterford Glass

Miroslav, feeling quite exhausted after his holiday, was happy to be back in Waterford. But things had definitely changed. As Bačik faded into the quietness of the office suite, Miroslav, also without a specific portfolio, found himself busier than ever. He was heartened by the obvious new investment that the new owners were making in the enterprise, and for the first time he could foresee a viable professional future in Ireland, even if he was not yet ready to imagine his personal future there. The mix of foreign and domestic talent that he and Bačik had assembled still needed his continued supervision and training, but he also had to work with Noel Griffin to set up the much bigger Johnstown operation and to recruit even more skilled craftsmen and new apprentices.

Miroslav's working relationship with Griffin was growing ever closer, even while his sentimental side wished that Bačik had not so quickly taken himself, or been forced, out of the front lines. He and Bačik remained congenial friends to the end of Bačik's life, always with that formality that was noted earlier, but they never again worked together within the Waterford Glass business.

Miroslav does recall a single occasion, not too long after the IGB takeover, when Bačik surprised him by dropping into the engraving department to inform him about a new automatic stem-making machine he had seen in a German-language journal of commercial glass technology. It was a very Bačik moment – all those linguistic, entrepreneurial and technical skills firing on all cylinders. But it was no longer a real moment, and Miroslav could see that his friend and former collaborator did not seem to be especially happy. Not long before, Bačik had returned from a holiday to find that his big corner office, one of the perks he had wangled from the IGB sale, had been handed over to one of the new Irish sales executives.

Now the big decisions on Waterford's future (and the assignment of offices) were being taken by Griffin, the young accountant-turned-glass factory leader. Indeed, to give a sense of how much of a youngster Griffin was at that time, he took the reins of Waterford Glass even while he continued to study for his final accountancy exams in Dublin.

Miroslav remembers Griffin as a constantly supportive presence after the Johnstown factory began its operations. Even more importantly to the yearning immigrant, Griffin understood Miroslav's legal (or illegal) position as, to use Miroslav's own expression again, 'a man in the air'. Although it would take close to another decade, Griffin was eventually to establish a formal design department at Waterford Glass, with Miroslav at its head as Chief Designer. This was a change which recognised what had in fact been happening for the first ten years at Johnstown. The factory had gradually re-organised into a system that began with good designs and detailed blueprints – the Orrefors model – and those designs and blueprints in turn managed the successive blowing, cutting and (eventually) engraving processes.

In modern corporate jargon, in the first decade of Waterford Glass, Miroslav was not only the company's chief designer but also its chief technical 'troubleshooter'. Sometimes he provided services that he probably shouldn't have, but which in the chaotic political climate of the post-war period were seen as acceptable or at least defensible. His calligraphic skills made him a superb forger, and from to time he did a little 'touching-up work' on the passports of the Continental blowers and cutters who were coming to Waterford Glass.

Most of these changes were fairly harmless, and usually involved extending the validity date of foreign passports that had expired. Miroslav would shine an intense light on the relevant page of a passport and gently remove the existing words or numbers with a sharp blade, carefully avoiding any scratches on the paper. Using special architect's inks, he would then insert the replacement information in the same style as the original. But he also could do more than minor alterations. He remembers one occasion when he actually created an entire West German passport for a Polish national who was being recruited to come to the blowing room. He asked a local German butcher in Waterford to provide him with an old or cancelled West German passport to use as his model for the forgery, and was surprised when the butcher sent him a packet of no fewer than seven German passports. Of course, it never occurred to Miroslav to use his talents to make himself a new Czechoslovak passport.

Miroslav's new Irish bosses were very aware of his key role in setting up the pilot factory, and were determined to retain his expertise as the Johnstown operation was being inaugurated. This attitude, however, is something Miroslav appreciates only as he looks back over the decades. His wartime experiences and his hard choices in coming to Waterford, as well as losing Rosa, pushed him towards the pessimistic side, forever clouding the sunny optimism of his youth in Czechoslovakia.

So, back in the early 1950s, Miroslav himself was never confident that he would be kept on. He found himself in the strange position of sensing that he would not soon be returning to his homeland, while at the same time hoping that the Irish, or at least the Irish entrepreneurs who were now running the company that he and Bačik had once run from a tiny builder's hut, would not throw him out.

After a few years of intense upheaval, the new Waterford Glass factory opened in Johnstown in October 1951. The era of producing soda glass at Ballytruckle had ended. Noel Griffin and Miroslav had many discussions as to the kind of glass-making process that would be developed at Johnstown. Griffin read and re-read Miroslav's reports from Orrefors and other Continental glass-making centres, and continued to accept (even if he had yet to act on it) that a functioning design department would be needed to steward the production of high-quality crystal.

Following the lead of Bačik some years before, Griffin himself went to Europe soon after he took over, to recruit more foreign glass-making talent in Germany, Austria, Italy and (ironically for Miroslav) Czechoslovakia. Anticipating the kind of enhanced production Miroslav was suggesting, Griffin was particularly looking for qualified stem-makers.

As ever, the presence of yet more foreigners, especially foreigners who were the masters to Irish apprentices, ignited some friction even on the factory floor. Nobody expected, however, that Joe McGrath himself would be responsible for stoking anti-foreigner sentiment. Yet, at the opening ceremony for the Johnstown plant in 1951, the elder McGrath took an apparent swipe at Waterford's Continental contingent, expressing the hope that 'only Irish workers' would eventually comprise the company's employees.

In fairness, McGrath probably intended his remark to be an optimistic forecast about the renaissance of indigenous glass-making skills rather than an attack on the foreigners who had revived Waterford Glass. And maybe, too, it was also a nativist reaction to some unpleasant developments in parts of the United States, where the acronym 'NINA' (for 'no Irish need apply') had begun to make its appearance.

Nonetheless, coming from someone who had held the labour and industry portfolios in Irish governments, the remark was considered sufficiently off-key that both McGrath and Griffin later felt the need to apologise to Bačik for it. Miroslav, never someone who would get unduly upset about the strange things people say in public speeches, had great respect for old McGrath, who had used his considerable wealth to invest in Ireland and the cause of Irish business. In that sense, he considered Joe McGrath, like McGrath's contemporary, Sean Lemass, who was then Minister for Industry and Commerce, to be 'a very progressive man'.

The opening of the new factory was Joe McGrath's first and only visit to Waterford Glass, although he later commissioned Miroslav to engrave his portrait in crystal. Still, Miroslav remembers that the foreigner issue was always a source of tension in those early days after the IGB takeover. Very soon after the transition to Irish ownership, he became personally embroiled in an unpleasant episode that revealed some of this tension very vividly. With new management coming in, Miroslav was being especially careful because of his uncertain personal status, and indeed he took responsibility for things that were clearly not his fault, rather than provoke confrontations.

One afternoon, he got a telephone call from Joe Griffin, Noel's father, who was now a director of both IGB and Waterford Glass. The elder Griffin told Miroslav that he needed to see him urgently at IGB headquarters in Dublin. Miroslav, terrified of what might be amiss, took the first train the next morning to Dublin. He was very familiar with the IGB facility, which he had visited some months before (again at Joe Griffin's request) to inspect some mould-making machinery that the company had recently acquired. He arrived in Griffin's office at ten o'clock. 'Miroslav, you will be in trouble,' he remembers thinking to himself. As Miroslav mentally went over some appropriate lines of apology, Griffin came quickly to his point. 'Mr Havel,' he said, 'I want to inform you that you are not to ask anybody in the Waterford Glass factory to identify their allegiance to any religion.'

Immediately Miroslav understood what had happened. He and Bačik had taken an employment application form that they used at Světlá, and Bačik had simply translated it into English for use at Waterford Glass. Asking for religious identity was an insensitive error, apparently, and one of the new Irish apprentice cutters had complained about the form directly to IGB management in Dublin. In Czechoslovakia, there were more than twenty-five religions, but in Ireland there was really only one (in the early 1950s, at any rate). Miroslav was sure that he had committed a capital offence, given the influence of the Catholic Church in every aspect of Irish life. He expected to be 'sent packing', he says. By sheer coincidence, Miroslav had one of the offending forms in his inside pocket, since he had been interviewing a new employee just the day before. He took it out and explained (in 'terrible English', as he recalls) what he and Bačik had done in pure administrative innocence. Griffin was sympathetic, replying that he understood the importance of having personal details about the employees, such as their addresses. 'But you must leave religion out of this form,' he told the young foreigner who was being held accountable for a decision that had been made just before Bačik's hopitalisation with peritonitis years before. The episode was another striking example of the rather wide scope of his duties as the company's 'Mr Havel'. Miroslav went back to Waterford feeling very relieved, but he had learned an important lesson in Irish business culture.

As the new factory got under way, it was finally possible for Waterford Glass, with its expanded furnaces at Johnstown (and the financial clout to purchase more costly raw materials such as silica sand and red lead), to create the kind of heavy lead-based crystal that Bačik and Miroslav had been planning several years before. Excited that Waterford Glass could now build a reputation that would have been impossible using only soda glass, Miroslav sketched designs for the first production of the new lead crystal.

The move to Johnstown allowed him to dust off his old National Museum drawings and to consider how the coming new generation of Waterford Glass products would bear its own signature styles, while reflecting also the heritage of the old designs. Again, he was forced initially to simplify his designs in order to match the learning curves of the apprentices. The masters, almost all of them foreigners, were still too few to carry the anticipated production entirely on their own.

And yet, as will be seen, this process of simplification was precisely how Miroslav managed to re-invent the old Waterford designs for a new age. Just as important as these design decisions, however, were Miroslav's many decisions on the technical and production side. As he once again examined his drawings at the National Museum of Ireland, and considered the lessons of his years of exposure to modern glass-making technology and the costs of modern production, he came to appreciate that most of the designs he had discovered in the Museum were 'useless', as he says, for commercial manufacture. Eventually 85 per cent of Waterford's catalogue during Miroslav's career would comprise his new designs, while the rest would be replicas (with technical adjustments) of old Waterford patterns.

All kinds of production decisions separated him from his Irish predecessors. The old Waterford glass-makers had focused very little on stemware, for example, and preferred to apply their very rich, elaborate and deeply cut patterns onto larger and sturdier items, such as butter dishes and bowls. When they did create a table-top suite, they typically produced only a decanter and one or two accompanying drinking glasses.

Old Waterford decanters had unusual embellishments, too, such as a set of three crystal rings, each of which was individually shaped from small lumps of molten glass and then carefully mounted around the neck of the decanter. Although the rings had a functional as well as decorative effect, allowing a better grip on the neck, the labour intensity of this kind of work would be commercially impossible in 1951. Miroslav's decanters would be blown in a single piece that included a straightforward neck section without added ornamental embellishments.

Moreover, for all its added weight, so different from the soda glass produced at Ballytruckle, the new Waterford heavy crystal was still not 'soft' enough, Miroslav recalls, for the minutely elaborate cutting and engraving practised in previous centuries. The softer the crystal, the trickier it is for the blower to handle, but the more susceptible it is to deep decoration by the cutters and engravers. As the years went by and Waterford refined its glass melting compounds, increasingly elaborate decoration would again be possible. Miroslav did eventually manage to replicate an occasional antique piece, particularly in his blueprints for Waterford's well-known table centrepieces. For the moment, though, he needed to think in terms of practical design solutions.

The production decisions that Miroslav did feel comfortable taking, however, were possible in the vastly improved technical environment of the Johnstown factory. The new facility had superior furnaces, expanded to ten pots in a line, operating with cheap gas from the local gasworks. Miroslav now had the support of a growing team of skilled mould-makers, such as Kurt Berger. The moulds are used by the blowers to shape the glass while it is still in its blazing-hot treacly state just out of the pot. Berger built his customised wooden moulds from ash-tree wood, using hundreds of special cut-out designs that Miroslav provided. Miroslav had recruited Berger a few years previously in Germany.

Moreover, the new factory, like its forerunner, was fortunate to have access to the busy shipping port of Waterford. The company ordered its upgraded raw materials, especially silica sand and red lead oxide powder, by the shipload, and it was a straightforward matter to transfer the freight quickly from portside to the manufacturing site at Johnstown. Simple economics dictated that easy access to the port gave Waterford Glass a sustained cost advantage over many of its inland-based Continental competitors.

On the production side, Miroslav was forced to replace the antique system of finishing the rim of the blown glass with a heavy metal scissors, a hugely time-consuming process, with a system of grinding which used cutting wheels to level the rims. The antique method gave a more rounded finish to the old Waterford rims, but was simply unaffordable in a modern factory. And the cooling process at Johnstown was incomparably superior to Miroslav's little pair of kilns at Ballytruckle. A single annealing oven, fifty metres long, received the glass on fast-moving conveyor belts direct from the blowing shops, and the old problems of exploding or fusing glass were virtually eliminated.

The most critical production change, of course, was the abandonment of soda glass. Waterford would now be making crystal glass with a 33 per cent red-lead content, much heavier than its Continental rivals (Czech glass, for example, used only 24 per cent lead). Red lead, from which lead crystal takes its name, was a much more expensive ingredient than anything used at Waterford previously. Lead is a very heavy substance which increases the density of the glass and raises its power to refract and disperse the light transmitted through it.

The departure from Continental standards of weight would create its own set of technical issues. The risk of impurities and imperfections is always present in glass manufacture, but the addition of more and more lead magnifies this risk. That was why the Continentals sacrificed a higher lead content (and therefore enhanced brilliance) in favour of more consistent quality.

The process of making, or 'melting', glass is known all over the world, Miroslav says, and is not a secret. The basic ingredients for making lead crystal were known to the Bohemians as early as 1676. 'What is a secret,' Miroslav adds, 'is how to keep the same type and quality of glass at all times.' If a customer buys a glass today, and then breaks it, the customer needs to know that exactly the same colour and quality and translucency will still be available in the marketplace even though lead crystal is made from a volatile mixture of ingredients including high-grade ultra-white silica (not beach) sand, potash and red lead.

Miroslav was conscious that Waterford Glass intended to market itself as a purveyor of crystal, and crystal, for Miroslav, was a glass of water-white clarity, resembling the natural stone, rock crystal. Indeed, for most of the history of the revived Waterford Glass, the pure sparkle of uncoloured crystal would be its signature – whiter even than the old Penrose product with its probably mythical bluish tinge. The quest for water-white crystal was technically demanding in itself. The quite ordinary materials used in making crystal – all that sand, lead and potash – create all kinds of possibilities of impurities in the melting process that will put tints into the glass (like the faint yellowish-green tint in the early Ballytruckle production). Iron oxide, for example, is an impurity found in all sand, even the higher grades of sand used in making crystal. As little as one part of this oxide to 5,000 parts of sand will give a pale sea-green tint to the finished glass.

To get these tints out and to purify the glass, various

decolourising agents have to be added through a patient process of trial and error. To illustrate the level of detail required, a pinch of manganese, for example, counteracts the green discolouration produced by even a small quantity of iron in the silica sand, and a pinch of arsenic reverses the tendency of manganese to give the glass a purplish tint. The irony, therefore, is that pure crystal glass is produced only by wiping out the colouring impurities that are naturally present when the ingredients are first mixed in the pots.

Waterford's decision to raise its lead content, therefore, would intensify the pressure to monitor the quality and uniformity of its melted glass. There would be much fiddling with the melting recipes to get everything right. But colour variations proved easier to deal with than the problem of bubbles. The molten glass in its fireclay pots, when it reached its maximum temperature in excess of $1,500°$ centigrade at about one o'clock in the morning, became a raging mass of bubbles. Miroslav says that the sight of this roiling, boiling, red-hot molten liquid was always 'terrifying'. From that time until the blowers' first shift at seven in the morning, the molten raw glass had to be very gradually cooled. A furnace worker checked the temperature hourly with a long metal thermometer. Although the bubbles died down as the liquid cooled, it was still necessary to eliminate as much of the residual unstable surface motion as possible.

When Miroslav first came to Waterford Glass, he used the time-honoured Bohemian method, which Bačik fully endorsed, of throwing turnips and potatoes into the pots. This vegetable tactic, tested by generations of Czech glass-makers, relied on certain predictable laws of physics which determined that these humble but heavy pieces of produce, which consist mostly of water, would plunge to the bottom of the pot, be consumed in the fire, and send water gushing upwards to dissolve the bubbles congregating on the surface of the pot.

The turnip and potato method was not foolproof, and tiny bubbles did appear in the blown glass. Nevertheless, Miroslav's vegetable trick survived for many years at Ballytruckle and Johnstown, before being superseded by mechanical (and eventually computer-programmed) processes which automatically feed the ingredients to the pots and minutely monitor the temperature to avoid any dreaded bubble formations. Miroslav has mixed feelings about the post-vegetable era. For him, the presence of at least some tiny impurities was a sign of an authentic handmade product. He always made what he thought was a key technical distinction between the clearest, brightest and most translucent mouth-blown crystal, which was his goal, and what he regarded as the almost inevitable presence of tiny imperfections such as bubbles.

Apart from these annoying issues of impurities, Miroslav later came to believe that the hand-and-wheel cutting at Waterford was superior to virtually all Continental cutting. One vital reason for this superiority was his continuing obsession with the techniques of polishing the cut crystal. An item of cut lead crystal glassware is typically given its crowning lustre by being dipped into acid. The mixture, a blending of hydrofluoric and sulphuric acids, strips a thin but uniform layer from the entire surface.

The deep prismatic incisions of wedge cutting (which is a Waterford signature) respond beautifully to the acid process. But acid is less effective on other types of cutting (flat cutting or a flat-cut variant called 'olive' cutting). These less penetrating cuts can be polished by wooden felt-lined wheels attached to a cutting machine, which are coated with a polishing powder and require the polisher to work against the motion of the wheel.

In the early days, Miroslav and his teams polished every glass by hand, dipping the wedge cuts into the acid in little baskets and busily polishing other cuts with wood-and-felt wheels. Timing on the acid dips was crucial, because naturally acid can quickly devour the delicate crystal rather than enhance it. Miroslav worked with all kinds of acid-based dips in his quest for the ideal polishing process, using trial and error to vary the strength and weakness of the solution and the length of immersion. Attention to polishing was even more effective for Waterford glassware because of its heavy 33 per cent lead content, which allowed sharper edges to the finished cutting, and therefore a much more intense gleam after the polish.

Using acid is a dangerous activity, and Miroslav was always careful to wear protective rubber gloves. But he recalls one afternoon, after he had been dipping the baskets into the acid for about thirty minutes, when he experienced 'horrible pain' in the fingers of both hands. After another short while, all of his fingers had swollen to the size of big frankfurters. He rushed to the doctor and was taken immediately to the city infirmary for a quick operation to remove eight of his fingernails. 'My hands were then like two bandaged bowls,' he remembers – a shocking sight for someone whose hands were so critical to his work.

The surgeon told Miroslav that the acid had visibly penetrated his rubber gloves and worked its way under his nails. Later, he discovered tiny holes in the gloves, even though he had just taken them out of their new wrapping. Miroslav was undeterred by his painful experience, however. He returned that afternoon to the factory to supervise his apprentice cutters, but it took three weeks before he could work again with his own hands.

When even Waterford Glass finally succumbed to the economic need for mechanised acid polishing, Miroslav never allowed an engraved or specially commissioned piece to leave the factory without being hand-polished by himself or one of his engravers. He usually used wood-and-felt wheels, but if he needed to give the piece a personalised acid bath, he did so. He would eventually acquire the reputation of being the world's best lead-crystal polisher.

Miroslav, always experimenting, did consider the possibility of adding colour to the new Waterford range, a decorative accent that was very much in the Czech tradition. Despite his obsession with water-white crystal, he was so technically curious that he conducted many months of trials to test whether some kind of light colouring could work in the very heavy lead product that the company was now producing. Even though he was very familiar with the rules of colour (adding copper to the melted glass produces red tints, for example, and a thousandth-part of gold produces a rose-coloured tint), he was never satisfied. The melting process somehow failed to synchronise.

He was even suspicious that the pots were being sabotaged in some way. This would have been relatively easy to do, because even a single copper penny dropped into the ferocious heat of those pots could cause an unappealing pinkish tint to disfigure the batch. If there was sabotage (and perhaps that's too strong a word), it was a sign of the times. Already Waterford Glass was developing a strongly unionised workforce, and Miroslav was beginning to understand that not every creative or technical decision that he might wish to make, or experiment he wished to conduct – including the addition of colour – was necessarily going to be implemented without opposition or dissent on the factory floor.

Little of this union opposition, as far as Miroslav could tell, was directed personally at him. Although he was never a member of any union, he typically was not identified as management either. He had a generally good rapport with the blowers, cutters and engravers, many of whom he personally trained in the challenging first decade of the company's existence. Perhaps his unwavering commitment to his craft, and his obvious enthusiasm for the magical chemistry and artistry of fine crystal, insulated him to some degree in an organisational hierarchy that increasingly divided the company's business managers from its craftsmen.

However, he did eventually have to bow to the union position on demarcation, which meant that his random but frequent appearances on the factory floor – to monitor production or, as sometimes happened, to perch himself beside a master cutter and to give instructions, or even to cradle the glass in his own hands to show the cutters how particular cuts should be made – were no longer acceptable practices. Given the highly informal way in which Miroslav's career with Waterford Glass had evolved, and how much of the production he had been responsible for over the years, he never understood why the unions were so reluctant to allow him to jump into the process whenever he saw the need.

For a long time, he was naively oblivious to these difficult issues of labour relations. Then, as the unions became more vocal, he told them that their opposition to his production interventions was 'ridiculous'. 'I told them that I was the designer,' he recalls, 'so they

25. A scale model of the Concorde, commissioned by Air France in 1974.

26. A crystal replica of the USF&G Falcon jet.

27. Paperweight commissioned for Pope Paul VI.

28. Paperweight commissioned for Pope John Paul II.

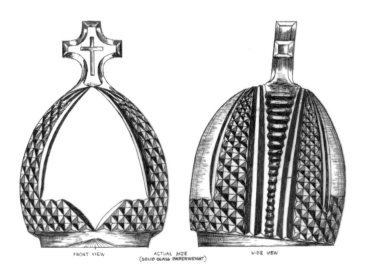

29. Original design sketches for the Pope John Paul II paperweight.

30. The Queen Margrethe Vase, which Miroslav designed for the visit of the Danish monarch to Ireland in 1978.

31. The trophy commissioned by the Wimbledon Lawn Tennis Association for the centenary of ladies' tennis at Wimbledon, and to celebrate tennis champion Billie Jean King's record number of tournament victories.

32. The unique personal trophy created by Miroslav for golf legend Sam Snead.

33. The 1976 *Daily Express* Cheltenham Triumph Hurdle Championship trophy.

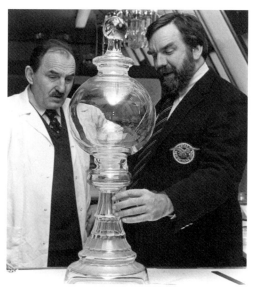

34. Miroslav and a USF&G official discussing the completed flat cuts on the stem of this golf trophy before the wedge-cutting of the bowl and the final polishing of the entire piece. Note Miroslav's trademark white laboratory coat.

35. The finished trophy.

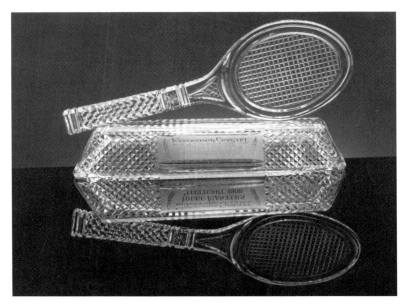

36. The mounted tennis racket sculpture, created for the Stuttgart 'Golden Racket' competition.

37. A football-shaped trophy commemorating the triumph of the San Francisco 49ers in Super Bowl XIX.

38.  A crystal golf ball and Number 9 club-face commissioned by Tony Jacklin and his wife to honour the performance of Bernhard Langer in the 1989 Ryder Cup.

39.  TV presenter Gay Byrne commissioned this piece to celebrate Maureen Potter's fortieth year on the boards of Dublin's Olympia Theatre. It shows Ms Potter's two young sons.

40. An oval bowl that briefly went into production, but proved too expensive to maintain as a regular catalogue item due to its specialised shape.

41. A horizontal cut vase.

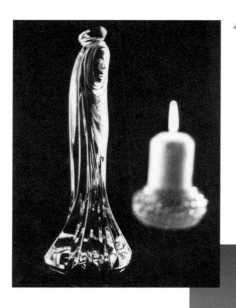

42. An abstract statute of the Virgin Mary cut from a single block of crystal.

43. This red jug from 1954 was a rare venture into coloured glass.

44. A vase from 1981 with free-flowing design.

45.   A 1984 bowl, showing a naturalistic design of
      a fish swimming through water.

46.   1985 sculpture of a fish.

47. A sailboat carved from a solid block of
crystal.

48. A 1980 bowl, with ball-wheel cutting on
the body and large diamonds below.

49. A 1980 vase, cut and polished into
vertical lobes and then wedge-cut.

50. A 1981 stem vase, where the flat surface
facing the observer reflects the deep
cutting on the other surfaces.

51. An Indian snake charmer.

52. An armadillo.

53. A Cinderella slipper.

54. A trilby hat made to anchor an exhibition on the history of hats at Bloomingdale's department store in New York.

55. Miroslav's crystal scale replica of the Statue of Liberty, which Taoiseach, Dr Garret FitzGerald, presented on behalf of the Irish people to US President Ronald Reagan on St Patrick's Day 1986, the year of the Statue's centennial celebrations.

56. In 1976, Taoiseach Liam Cosgrave celebrated the US Independence Bicentennial with this Waterford Crystal presentation to President Gerald Ford.

57. Taoiseach Dr Garret FitzGerald, President Ronald Reagan and
Miroslav Havel on the White House lawn on St Patrick's Day
1986, following the presentation of Miroslav's crystal replica of
the Statue of Liberty to the US President. In the background is
Patrick McKernan, then Political Director of the Department of
Foreign Affairs, and later Irish Ambassador to the United States.

thought I should stay in my design department.' Among the union positions he strongly opposed was the insistence that no cutter could do both wedge and flat cutting. This was a demarcation decision that contradicted his experience from the Bohemian tradition.

Sometimes Miroslav's willingness to ignore union rules could have positive outcomes for the business. Fred Curtis, who later became one of Waterford's top designers, got his start because Miroslav had such an independent streak. Curtis was originally a cutter, but sometimes on the job he took a little time to work on special pieces he had designed himself, like an elaborate crystal sailing ship. This work caught Miroslav's eye as he swept to and fro past Curtis' cutting station and Miroslav encouraged Curtis to keep doing it. After being warned repeatedly by his cutting room superiors to stop working on special pieces, one day Curtis was suspended because of the time he was dedicating to what they considered non-production activity. When Miroslav heard about the suspension he went to Curtis' house and asked him to come back as a member of his new design and sculpting department. Miroslav justified this unilateral hire, a clear violation of union practice, by saying that he needed someone to work with him because his hands were shaking, he was getting older, and any number of other excuses that no-one felt able to protest.

Occasionally, Miroslav's flashes of artistic impatience would make themselves felt in situations where he thought administrators were needlessly interfering with the creative work of the factory. His former engraving colleague, Jim Burke, recalled one day when a particularly officious group of managers from quality control were walking around the engraving department, checking the items they found against a list of finished inventory.

Outside Miroslav's office, they discovered a box of working samples. 'We have no record of these items,' one of them shouted in to Miroslav, sounding for all the world like a typical Communist bureaucrat. Furious at the sudden interruption, Miroslav abandoned his engraving wheel and came outside his office. He picked up the box of samples, smashed it defiantly to the ground, and declared as the startled managers surveyed the wreckage, 'Now you have no problem.'

Just as Miroslav had once travelled to Sweden to gather and to poach ideas on glass-making techniques, so the Waterford plant's success was itself attracting interest from overseas manufacturers, including the Swedes and Finns. But the Irish government still had something of an inferiority complex about the strength of foreign competition. On the initiative of some bright official in the Department of Industry and Commerce, in 1957 the Scandinavians were invited to send a team of six experts to Dublin to make presentations to local Irish industrialists on a number of contemporary manufacturing processes, including glass-making. The gathering was billed by the government as an opportunity for Irish factories to learn ideas from the Swedes and Finns about how to become more efficient and market-savvy. As such, it had already caused some of the invitees to bristle at its blatantly condescending purpose.

Waterford Glass was represented at the meeting in a Dublin hotel by Miroslav and Dr Franz Winkelman, a Belgian-born Irishman who had recently joined the glass factory as head of production. Winkelman was the second qualified glass-making technologist at Waterford Glass (after John Barraclough), and he was steeped in a family tradition that included a glass-making business run by his uncle in Italy. He himself was a PhD graduate of the prestigious Department of Glass Technology at Sheffield University.

To Miroslav, Winkelman was the first big Western European glass 'name' that the factory had been able to attract. He and Winkelman had an excellent rapport, and it was Winkelman who eventually pushed Griffin to make good his promise to give Miroslav an autonomous design department. Winkelman, a seasoned traveller, was also one of Miroslav's best sources for his comprehensive stamp collection, which he had re-launched in Ireland after being forced to abandon his original collection in Czechoslovakia. Winkelman made a habit of posting special first-day-of-issue envelopes to Miroslav from all sorts of exotic places.

Miroslav was pleased to be on Winkelman's right side, and particularly so on the day of the Dublin presentation. The

Scandinavians had laid out a collection of Irish-made products on some tables in the meeting room. They walked around the room, pointing to the various samples of tea-towels, Aran sweaters, linen, pottery, and of course hand-made crystal glass, and made some negative comments on what they perceived as the marketing strategies for these products.

'You Irish do everything with shamrocks,' one of the Swedes remarked in a provocatively uncomplimentary way. In one sense, his statement was pretty accurate. Reliance on Irish and Celtic associations, after all, was already a critical part of Waterford's sales pitch to the American market. But the speaker became even more daring. He picked up a crystal drinking glass and declared that 'This should be much better to suit its function.' Since Waterford was the only Irish crystal factory, Winkelman felt compelled to respond to the Swede's strange but probably unflattering remark. 'What would you do with a drinking glass?' he asked. 'What would you change to make sure that it serves its function of being a drinking glass?'

The Swedish expert, not expecting such effrontery from the Irish he had come to instruct, replied, 'It depends on how much you pay me.'

'Well, I don't need to pay you to tell me that a drinking glass holds a certain amount of wine or beer and that's that,' Winkelman shot back.

The exchange cast a pall over the meeting. Miroslav was sitting beside Winkelman in the audience and reddened with embarrassment, but he knew exactly what was going on. A bold and brash new generation of Irish industrialists was beginning to make its appearance, and Winkelman, like Noel Griffin, was one of its advance men.

# A New Design Philosophy – 'Lismore'

For Waterford Glass, the move to Johnstown meant that the era of barrel-chested beer glasses was finally over. The products from the new plant started with less complex shapes, such as salad bowls, vases and plates, all of which had wide spaces that could be cut with relative straightforwardness even by younger apprentices. But Miroslav, without much attention to the fashions of the times, quickly went much further.

Anticipating continued sophistication in the company's skill sets, especially as some of the first generation of apprentices graduated to the rank of master, he conceived the idea of the extended Waterford Glass 'suite', and plunged into the design of complexly cut table glasses in full sets, 'from the liqueurs to the tall champagnes', as he puts it. Miroslav's suites were comprehensive, but also, from a sales and marketing perspective, a complicated product idea. Each suite was anchored by a large stoppered decanter, and also comprised a matching series of at least eight drinking glasses.

Miroslav, excited by the factory's growing bevy of qualified stem-makers, developed stem-glasses for port, sherry, white and red wine, cocktails, and water, as well as low-stemmed liqueur glasses, round-bottomed glasses for whiskey and other spirits, and low and tall champagne glasses. Depending on the suite, his chosen stem sizes could be tall, mid-level or low. The size of each glass was matched mathematically against official domestic and international measures for liquids. The rich variety of items in each suite already represented another departure from the French and Swedish industry standard. The Continentals tended to use a single glass for several purposes. For example, sherry and port would have one glass, and a single tall-stemmed glass could do duty for red and white wine and water.

This burst of activity was the single most intensive period of Miroslav's working life, since his task was to generate a vast array of designs that would then be culled, by himself, by Griffin, and by a new generation of post-Marckwald salesmen, to decide what would go into production. Over fifty of Miroslav's patterns were approved for manufacture during this classic period. In addition, over the coming years, he developed designs for over a hundred different items of crystal giftware, from globes marked with accurate lines of longitude and latitude, to scent bottles, ship's decanters, glass bells, ring-holders for dressing-tables and carriage clocks. He 'doodled' thousands of ideas, of course, but only a fraction could ever reach production.

Miroslav was adamant, moreover, that Waterford Glass could avoid being a mere imitator of its Continental rivals. Some of the new company directors had visited German or Scandinavian factories and were enthusiastic about Continental-style glass. But Griffin, who made caustic remarks about not producing 'what the boys saw on their holidays', allowed Miroslav a total free hand.

Even with many technical challenges still to be met, Miroslav's expectations for better things were soaring. He was particularly excited that a higher quality of crystal would gradually deliver him from what he considered to be a glass designer's nightmare – the need to cover up all the 'miserable' defects in the blown glass with extensive cutting. Now he could boldly experiment with undecorated blank areas that would serve as a kind of negative space to enhance the delicacy of his designs. Miroslav believed strongly that as much free space as possible should be allowed on a glass, but that is possible only when the crystal is of reasonably high quality. Old Waterford and Bohemian glass-makers, he noticed, rarely took that chance. They used extremely fine cutting stones to fill up empty spaces, even the small spaces between wedge cuts, with tiny cross-hatched cuts and fields of very fine diamonds. Nineteenth-century Bohemian glass was particularly known for covering up every available square inch of glass surface with extravagant decoration. And Miroslav noticed that the tiny cuts found on so much old Waterford and Bohemian glass blocked rather than admitted light. He preferred a vocabulary of much larger prismatic cuts that would enhance the sparkle of Waterford's higher-quality crystal.

Miroslav had also grown to dislike the unpolished glass that dominated the Continental glass industry, which he felt could not do justice to the natural luminosity and translucency of high-quality crystal. He wanted the new Waterford Glass range to be distinguished by a high degree of gleam and lustre. And that meant that the pieces would be even more highly polished than anything in the old Waterford collection.

To a great extent, Miroslav's ideas of good glass design can be traced back to his training under Přenosil and Brychta at the Železny Brod school. These artists had emphasised a more harmonious balance between form and decoration than they considered Bohemian glass-makers to have achieved in the nineteenth century.

Nonetheless, he was still captivated by his National Museum sketches and his early work in Waterford. He never intended to bow to the Scandinavian 'cult of plain glass' by eliminating most decoration and relying for design innovation and appeal almost entirely on variations in glass shape, size and thickness. Even though Waterford Glass itself went in that direction after his retirement, he still believes that lead crystal's hallmark is the sparkle and glitter that can be produced by decoration. 'Natural plain glass doesn't shine,' he says.

The alternative to deep-cut decoration is to play with the shape, as the Swedes did. Relying on shape is much cheaper, of course, than relying on decoration, and Miroslav knew from the very beginning that the reborn Waterford Glass was headed toward a more expensive method of production. 'But even the Swedish are introducing more cutting these days,' he says today, 'trying to give their glass a little sparkle.' Still, shape and form would also be very much a part of his new design ethos for Waterford Glass.

Griffin still wanted the Bačik–Havel vision, of Penrose reborn, to drive the new factory's production. Miroslav agreed, believing that the old Waterford influences would be much more commercially interesting than a jumble of patterns borrowed from German, French and other Continental sources. His designs, therefore, prominently featured the diamond-shaped wedge cutting – echoing the old Penrose styles – that would become new Waterford's most identifiable (and itself much-imitated) characteristic. Wedge cutting requires the craftsman to make three incisions into the surface of the glass with a cutting wheel – a very deep cut and two shallower lateral cuts that form a 'v' shape on the surface of the glass. The accumulation of cuts creates a distinctive cross-hatched or diamond pattern. Wedge cuts assembled into these patterns are prismatic and give Waterford's crystal glass its characteristic glittering effect. 'Flat' cuts, in contrast, use the hardness of big carborundum wheels, in effect, to slice or peel indentations on the glass. A sandstone wheel then gives a smooth finish to the cut. Flat cutting, which is broad and without detail, is used on all stems.

As Miroslav is the first to admit, the success of his designs came not from the use of these cutting styles, which have been known and practised for centuries. What eventually captivated the marketplace, rather, was how Miroslav assembled these signature cuts into combinations of rich but uncluttered patterns, enhanced by the resilience and gleam of Waterford's heavy crystal and the attention that he paid to the art of polishing.

As he is also quick to point out, however, he always understood that his position at Waterford Glass was not that of a professor of design at the Umprum school in Prague. He was, rather, a creative artist who was compelled, and felt compelled himself, to re-mix his creative juices to accommodate not only the limitations of production but also the demands of that unpredictable tyrant of production – sales and marketing. Thus, as he and Noel Griffin worked to organise production, in the mid-1950s other ambitious Irishmen were arriving at Waterford Glass to help build the company's sales and marketing prowess. Miroslav remembers particularly the energy of Cornelius (Con) Dooley, Griffin's hard-driving cousin, who, by as early as July 1952, was in the United States dealing directly with the big US department stores – like Marshall Field's in Chicago and B. Altman's in New York – that would eventually become the primary stockists for the Waterford Glass product.

Miroslav made about twenty or thirty designs for Dooley to take on his first American expedition, so that he could give potential distributors a sense of what the factory intended to do. It was a daring mission for Dooley, and not just because he had to take a fifteen-hour flight on one of the old DC-4 aeroplanes. The US market at the time, Miroslav recalls, was flooded with French, German, Spanish, Czech and even Romanian high-quality crystal, and Waterford Glass had no special expertise in how to promote a new glass product. Someone even told Dooley that he was wasting his time because Americans, especially Californians, didn't even use glasses or drink wine – they sat on their beaches and drank coffee out of paper cups. One nice touch was that the Irish government's export agency, Córas Tráchtála, hosted a reception at Ireland House in New York City to publicise Dooley's arrival in America.

The benign nepotism of how Griffin and Dooley got their jobs was hardly noticed in those days, but in any event their success cannot be denied. Dooley 'blossomed' in the gritty US retail market, Miroslav recalls. He had the advantages of an oversized personality and, at least at the beginning, the fact that Noel Griffin's father, Joe, was a well-known horse breeder and trainer who had excellent contacts with this blue-blooded and wealthy sport in the United States.

However, it was not just a matter of big personality and good contacts. Dooley himself was always inventive in finding clever ways to crack this huge market. He asked Miroslav to design a series of big colourful posters which he managed to have placed in several large retail outlets in big cities across the United States. Underneath the posters, Dooley displayed specimens of new Waterford drinking glasses on a little stand, and beneath the stand was a suggestion box inviting the public to submit comments on the design. The posters struck a chord with the Irish-American community, and word began to filter out of a terrific new luxury crystal collection coming from the old country.

By the beginning of the 1960s, Waterford Glass was beginning to get more than a toehold in the American market. 'We were really making some money,' Miroslav recalls, and, for the first time, the factory paid a Christmas bonus to all of its employees. The race to greatness had begun. By 1970, the company, re-styled as Waterford Crystal, would have nearly 3,000 employees working in the world's largest crystal glass-making facility. The new facility would occupy forty acres in the townland of Kilbarry, about three kilometres south-west of Johnstown, at what were then the very outskirts of Waterford City.

Miroslav always believed – and Con Dooley and the Waterford Glass sales team continually proved him right – that a twentieth-century re-interpretation of the classical Penrose designs, laden with the mystique of Irish history, would appeal to the huge and increasingly wealthy Irish-American marketplace. Years later, Dooley would recollect that the revival in the general use of heavy crystal began with Waterford, and with Miroslav's re-interpretation of the old Penrose heritage.

In the beginning, however, Miroslav's patterns were commercially risky. Even though he was creating new ways of expressing the classical Penrose designs, he was aware that, by the close of the nineteenth century, the extravagance of Waterford-style cut crystal had fallen victim to the popularity and cheapness of the mechanised methods of pressing glass developed in America. Also, the Modernist movement in early twentieth-century art tended to favour unadorned or lightly decorated crystal. The commercial effect of Modernism was felt most strongly in the second half of the twentieth century – exactly the time when Waterford Glass was revived – in the rise in demand for well-designed, inexpensive, utilitarian industrial products. Manufacturers of furniture, textiles and glassware were all affected by the ripples from this new preference for simplicity and low cost.

Miroslav's design solution to these tough market challenges was clever. He clearly intended to scale back the heaviness and intricacy of the Penrose style. But he was confident that the glitter and sparkle of cut crystal could still prove appealing when combined with a more harmonious appreciation of the form and shape of the glass. Miroslav, in other words, intended to re-balance the Penroses' Victorian preference for showy decoration over form. His designs would have utilitarian appeal to satisfy the modern preoccupation with functionalism, but they would also echo an earlier age of luxury and refinement. The best expression of Miroslav's design philosophy in those critical early days – the combination of delicate decoration and purity of form – is to be seen in the Lismore suite.

In 1952 and 1953, during that intense period of design activity noted earlier, Miroslav worked hardest on five variants of what he called, using the simple sequential numbering system devised by his new design assistant, Frances Cahill, Design Number 600-318. The 600 represented the shape and the 318 identified the cutting pattern. Miroslav, incidentally, had hired Frances, who worked in a local art shop, when he called to the shop to buy a stock of pencils and drawing paper for his late-night design marathons at Portree House. She had an art background, and he trained her to execute exact copies of his designs for his master catalogue. Frances remained his right-hand person for over forty years until his retirement.

Miroslav is characteristically modest and non-committal when he speaks of his work. He will say only that Design Number 600-318 was a 'straightforward stem glass' enhanced by fine and uncluttered wedge-cut diamond cuts at the bottom of the glass bowl, paired with a series of upward perpendicular cuts which did not 'disturb' the distinctive conical shape of the glass. In fact, what he thought was most appealing about Design Number 600-318 was how it achieved the designer's holy grail of matching the design to the shape of the glass. He imagined the shape first, and then designed the cut to suit that shape – not, as one might expect, the other way around.

Other than the neck of the decanter and the stems of the glasses, the pattern avoided the complexity of flat cutting. To the bottom of each stem in the suite he applied his characteristic starburst design, which ran to about a quarter of an inch from the edge of the foot of the glass. It would have been 'awful', he recalls, to run the design to the very edge, as some glass manufacturers did, because the pleasing impression of the star as a coherent free-standing pattern (visible through the bowl of the glass) is then distorted. And the star pattern had another, very practical, advantage. Because mouth-blown glass has a little natural unevenness on the bottom, the geometrical slices of the star pattern gave the glass an extra stability against wobbling.

And Lismore had the critical commercial advantage that the cutter needed to use only one carborundum cutting wheel for the entire process. 'The boys loved that cutting,' Miroslav recalls, always thinking of how his ideas were actually put into effect on the factory floor. For craftsmen paid at a so-called piece rate – in other words, by the number of glasses they finished – an efficient single-wheel pattern like Lismore was a financial godsend. Miroslav always designed with the idea that at most two or three wheels would be used by the cutters, since changing wheels takes time and is therefore inefficient.

Speaking again of Lismore, he remembers that another commercial bonus was that the pattern was equally adaptable to all elements of the suite, from liqueur to wine glasses. Miroslav was particularly pleased with his decanter, a classic shape which narrowed and flowed elegantly from the base up towards the neck, with no sharp turns. There was a series of delicate flat cuts around the perimeter of the neck, but otherwise only the characteristic vertical points of the Lismore pattern indicate any cutting on the top two-thirds of the decanter. The accompanying suite of drinking glasses concentrated the wedge cuts in the lower part of the bowl. 'Lots of cutting would have been ugly,' he says with his usual artistic directness. And the stopper had a variation of that 'upside down' look that he so much liked in his National Museum sketches (see photograph 8).

As Miroslav appreciated very well in those experimental years, as in all product development it would be hard to predict customer reaction to any of his design ideas, and especially to the development of Waterford's comparatively extensive suites. From a practical point of view, Griffin still had to gear up the mould-makers and craftsmen to manufacture a product that might or might not capture market attention. But, unless the glass existed and could be held in a customer's hands, designs on paper could not make any money. Miroslav constantly put what he called 'sample ideas' down on paper, and he attended countless meetings where management and sales executives would debate their likelihood of commercial success.

Miroslav's personal catalogue of his unproduced designs comprises an art collection in itself, since his draftsmanship was so impeccable. Some examples of these remarkable freehand creations, a collection of design sketches for vases, can be seen in photograph 9. It is hard to believe that these are freehand drawings, since not only do they display accurate geometrical formations, but Miroslav's ability to capture perspective in his drawings reveals the physical roundness of the crystal vessel, and therefore exactly how the patterns would look to the real-life observer.

His 1979–1980 sketches for special presentation decanters (see photograph 10) reveal that, despite his usual avoidance of elaborate traditional cutting, if cost permitted he liked to experiment with complex neck shapes and rich cutting 'to give dignity' to a unique decanter. For these presentation pieces, cost was not usually a restriction, and he thought that the detailed patterns would not work as well alongside plain uncut sections and the necessary inscription panels on the front of each piece. The 'complementarity' between cut and uncut glass worked better, he felt, in small pieces such as his suite glasses.

Design Number 600-318 was just one pattern in the great outpouring of suite designs from the early 1950s. It did not receive any special attention as Miroslav progressed through many different designs for many different types of product. 'I design it normally,' he recalls. Griffin liked Design Number 600, but he also liked many of Miroslav's designs and, like so many other designs, it didn't go into immediate production. It was not until Con Dooley saw it, and fell in love with it, that its true commercial potential could be realised.

Unlike Miroslav (and indeed unlike Griffin himself), Dooley had a natural marketer's flair. Miroslav, ever the artistic dreamer, would have been happy to market this product, with which he was quietly satisfied, as 'Design Number 600-318'. Dooley, however, had a much different intent. His desk was littered with ideas for naming Miroslav's suites in a way that would evoke the homeland for the forty million or so Irish descendants living in America. He pored over lists that he made from historical maps of Ireland, books of potted Irish history, and a variety of Celtic and Irish-oriented dictionaries, encyclopaedias and almanacs.

One afternoon, Dooley was sitting at his desk, glancing over a new map of County Waterford, published by the Ordnance Survey, when he found himself drawn to an ancient name that combined in one market-efficient package an Irish town, a famous Irish castle and a famous Irish landmark. 'I've got an idea for 600-318,' he told Miroslav the next morning. 'We'll call it "Lismore".' The new pattern hit the market on 23 October 1952 (see photograph 8).

Here is the advertising copy that Dooley later drafted to link Miroslav's pattern to an Irish mystique (the capital letters were used in the original):

Lismore, with its ancient turreted Castle, seat of the Dukes of Devonshire, crowning the wooden slopes of the great river Blackwater, is a pretty little village famous since the eighth century for its illustrious school of learning, which produced the Book of Lismore. Illustrious, too, is the Waterford Glass Lismore suite with its restrained and elegant pattern – a border of diamonds finished with vertical incisions. The Lead Crystal content gives unequalled lustre and sparkle. The glasses have delicately tapered, faceted stems and sun-burst bases.

Dooley actually used to suggest, with a leap of his imagination, that Lismore's diamond cuts represented the leaded windows of the castle and the perpendicular wedges its turrets.

By 1965, no fewer than five of Miroslav's stem-glass designs, including Lismore, were listed in the top ten best-selling crystal patterns in the United States. Lismore, in fact, had taken the number one slot. As he remembers it, Lismore's success was 'a craziness', even in the overheated American marketplace.

In the 1950s and 1960s, therefore, through a happy conjunction of great designs and clever marketing, Waterford Glass was able to respond like no other Irish company to a booming post-war American consumer society that was ready to risk some indulgence. The Waterford Glass factory that was emerging in the early 1960s was leading Ireland out of an era of shamrocks and tea-towels and table linens, to a new, more sophisticated appreciation of brand and product positioning.

Indeed, while Con Dooley's Irish twist on Design Number 600 may have seemed overly sentimental to some, it proved to be such an ingenious and effective marketing concept that he kept coming up with cute historical associations (more towns and castles and Gaelic female names) to adorn the designs to which Miroslav himself applied only Frances Cahill's numerical identifiers. 'I did not say, go and cut the Lismore suite,' he remembers. 'I said, go and cut suite 600-318.'

Miroslav always thought of himself as primarily an industrial designer rather than a studio artist, and the difference is nicely captured in his insistence on referring to his celebrity Lismore suite as simply '600-318'. Dooley, of course, had a dramatically different perception. Through his marketing wizardry, cutting pattern Number 786 became Ashling, Number 854 became Kenmare, Number 927 was transformed by his wordsmithing into Rosslare, and so on.

Although Miroslav was pleased by Lismore and its rapturous reception in America, he never counted it among his very best patterns in the frenetic work environment in which he created it. He had a softer spot for Design Number 602-137, which Dooley christened the 'Colleen' collection (after the Irish word for a girl) – a low-stemmed suite with a dramatic mixture of wedge and olive-shaped flat cutting (see photograph 11). The suite's name also allowed Dooley to teach Miroslav his only Irish expression: *Cailín deas is ea í* ('She's a pretty girl'). Dooley's copy for Colleen was similarly hokey but worked well in a different era:

> Colleen ... Who has not heard of the beauty of an Irish colleen? Here is a Waterford Crystal suite that holds a charm as bewitching and as magical as a fair girl's loveliness – intricate diamond cutting offset by gracefully fluted ovals, with a close diamond pattern on the knobbed stem.

Despite this gushing prose, Colleen did not, however, maintain its initial commercial popularity. Miroslav reflects, matter-of-factly, that tastes and fashions have changed, and, as an industrial designer, he accepts that these changes must and will continue to occur. Colleen fell victim to a growing preference for tall-stemmed glasses: 'Suddenly everybody wanted only tall glasses, tall stems, tall champagne glasses,' he recalls.

He also liked the 'Sheila' collection (Design Number 604-175), which was his only suite designed entirely with flat cuts (see photograph 12). In its early days, Sheila was almost a monopoly for Waterford's Italian flat-cutter, Giacinto Carelli, whom Miroslav remembers as a superb craftsman but also a dedicated teacher. Leafing through a catalogue of his suite designs, Miroslav also spots the flat cuts of the 'Curraghmore' collection (690-127), which Dooley named after the family seat of a surviving aristocrat, the Marquis of Waterford. He is intrigued again by Curraghmore's stem, a departure from his usual straight up-and-down patterns, which bears a distinctive wedge-cut 'knop' just below the bowl of the glass (see photograph 13).

Another intriguing pattern is 'Hibernia' (603-140), the Greek and Roman name for the island of Ireland, which represents Miroslav's only explicit attempt to imitate the dense wedge-cuts in tall rectangular boxes that he saw on many of the old Penrose designs. As noted earlier, the distinctive ornamental rings on the neck of the Hibernia decanter were blown in a single mould, unlike the Penrose original where each ring was moulded separately and then fused over the straight neck. Miroslav's much cheaper 'one-shot' product is nevertheless almost indistinguishable from the Penrose decanter. And Miroslav went much further than his predecessors, who produced only a single glass to accompany their decanter, by developing an entire Hibernia suite – from liqueur to tall champagne (see photograph 14).

Perhaps Miroslav's fondness for Sheila and Curraghmore also reflects his sensitivity to the fact that flat-cutting, despite the demanding skills it involves, usually had a much less glamorous role to play in his design universe. In Miroslav's suites, flat cuts were featured only on the stems of the drinking glasses and on the necks of the decanters.

And, as always with Miroslav, there was a practical undertow to this creative decision. Stems are made from melted glass which is not blown and so relies for its shape on the dexterity of the stem-maker. Working with handmade as opposed to mechanically pressed glass, the stem-maker could not physically produce identical stem thicknesses every time. The flat cuts effectively camouflaged the minor variations in thickness that might exist among handmade stems even in a single set. When consumers buy products made of real leather or cherry wood, for example, they willingly accept that variations and even manifest blemishes are a natural consequence of using authentic materials. Mouth-blown glass is similarly authentic, Miroslav notes, but the public always seemed to resist the idea that stems might not be uniformly thick or that there might be tiny bubbles locked into the finished glass.

Dooley probably should have pitched these variations as a desirable enhancement, Miroslav laughs, but he never did. The competition wouldn't have allowed it, anyway. The prestigious Riedel Glass of Austria boasted in its US advertising that any glass with a bubble would be considered flawed and discarded as a 'second'. Indeed, Waterford Glass seemed to have a constant public relations battle with the issue of bubbles. Miroslav, as noted earlier, considered these tiny globular imperfections as simply a natural phenomenon of mouth-blown glass, and not the result of craftsman error or laziness.

Miroslav gives great credit, too, to the Waterford Glass blowers, who responded to his pioneering but challenging insistence that they should manipulate the molten glass from the furnace to produce a blown piece of crystal that was relatively thin on the top but gradually thickened towards the base. Continental blowers did not typically try to vary the density of the glass in this way, preferring a uniform thickness. The thicker base of the Waterford product allowed Miroslav to design much deeper, and therefore more characteristic, wedge cuts on the lower parts of the bowl of a suite glass and to allow a graceful undecorated surface around the thinner upper area. This was really the design secret of Lismore.

The heyday of the great Waterford suites is past, Miroslav freely admits. He can still reel off all of the different types of drinking glass that might comprise a suite, including (in addition to the eight standards mentioned earlier) goblets, sherbets, claret glasses, Continental and saucer champagnes, hocks (designed specially for dry white wine), highball cocktail glasses, brandy balloons, cordial glasses, and even (he says) 'for the person who does not drink', tumblers in sizes from four to fourteen ounces.

He was proved right that consumers would not buy wine-specific glasses (for Burgundy or Bordeaux, for example), an idea promoted by Riedel Glass that was allegedly based on scientific studies of how specific wines respond to the particular size and thickness and shape of a glass. But he had other ideas for extending the ranges of his suites. The larger suites, like 'Kathleen' (Number 602-178), also expanded to footed juice glasses, grapefruit bowls, ice plates, salad plates, finger bowls and jugs.

Consumers at the time were 'delighted', Miroslav remembers, to collect the full complement of a suite, and even to have multiple suites. It was a marketing coup – the more Waterford implanted the idea of the collection, the more items could be added to a suite.

According to a 'suite card' issued by an Irish distributor for the Kathleen collection in 1953, the suite items sold for about £1 each, although decanters, goblets and jugs were most expensive. A decanter cost just over £5.

Waterford Glass suites were proudly displayed on well-set dining tables, and also used as decorations without ever being contaminated by a real drink. But consumers today, according to Miroslav, have no difficulty in using just one or two white wine glasses, and maybe a whiskey glass, for every kind of purpose. And even the look of that lonely white wine glass has dramatically changed. Miroslav designed relatively small wine glasses, because the custom was to pour just a little wine at a time. Now, he says, 'it is the fashion to drink wine from a big lovely bowl.'

Still, the endurance of the Lismore pattern continues to be a source of great pride for its designer. To have created a design that has become an industry standard, and that remains Waterford's most popular and distinctive pattern, even after the passing of over fifty years and the rise of a marketplace that turned against showy complexity, is something that even the demanding Professor Štipl might have conceded as a remarkable achievement.

# The Chandelier Man

Labour and administrative issues never deterred Miroslav from his growing commitment to design. He continued to be brimful of good ideas. However, he remained unhappy that his independent design department still had not formally materialised. But, as is so often the case with creative people, his mixed personal feelings unleashed a blaze of creativity when he sat down to work.

Even while he was concentrating on his extensive new suites, he was still studying the Waterford originals of a hundred years earlier. Now he turned his attention to the old Penrose chandeliers. As mentioned earlier, America in the early 1950s had some specimens of these large chandeliers. Philadelphia's Independence Hall (as Bernard Fitzpatrick had once noticed) had a famous replica of an old Waterford chandelier, beneath which the Declaration of Independence was signed. Other examples could be found in the grand private apartments surrounding the city's wealthy Rittenhouse Square. Washington, DC, too, reputedly had some fine examples of these complex and intricate masterpieces of the eighteenth and nineteenth century glass-makers.

Noel Griffin had never anticipated that the revived company would get into the chandelier business. To some extent, he still thought of Miroslav's fancy wine suites as beer glasses on stilts. One can imagine his amazement, therefore, when he saw the huge tiered 'wedding-cake' chandelier that Miroslav assembled in another one of those little storage rooms that he was always colonising at the Ballytruckle and Johnstown factories.

Miroslav had made all of the hundreds of faceted drops and buttons himself, from design to cutting to engraving. And he retained as a design feature the traditional crystal saucers that, before the coming of electricity, caught the melted wax from the candles. Although he was not a trained electrician, he had managed, with the help of a few of his engravers, to coax a thin electric cable through the central metal pillar of the chandelier.

Griffin, however, was not so amazed with this creation that he couldn't think of what to do with it. Within months, Waterford Glass had sold its first chandelier, an eight-foot tall, four-foot wide monster, to Dublin's Ambassador Cinema. Miroslav soon made the first of what would become a lifetime of on-site installation visits. He installed his chandelier in the cinema's lobby, a lofty hall, eighty feet in diameter, known as the Rotunda in homage to the Rotunda Maternity Hospital next door. He was delighted that the roof over the lobby ceiling was already equipped with an elaborate system of pulleys – a legacy of the old lighting fixtures – which allowed him to raise the chandelier fully assembled from the floor.

When Griffin enquired how Miroslav had built such a huge thing without any detailed plans or specifications, Miroslav replied that he had looked at some pictures of the massive old Penrose creations and had then basically done it 'from the head'.

Chandelier-making actually became a Miroslav Havel speciality in the years to come. Despite his instinct for scaling back the elaborate decorations of the classical Penrose era, he disliked the metal supports that chandeliers required, and so he happily concealed them under masses of buttons and drops and other decorative motifs borrowed from the eighteenth century. In his zeal to reduce the quantity of metal, he relied more and more on the density of Waterford's new lead crystal to replace the old metal supporting arms of the classical chandeliers.

Indeed, avoiding any metal on the arms of these crystal beasts was an innovation that even his forebears in the Penrose era had been reluctant to attempt. Miroslav was always concerned about the problem of the heavy weight of the chandeliers, and making the arms out of solid crystal worked well in confining to the core of the assembly the heavy metal that had to be used in construction. Also, he designed the signature sweeping low curves of the crystal arms to avoid the problem of the concentrated heat of all of the lights damaging (or even igniting) whatever ceiling material might be above the fixture.

The distinctive low curvature, which therefore had a distinctly practical origin, was so appealing that it remained integral to Waterford chandeliers. But these curved arms were initially a technical headache because it was so difficult to blow them all to the same thickness. Eventually Miroslav decided that the arms would not be blown at all but only shaped from molten crystal in custom-made wooden moulds. Miroslav worked closely with Kurt Berger, one of Waterford's best mould-makers, to solve that problem.

Miroslav gradually pared back the grand scale of his chandeliers so that he was able to develop a collection that could be suspended from the lower ceilings found in ordinary homes. While he matter-of-factly describes these home lighting systems as 'low chandeliers that you can still walk under', he warns that he often found that builders cheated in stating ceiling height – an eight-foot home ceiling was just as likely to measure seven-and-three-quarter feet when the time came to install the glittering new Waterford chandelier.

The home chandeliers, in any event, were a marketing bonanza for Waterford Glass or, as Miroslav puts it, 'It catch.' In the late 1950s, American consumer magazines like *House and Garden* started to publish lengthy colour spreads featuring the hot new idea of in-home crystal chandeliers. And this business-driven miniaturisation of scale, from industrial-strength to compact home-friendly, continued as Miroslav further reduced even his domestic chandeliers into a series of wall brackets that became one of Waterford's most popular home products.

The whole chandelier concept that Miroslav developed like a

secret nuclear weapon in the bowels of the Johnstown plant eventually grew into a huge business for the company. By the middle of the 1960s, Miroslav had a team of twenty specialists whose only job was the installation of all shapes and sizes of chandelier. As he points out, it was never possible simply to put a pre-assembled chandelier into a box, with its profusion of arms and buttons and teardrops already mounted in place, and have it delivered through the post office.

When Miroslav thinks back on his chandelier experiment, he has an especially fond remembrance of his grand commissions. There are enormous Miroslav Havel chandelier installations in public and private buildings all over the world. His signature lighting creation, in his view, is the chandelier that sits in the President's Lounge of the Kennedy Centre in Washington, DC. He supervised its installation during his first visit to the United States at the end of April 1971. Until that time, in fact, Griffin had insisted that it would be uneconomical for Waterford to supply chandeliers of any kind to the US market. Miroslav's celebrity chandelier at the Kennedy Centre utterly changed that short-sighted calculation.

Even before his first American commission, Miroslav had led the Waterford chandelier revolution into the lobbies of Ireland's greatest hotels – the Shelbourne and the Gresham – and across the Irish Sea to the majestic central nave of Westminster Abbey in London. As Noel Griffin liked to add at the end of his marketing speeches, the little company that made beer glasses for Waterford bars and pubs ended up putting giant chandeliers in Westminster Abbey and the Kennedy Centre.

# Becoming an Irishman

With the Johnstown plant in full production, growing consumer enchantment with the Lismore collection and his chandelier creations, and the opening of the American markets, it suddenly struck Miroslav that he had spent close to seven years in Ireland. What had happened to his three-month student internship with Mr Bačik? Bačik himself, despite his loss of control at the Waterford Glass factory, could never entertain thoughts of returning to Czechoslovakia. There were too many grudges against him, and too much history. He died without ever returning to his native land. How he felt about not being able to go back, about never seeing Světlá again, was something that he chose not to share with Miroslav. And Miroslav, in turn, could not discern anything about Bačik's deepest feelings, despite many conversations about their shared past in another country: 'You cannot read him if he was sad,' is how he puts it.

Miroslav remained convinced that he himself had been put onto some kind of blacklist just because he had left Czechoslovakia, lost his passport in cloudy circumstances, and had not gone back. He always held out hope that eventually he would get permission to return and that he would do so even though his many letters to successive Czechoslovak authorities had gone unanswered.

When he finally wrote his farewell letter to Rosa in 1951, much time had already slipped by, and he had given almost no thought to his personal life or to where or how he would spend his future. Since then, he had been so fully immersed in glass-making that his emotional investment in building the new Waterford Glass company had been all-consuming. As he anticipated the time when he would mark a full decade in Ireland, probably still without a passport, and no longer romantically connected to Rosa, he was (he recalls) in a state of 'not good thinking'. He was, in fact, about to meet his future wife, but marriage to an Irish woman was just about the remotest thing from his mind at that time.

Miroslav claims today that he was not looking for a girlfriend, that he had 'no interest' in women in Ireland. This was true in large part, of course, because he was so obstinately certain that at the first opportunity he would be returning to Czechoslovakia. He speaks mischievously of the 'chances' he had, but then talks about taking a girl 'once or twice to the pictures'. Miroslav has always been, above all, a loyal man, a man who would keep his word, and he was determined not to betray Rosa.

Eventually, he and Rosa accepted that destiny had turned against them and against the fifty or so hopeful letters he wrote to her from Ireland, and she finally married her forestry worker. Still, even after Rosa, he was not seriously contemplating marriage in Ireland. He had encountered a little of the hostility to foreigners that the factory had exposed, and he just didn't think a match would be very likely: 'It is always very difficult for a foreigner to understand the nature of people from another country,' he says defensively.

Miroslav certainly had a number of younger female friends who were quite happy to accompany him for a night out. After all, with his moustache, his navy blazer, and his Central European accent, he must have been an exotic and interesting presence in Waterford in the 1950s. The big social events of the time for young people were showband dances. The famous Royal Showband was actually based in Waterford, and its former lead singer, Brendan Bowyer, is still a well-regarded crooner in Las Vegas. So, while Rosa was teasing him in her letters that he was missing out on all the fun at the weekly

'Socialist Balls' which were being held in every Czechoslovak town and village by the Communist Youth Movement, Miroslav, despite disliking noisy congregations because of his hearing, was attending some dances in Waterford, and enjoying the frenzied pace of non-Communist showband dancing. He found plenty of friendly attention at these events, but he always felt a bit older than the usual dance crowds (which, of course, he was, since he was now well into his thirties).

If Miroslav had decided that he was in the market for an Irish marriage, his prospective spouse would most likely have come from among the small circle of local people with whom he forged close friendships in his first decade in Ireland. At the centre of this circle was a prosperous County Waterford farming family, the Richardsons. Miroslav was introduced to the Richardson clan by Billy O'Connell, an engineer who was his co-resident at Portree House on Mary Street and with whom he became friends. O'Connell, a wisecracking Dubliner, was on assignment in Waterford as part of a team helping to construct one of the city's new wharves.

When O'Connell met Miroslav, he was seeing Breda Richardson, the eldest daughter of the Richardsons, and gradually Miroslav became part of the convivial group that assembled almost every weekend in the family's grand farmhouse at Rosduff near Woodstown (a seaside hamlet later to become world-famous as one of Jacqueline Kennedy's retreats after her husband's assassination). Eldest son Jay Richardson was a devoted cricket player and even persuaded Miroslav, who missed the active sports life of his youth, to don whites for the Waterford team against a visiting Scottish side.

Billy O'Connell was also responsible for an important move Miroslav made around this time, taking himself out of Mrs Cronin's cramped quarters in The Glen and into a flat in Ferrybank, across the river from the main city quays and just a short walk up from the little railway station where he had arrived, bleary-eyed and hungry, several years earlier. O'Connell came into the factory one day with another former Portree House resident, Tom Scanlon, and told Miroslav that they were going to look at some flats in Ferrybank after work and that he should join them.

The Ferrybank flat that they found that evening had three large and beautiful rooms, as well as its own little (indoor) kitchen. It was nicely decorated, and Miroslav and Scanlon, who became his new flatmate, even had the use of a beautiful silver teapot and little silver cups and saucers. They often entertained friends to dinner and cards there, although Miroslav remembers that quite a few of his dinner guests in those years were separated from their spouses, so marriage once again stayed largely off the agenda even in the informal chatter of dinner-party conversations.

Scanlon worked in a local coal company and was, as Miroslav tells it, something of a 'holy man', devoutly kneeling and saying prayers after his day's work. Miroslav, whose upbringing had only barely been touched by religion, was always amazed at the level of devotion to the Roman Catholic Church, and to religion in general, that he found in Ireland. It was a reason for a foreigner like himself to tread carefully, but it was also the very reason why he was so susceptible to Fr Hallinan's efforts to convert him.

As things turned out for Miroslav, his break-up with Rosa did not spell the end of his hopes for a great lifetime romance. He might have thought that it did, and that his biggest 'chance' had passed him by, but fate had one more surprise in store for him. Mary Bridget Storey, known as Betty, was a 22-year-old Waterford native who had returned from working in England a few years before and had taken a job at the Waterford factory. Betty remembers how the new glass factory was creating a lot of expectation in an economically depressed city, and how she applied for and landed a job in the quality-control department. Like almost all Irish women of her generation, she was working as a way to bridge the years to marriage and a family.

Betty also had in mind that she might return to England in a few years' time, mirroring Miroslav's own doubts about whether Ireland was really his final destination. From time to time, Betty went out with some of the eligible local men, and she paid only as much attention to her factory job as she needed to. This was still the age of

Eamon de Valera's Constitution, which proclaimed the traditional message that 'By her life within the home, woman gives to the State a support without which the common good cannot be achieved'.

Miroslav and Betty started going out together in 1954. Their romance suggests that Miroslav was not quite as unwilling to think about dating Irish girls as he now remembers. For a while, he and Betty exchanged interested glances as he passed by her quality-control station, which conveniently was located mid-way between the engraving department and the largest cutting shop. She remembers how he wore his spotless white laboratory coat, and how the breast-pocket of the coat was always stuffed with assorted pencils and brushes and metal measuring instruments and God knows what else. With his trim moustache and distinctive swept-back hair, he was well-known among the non-craft factory staff as the young and handsome 'foreigner' who had come over with Mr Bačik to start the original factory at Ballytruckle. Miroslav, for his part, remembers that he immediately noticed this attractive, fair-haired young Irishwoman.

One day, while ferrying one of his glass creations from cutting to engraving, Miroslav paused for just a moment at Betty's station and asked her, with an impulsiveness that stunned both of them, if she would like to go to the pictures. In the city of Waterford in 1954, that meant seeing a sugary Clark Gable romance at the local Regal Cinema – or the 'picture house', as it was called back then.

Betty blushed deeply and said yes, even though at the time she had been seeing someone else for a few months. She was more than intrigued by this sudden invitation from 'Mr Havel'. That evening, she broke the news excitedly to her mother, her father and her two younger sisters, Angela and Margaret. 'He's from Czechoslovakia,' she announced with some pride, an assertion which must have sounded about as strange to them as 'Éire' had sounded to Miroslav when he had received his first letter from Charles Bačik.

Meanwhile, Miroslav, the stateless person without a passport, was beginning to show real signs of putting down some roots in Waterford. In June 1953, he had acquired something considered very unusual in the city at the time – his own car. It was a Fiat Bambino, just about the smallest passenger vehicle ever built by modern civilisation. At £500, it was, nevertheless, an expensive acquisition. Miroslav, who loved cars, bought it through Dick Wright's all-purpose motor car, motorcycle and bicycle emporium, just off the main quay.

Old Wright was either a foolish businessman or a very shrewd one. 'Don't you worry about the money,' he assured Miroslav. 'Just take the car.' He made a deal with Miroslav to pay £5 a week for the vehicle – a primitive form of hire purchase and done without any documentation. From Miroslav's perspective, the deal was both attractive and perhaps a little too ambitious. He was being paid about £15 a week and would be paying a third of it for the car.

Miroslav confessed his plight to Bačik. It was long past the time when Bačik had the power to give Miroslav a raise, but he did the next best thing. He used his bank connections to enable his protégé to get an overdraft facility at the local Munster & Leinster Bank (now a part of Allied Irish Banks). In those days, an overdraft was a mark of high status, and Miroslav was extremely gratified that he now had something that to most Irish people at the time would be vastly more impressive than any passport.

Having made this wonderful accommodation, Bačik immediately took advantage of his own generosity by borrowing the car to drive to Midleton, County Cork, where he was to be the guest of honour at a reception being hosted by some Czech visitors. Miroslav happily lent the car, wondering all the while why Bačik didn't drive his own more ample vehicle. In any event, the older man's powerful six-foot-four frame was a comically bad fit with the little Bambino. When the car was returned, the top of its black canvas roof had a very visible, and unfortunately permanent, bump where Bačik's great head had pressed against it for the journey to and from Midleton.

Meanwhile, Miroslav was 'doing a good line' with Betty. Actually, the way Miroslav says it might be even more evocative: 'We were in the good line', he recalls. 'We were going with Betty, and suddenly

I realise I like her very much. She was very keen on me, too.' They went out together for three years and took many little trips together in the Bambino, including a delightful, sun-kissed few days in one of Miroslav's favourite spots in Ireland – the town of Killarney.

The Bambino, as Miroslav had feared, proved to be a burden as well as a pleasure, and by 1957, he realised that he was going to have some trouble making his income tax payment that year. He calculated, however, that he would get a small income tax break if he married Betty just before the tax deadline, and for that reason he picked Saturday, 2 March, as the wedding date. Miroslav's interest in that particular date was entirely fiscal, and not religious, even though it was close to Easter that year. Irish people in those days, as he knew, did plan events in terms of coming religious holidays, and that is exactly how he sold the date to Betty.

Miroslav never actually proposed to Betty. 'She was taken by surprise,' he remembers. 'And in fact she was amazed.' Nor did he ask Betty's parents for permission to marry. Jimmy Storey, Betty's father, was a retired Irish Army quartermaster, a true 'quiet man', and never raised any objections to his daughter's marrying a man he truly liked and respected. Betty's highly strung mother, Bridget (Biddy), on the other hand, was more of a force of nature – to the end of her long life blessed with a healthy suspicion of other people (and not just of foreigners). But Biddy, too, always had a soft spot for this man from a far country. She also had an innate sympathy for his poor hearing, a disability she shared as the result, in all probability, of an untreated fever in her youth.

Biddy was certainly a bit concerned that Miroslav was a foreigner, but in reality she was more troubled by his age than by his country of origin. He was now approaching 36, while Betty was still only 25. An eleven-year age gap was quite unusual in Irish family circles at the time. And one other thing made her uncomfortable – Miroslav, as far as anyone knew, might not be a Roman Catholic.

Soon after, Betty popped that question herself to Miroslav. She was delighted to learn that he was indeed a member of the Church, the result of Fr Hallinan's efforts back in the late 1940s. There would therefore be no question of the scandal of a 'mixed' marriage for Betty and her family. Fr Hallinan, who had introduced Miroslav to the delights of the Cronin household, had taken charge of Miroslav's religious welfare shortly after that introduction. He haled from a village in County Waterford, but had spent most of his clerical career in Scotland. He saw Miroslav as his best (and maybe his only) chance for decades to score a victory for the Vatican. The zeal of the convert struck Miroslav pretty quickly, and he became a devout member of his new religion in a way that Franta could never comprehend. Even before his conversion, in fact, Miroslav had attended an occasional Sunday Mass at the Dominican Church with his room-mate Tim Scanlon (the 'holy man') and his friend Billy O'Connell. 'There was no control on the gates, so I just went in with them,' Miroslav remembers. But he did not receive Communion ('I was not that pious yet').

On one occasion during the conversion process, Fr Hallinan dragged Miroslav up into the Comeragh Mountains in west County Waterford, past the county town of Dungarvan, to meet his parents in their tiny country cottage. Miroslav entered a living room filled with the yelping and screeching of what must have been a dozen dogs and cats (and maybe even a fine fatted pig). Old Mother Hallinan herself was an antique well into her eighties; she had never seen a train in her life, and she and her even older husband had no idea that the noises they sometimes heard from the sky overhead were actually aeroplanes.

Miroslav found the old couple delightful. Mrs Hallinan, unlike her husband, had a fine set of her own teeth, and was able to chomp down lustily on a massive side of ham on the day that Miroslav visited. Maybe this meeting was part of Fr Hallinan's strange ritual of conversion, which also included a weekly dose of catechism training which Miroslav received for a full year at the priest's house back in the civilised city.

As Miroslav explained to Betty in what turned out to be a long conversation about his religious induction in Ireland, he accepted Catholic doctrine with little dissent, except that he never really overcame his doubts about the notion of angels. Eventually, Fr Hallinan took him to the bishop's residence to see Bishop Daniel Cohalan, the formidable and long-serving senior prelate of the ancient diocese of Waterford and Lismore. Miroslav told Bishop Cohalan (or maybe the Bishop told him) that he was ready to be taken into the bosom of the Roman Catholic religion. Bishop Cohalan granted permission for Miroslav to be baptised.

The new convert asked his former landlady, Mrs Cronin, to be his godmother and Mr Bačik to act as his godfather. On Sunday morning, 18 March 1949, as Miroslav told Betty, the three of them had appeared at the baptismal font after Mass at Waterford's Cathedral of the Most Holy Trinity. Miroslav recalls that several churchgoers had the impression that Mrs Cronin and Mr Bačik were there to get married, since they were standing solemnly side-by-side and there certainly wasn't an infant child anywhere to be seen.

And then something even more extraordinary happened. The sacristy door swung open and His Lordship, Bishop Cohalan himself, showed up to perform the ceremony. It was his first baptism of an adult, he said, as he splashed some water behind Miroslav's neck instead of dunking him in the font. Apart from the confused bystanders, the person most unsure about the occasion was poor old Mrs Cronin, a petite five-foot-three, who found herself joined in prayer and devotion beside the massive presence of her fellow godparent, Charles Bačik.

Very shortly afterwards, Miroslav told his wife-to-be, he completed his rapid induction into Irish Catholicism by appearing for his Confirmation. To be confirmed, he took his place in the cathedral in the middle of a long line of over 180 low-sized children. He remembers wearing a new suit that he had bought specially for the occasion. Like the suit he wore all those years before with his parents at Luhacovice, it was a brilliant white.

The congregation of Waterford people, subjected for the second time in as many years to the sight of a full-grown adult receiving the sacraments usually associated with childhood, observed the very tall man in the white suit with great interest. 'What is that fella doing there among all those children?' he imagined them saying. He processed eventually to the front of the line and stood before Bishop Cohalan, who was seated on his throne. They recognised one another, but neither displayed a trace of emotion or even of slight amusement. As part of the ceremony, the Bishop had to rise from his throne to place the sacramental oil of chrism on Miroslav's forehead. Normally, he bent down to the kneeling children to apply the oil, so the wonder of the crowd was even more perceptible when the Bishop rose to meet Miroslav eye-to-eye.

Miroslav had planned to take as his confirmation name the same name, Bohomil, that he had adopted at a Czech confirmation ceremony which he vaguely remembered from his childhood. It was also the first name of the man who had been his godfather at his baptism ceremony in the Czech Church, Bohomil Mrklas. The name, appropriately, means 'lover of God'. Perhaps fearing a citywide riot, or maybe just the prospect of hopeless mispronunciation, Bishop Cohalan told Miroslav a few weeks before the ceremony that Bohomil would simply not work and that he must take the name of an Irish saint. The Bishop recommended Patrick, which he explained would allow Miroslav to give honour to St Patrick, the patron saint of Ireland and a most respected leader of the ancient church. Not only that, the Bishop proclaimed, but Patrick (and Paddy) were very popular names in Miroslav's adopted country and His Lordship would be proud to put oil on the forehead of a man called Patrick.

Miroslav had never heard of either of these names while he was in Czechoslovakia, but he was shrewd enough to appreciate that the Bishop really did have a serious pronunciation problem with Bohomil, and he bowed without further discussion to the higher authority. He never had a middle name in his country of origin (that was not the custom), but from the moment of his confirmation in Ireland, he styled himself, 'Miroslav P. Havel', the 'P' of course standing for Patrick or Paddy.

Miroslav suspects that word of Bishop Cohalan's recommendation or command that he be confirmed as Patrick must have filtered back to the factory. Maybe some of his fellow employees were among the sponsors standing behind him at the altar when Bishop Cohalan loudly proclaimed 'I confirm thee as Patrick'. Soon afterwards, in any event, some of his fellow employees at Waterford Glass (or at least the Irish employees) started referring to him by the friendly nickname, Paddy. Maybe they preferred to use that name because, like Bohomil, Miroslav (or even the shorter Mirek) is not a straightforward pronunciation for the Irish. Miroslav is doubtful about this explanation, however, because he points out how beautifully his nurses and doctors today pronounce his full Christian name. For some natives of Waterford, calling this man Paddy Havel made him truly sound one of their own, and the name stuck throughout the remainder of Miroslav's career at the factory. Miroslav never used his nickname in referring to himself, but some of the Waterford Glass executives sometimes called him Paddy, notably Con Dooley. The workers in the blowing and cutting shops always used the nickname when they were talking about him in the third person (or when they thought, or rather knew, that he couldn't hear them as he passed by their work areas). Noel Griffin, on the other hand, never called his top designer by any name other than 'Mr Havel'.

But at least his last name caused no problems to the Irish ear. Here is what he told an interviewer in 1981:

Since I came to Ireland I have always been happy that my last name is Havel. It's easy to spell and pronounce, not like some Czech names which play havoc with your tongue. In fact, it's well-designed!

According to some sources, the name Havel is, in fact, a Slavic corruption of 'Gall', as in St Gall, who left Ireland in the seventh or eighth century and founded a monastery beside Lake Constance, in Switzerland, from where he converted the inhabitants of (among other places) the Czech lands.

Betty, in any event, told her parents the good news that Miroslav was a Roman Catholic, and a devout one. As March 1957 approached, Miroslav assembled his bachelorhood cronies to prepare for the wedding. He picked his pal and golf companion, Teddy

Hughes, to be his best man, and Teddy was accompanied by groomsmen Tony Fennessy, Jay Richardson and Jim Sheedy. Miroslav remains in touch with all of them, except Fennessy. Tony worked at a local plastics factory which was closed down a year or two after the wedding, and he disappeared without trace to England.

Miroslav agreed with Fr Hallinan that the wedding should be at St John's Church, Betty's local parish church, just a stone's throw from the Johnstown factory. Saturday, 2 March 1957, was a fine day, unusually for that showery time of year in Ireland. Miroslav and his best man and groomsmen arrived about an hour before the ceremony, packed into the little Bambino in their top hats and tails. For the little group, it was quite a nostalgic drive – a final reminder of good times when Miroslav (when he wasn't out with Betty) would take them for weekend 'spins' all over the mountainous countryside of west County Waterford. At nine o'clock in the morning, Miroslav Havel of Držkov, Czechoslovakia, stood at the high altar of St John's Church, Waterford, and waited for his Irish bride.

Many thoughts filled Miroslav's heart as he prepared himself to exchange vows with Betty in the traditional all-Latin wedding ceremony. He was taking a huge step in his life. And he was doing it without Franta and Anna, whose existence was now so far removed from his own that he was having trouble imagining, as he committed himself to marriage in Ireland, that he had spent the first twenty-five years of his life with them.

Rosa had predicted and feared that things might turn out this way. 'Everywhere I go I think about you but you are in a different world,' she wrote in July 1947 in one of her earliest letters after Miroslav left. 'You are seeing all these new things and new people, learning a new language, everything about a new country ... and maybe your whole country, your family, and I will disappear, and you will remember us only as a dream.' She finished the letter with her typical candour: 'Or am I wrong?'

Nearly a decade later, it appeared to Miroslav that Rosa had not been wrong. As he reflected on her words, he looked over to Charles and Edith Bačik. No doubt he had a peculiar feeling as he gazed at his old mentor, also removed from a past that he would never revisit. He thought again of that fateful letter that had brought him to the land of bananas and oranges, almost exactly a decade before.

Fr Tom Power conducted the wedding ceremony, and, as was common at the time, there was no music, and photographs inside the church were strictly forbidden except for a single shot of the signing of the marriage register in the sacristy. The reception, then called the wedding breakfast, was held at the Adelphi Hotel at the south end of the main quay. The hotel has long since disappeared and been replaced by the nondescript modern block of the Tower Hotel. As Miroslav left the hotel with Betty after the reception, he gave his new father-in-law an envelope of cash to pay the bill, which Miroslav had been handed by the hotel manager as he came out through the lobby. No such thing as credit cards in those days, of course, and new husbands and wives were expected to pay the reception charges as soon as the limousine pulled up to begin the honeymoon. Miroslav still has the original bill, which was for £30–19s.–6d. The bill included about £20 for what it called 'intoxicants'.

There was one special aspect to the ceremony and reception that was very unusual at the time. Jay Richardson had a friend who was the operator for the projectors at the Coliseum Cinema and who had a very old-fashioned 16mm cine-camera. Jay persuaded his friend to come along to the church and the Adelphi Hotel, to set up the camera and to shoot some film. The resulting product, a glorious black-and-white snippet of history, was shipped to Anna and Franta (despite the risks of seizure and confiscation), who booked the local cinema in Držkov for a special screening – attended by almost the entire village – of Miroslav and Betty's 'wedding video'. The film could be shown only by mounting it on the massive reels used at the time by the cinemas, so it was obviously a thrilling occasion for Franta and Anna and their guests. It was not until 1996 that the film was transferred to a modern video-cassette tape and could be viewed by a new generation on an ordinary television set.

The film quality is jerky even on video-cassette, and the

members of the wedding party flicker across the screen with the exaggerated speed of an old silent Chaplin or Keaton movie. It is particularly funny to watch the guests, irrespective in several instances of quite advanced age, swooshing madly up and down the great front steps of the Adelphi Hotel. But it is a touching memento of the day, and it concludes with a vignette (added just before the first viewing) of Betty looking out through the window of her new kitchen and Miroslav waving a single pound note – part of his first payment towards the mortgage. Thus were the respective roles of a husband and wife in 1950s Ireland vividly captured in celluloid.

The honeymoon was not particularly grand. Miroslav had decided to take Betty to Dublin for the remainder of the weekend – the only trip he really could afford. They got the train from Waterford to Limerick Junction, and changed there for another train to Dublin. At the time, there was no direct train link through the southeast between Waterford and Dublin. Two of the train's carriages were carrying cattle to market in Dublin.

By the time they reached their destination, the rain was belting down in great sheets, weather that was much more typical of an early March in Ireland. And there was no relief. The only photograph from the weekend shows the rain-drenched newlyweds huddling under a huge umbrella with their raincoats belted tightly around them. They stayed at the Four Courts Hotel on Dublin's Ormond Quay for two nights, and came back to Waterford on the following Monday morning. A good chunk of the mini-weekend was spent around the casualty department at St James's Hospital because Miroslav apparently got food poisoning. Betty still doubts that he had anything wrong with him, but she does recall that she and her new husband had hardly arrived in the capital before they began hunting in the drenching rain for emergency medical treatment. Miroslav, perhaps as a legacy of his very long bachelorhood, would be a lifelong hypochondriac. By Tuesday, nonetheless, he pronounced himself fully recovered and was back in the factory as usual. Betty, meanwhile, was taking charge of their newly built house at Grange Lawn, located just under a kilometre from the gates of St Otteran's psychiatric hospital, the institution which Miroslav had once mistaken for the Bačik glass factory. Grange Lawn was one of the first new housing developments outside the inner-city area.

For Miroslav, married life was a bit of an adjustment. He had been a very contented bachelor, cooking, playing cards and even sometimes strumming a guitar with his friends at the flat in Ferrybank, all of them blissfully unaware of the absence of that wonderful invention for passing long winter evenings, the television set. As he now recalls, he needed a 'little push' to get himself out of that lifestyle, and Betty gave him the push he needed.

But he also pushed himself a little bit, because he bought his new house even before he had settled finally on the idea of getting married. And, although he and Betty had been 'doing a line' for almost three years, in those days men (and husbands) took proprietorial charge of all major purchases, and so he hardly consulted her at all on his big decision. He found a nice bungalow at Grange Lawn, just across from Con Casey's grocery shop.

Casey, recently retired from his dual responsibilities as a railway executive and town commissioner in Tramore, was planning to spend his golden years (and some part of his considerable wealth) running the shop, and he strongly recommended the new development to Miroslav. 'You're a single man,' Casey said to Miroslav one day in his shop, gesturing across the street towards the new construction. 'And you should invest in one of those new houses.'

The two men had first met about a year before at a dinner held in Casey's honour at the Majestic Hotel in Tramore. Casey received an award, a fourteen-inch Waterford Glass plate engraved by Miroslav, which he carefully placed behind him on his chair as he rose to deliver some remarks of appreciation. After he had read his speech, and was making a few off-the-cuff comments in conclusion, he threw his notes back onto the chair, covering the plate. When the applause subsided, Casey sat down, and the plate cracked into smithereens beneath his ample bottom. The speaker was not hurt (protected by the notes of his lengthy speech, most likely), but the audience was caught between horror and hilarity. Miroslav, of course, immediately engraved a replacement plate. Throughout his career, he would receive anguished calls from organisations whose guests of honour had cracked or dropped a signature piece of Waterford Glass. Old Casey's misfortune was just a very early example.

Miroslav realised that a brand new house was outside his budget, but he had become accustomed to living life on the wings of his prestigious overdraft. As to the house itself, he really didn't have a clue about investment values or even what kind of property would best suit him. But, as often in his life, he responded instinctively to the counsel of people he truly liked, and so he followed Con Casey's advice, walked up and down the gentle slope of the hill that comprised Grange Lawn, and finally picked a site that was almost directly across the street from Casey's shop.

For the next few months Miroslav showed up at the site every couple of days, revealing an interest in his purchase that surprised even himself. One morning, as he was watching the finishing touches being put to the roof, he was greeted over the freshly built garden wall by his new neighbours, Donal and Mona O'Keeffe, who had just moved in next door. Donal was about to begin a forty-year career as a secondary teacher at the De La Salle boys' school. Betty and Mona would become lifelong best friends.

The new house cost £2,100. Although the property was simply designated Number 6 Grange Lawn, Miroslav pulled a Con Dooley by giving it a proper name. He called the house *Domov*, the Czech word for home. The young man from Czechoslovakia was finally coming to terms with his altered status as an Irishman.

The Marckwalds, who had no children of their own but always treated Miroslav as a kind of surrogate son, gave Miroslav and Betty a wardrobe and a large marital bed to get them started. To raise some extra cash, Miroslav reluctantly sold his beloved Fiat Bambino to 'some fella in Piltown', netting a respectable £80. He retrieved his old bicycle from the back of the garage at *Domov* and for two months he cycled to and from the glass factory.

But he was a man in his late thirties, and he soon found that pumping the pedals on the old bike was much more of an ordeal than he might have imagined. So, he went to Noel Griffin and said, with a good deal of innocence, 'Mr Griffin, cycling to the factory is not the best thing for me. I need a car.' He caught Griffin at a particularly tense moment, and the general manager expressed his positive response with a low growl: 'Well, why didn't you say so before? I'll arrange a bank loan for you.' Such was the way business was done in those days.

Miroslav's generous bank loan, which threatened to send his overdraft into the stratosphere, allowed him to buy a new dark-green Ford Anglia, the original version of what is today called the Taurus. Now Miroslav had a new wife, a new house, new furniture, a new car, new neighbours, a new religion and an overdraft, all in the Republic of Ireland. All he needed, he thought, was a new passport, and a chance to return again to see his parents.

# Two Visitors from Bohemia

Back in Czechoslovakia, for the same period of ten years that Miroslav had been in Ireland, Franta and Anna had not seen their only son. Nor indeed had they spoken to him – the age of regular transcontinental telephone contact with one's relatives was still many years in the future. With Franta still away working in the mines, Anna had taken a clerical job at a local glass factory that manufactured small medical instruments. She continued to write regularly to Ireland, defying the censors who were obviously ripping open her letters and taking a look at her little words of personal affection to Miroslav. Often, the letters arrived in Ireland with the top of the envelope crudely glued or taped back together.

Miroslav supposed that the same thing was happening with his letters home, which sometimes included a few of the photographs he was now constantly taking of Betty and his growing family. Anna missed Miroslav terribly, but she was a very strong person, not given to emotion (or at least to visible emotion), and always had a clear and confident idea of what might be for the best. In Miroslav's case, she had come to the unshakeable view that he was better off in his new country.

Anna never mentioned the Communist regime explicitly, but she repeatedly assured Miroslav in her letters that there would be 'no life' for him in Czechoslovakia. He understood precisely what she meant. As he puts it, being the son of a marked bourgeois, even after ten years of Communist rule and despite the contribution he might have made in Czechoslovakia following his years of training, would still have carried a stigma that was like 'the measles'. And, although in the beginning Anna had often urged him to come home soon, as the years passed by, she never once complained about his long absence from Držkov. 'She was great woman – she support me with every letter, and never said one word that I did wrong,' he remembers. 'She was only concerned that I am all right, that I have everything that I want in life.'

When he was back from coalmine duty, Franta would occasionally pen a few lines at the end of one of Anna's letters. He was not much given to detailed correspondence. Once he reported (which she would not do herself) that Anna had been named Socialist Worker of the Year at the glass factory and had received a glossy certificate at a ceremony held on the most recent first of May Labour Day holiday, the holiest day in the Communist calendar. Franta, who saw himself as resolutely bourgeois in spite of his post-war confinement to the mines, was amused by the irony of his wife's achievement.

But it was sad for Miroslav and his parents, nonetheless. Good years were slipping by. Miroslav was already entering his forties, and his parents were at the cusp of old age. He was still routinely making his requests for permission to return, and just as routinely they were being denied. He decided, with Betty's support, that he would try to have his parents emigrate to Ireland. He asked Anna to see whether they could both get out at the same time, since he thought that if they could leave together, they could then both stay in Ireland, regardless of what the Czechoslovak authorities tried to do. And would the authorities really care about an ageing couple leaving to join their only child for the remainder of their years?

As it turned out, the authorities in Prague cared very much. Even though she had nagged the Mayor of Držkov into giving her a favourable letter, and wangled the support of two or three key officials in Semily, the regional administrative capital, Anna's careful negotiation through the thickets of the Communist bureaucracy ended abruptly at the Ministry of Foreign Affairs in Prague. In a few unpleasant lines, the letter from the Ministry advised her coldly that she and Franta would never get permission to leave as a couple, and that the State records continued to show that her son had 'misused' his passport to abscond from Czechoslovakia and had never come back.

While Anna and Franta were vainly shaking the Czechoslovak emigration tree, Miroslav himself was moving toward a final resolution of his status in Ireland. By now, he had abandoned any hope of restoring his nationality in Czechoslovakia. Too much time had passed, and his name was obviously blacklisted a hundred times over in the Communist system. Noel Griffin was sympathetic, not least because without a proper passport Miroslav was unable to leave the country to keep his designer's eye on the increasingly tough glass-making competition. His earlier visits to the Continent had been facilitated through Bačik's Red Cross connections, but that was an emergency post-war accommodation which was no longer available.

Griffin, too, was a man with excellent contacts in the Irish political and business establishments. His father, Joseph, had close connections to old Joseph McGrath at IGB, and both Joe and Noel Griffin were deeply involved with Fianna Fáil, the political party which held power in Ireland through the 1960s. At Noel's urging, Griffin senior had a 'chat' with the then Irish Minister for Industry and Commerce and future Taoiseach, Seán Lemass, about the brilliant Czechoslovak designer whose work was energising the success of Waterford Glass.

And Noel Griffin himself introduced Miroslav to Lemass at a luncheon to celebrate the opening of the Johnstown factory, at the Grand Hotel, Tramore, on 24 September 1952. Lemass was the guest of honour, and his toast to Irish industry was responded to by the then Mayor of Waterford, Alderman Martin Cullen. According to the souvenir programme, the luncheon featured 'glass by Waterford'. Griffin told Lemass at the lunch that Miroslav's stateless position was hurtful to the company. Lemass was the hero of modern Irish industrialisation, and very receptive to these pleadings on Miroslav's behalf. Unlike many, including some members of the Waterford city clergy, he was not the kind of man to treat foreign talent with immediate suspicion. Lemass agreed to 'have a word' with the Department of External Affairs about issuing Miroslav a passport. Under Irish law at the time, marrying Betty did not guarantee a passport to her husband – the old unity of domicile law provided that the wife's nationality automatically became that of her husband upon marriage, but not the other way around. Lemass had his word with the department, but the Irish bureaucracy was exceedingly slow. Nearly five years later, and over a year after Miroslav married Betty, the government of Ireland issued him a certificate of citizenship on 13 May 1958.

The entire certificate was printed in Irish, so Miroslav had no idea what it was when he opened the letter from the Department of Justice. Only when he looked at the bottom of the certificate, where he saw the big green wax seal with a harp in the middle, did he have a clue that his quest might be over. His passport arrived a few months later. His name, as stated in that first Irish passport, was 'Miroslav Patrick Havel'. Ever after, Miroslav's unfailing sense of loyalty obliged him to vote for Lemass's Fianna Fáil party.

Recognising that the Communist government would never permit his parents to leave together, or allow one to leave while the other was still overseas, Miroslav decided that he had no choice but to bring them separately for extended visits, if he could. Coincidentally, Bačik had told him that the Czechoslovak government, in one of its periodic fits of mild liberalisation, had passed a law that would allow the parents of émigré Czechs and Slovaks to visit their children abroad for a limited period, provided that only one of the two parents travelled.

Anna's early efforts to take advantage of this law were in vain. In October 1962, she received a stern letter from the Czechoslovak Ministry of Foreign Affairs, stating the following:

> Your request for permission to travel to Ireland cannot be granted for the reason that your son violated his permission to travel and stayed permanently in a foreign country.

In the summer of 1964, however, the effects of the relaxation law were beginning to be felt. Anna received an exit visa to visit Ireland for three months, but only on the express condition that Franta remain behind.

Given that there was no direct air-passenger service between Ireland and Czechoslovakia, Anna had to become very inventive in figuring out a way to get to her son's adopted country. As it turned out, she flew in the jump-seat of a Cuban cargo plane from Prague that was making a refuelling stop at Shannon Airport, en route to Havana. The Cubans operated regular international air cargo services between Havana and almost all of the Eastern European capitals. The Czechoslovak and Cuban governments were closely allied as partners in the march of world Communism, and the Cubans traded their fine cigars for Czech-made precision medical equipment.

Anna was delighted that she had found a very convenient and inexpensive option that would avoid the horror of trying to change planes to make connections, which would have required multi-carrier flights via Frankfurt and Heathrow. Like Miroslav when he had first begun his trip to Ireland, it was her first journey of any kind outside her homeland.

Her plane touched down at four in the morning on the tarmac at Shannon. The door of the aircraft opened and a set of steps was rolled from the terminal to the front of the plane. A straight-backed, ruddy-complexioned, beaming woman in her mid-sixties, made conspicuous even in the half-light of the early morning by the bright silk headscarf she wore tightly tied around her neck, was the only passenger to leave the plane and to walk down the steps and across the tarmac into the terminal. Miroslav, watching inside from high in the viewing gallery, saw his mother leave the plane and walk towards the building. He ran down to meet her.

'It was a most affectionate meeting,' he recalls with considerable understatement. Mother and son threw their arms around one another, and just stood there in silence, Miroslav remembers, 'for minutes and minutes and minutes'. Fifteen years had passed since they had last seen or even spoken to one another. They were two people meeting again who had known each other in another lifetime, yet they were also mother and son. He thought she looked wonderful; she thought he looked too thin.

The special moment was soon disrupted, however, by the kind of transportation headache that Miroslav seems often to have encountered in Ireland. His mother's luggage had not materialised, and he started complaining to the only airport official he could find at that ungodly hour. One of the Russian pilots of the Cuban aircraft then showed up in the desolate terminal, evidently on a hopeless quest to find a cup of coffee before continuing to Havana. He overheard the conversation (in English, which he understood) about 'Mrs Havel's luggage'. 'Oh my God,' he said to Miroslav. 'We have packed the whole plane with freight for Cuba, but your mother was our only passenger getting out here.'

In other words, nobody in Prague had thought to put Anna's luggage in a convenient space in the hold for the stopover in Shannon. Still, the pilot was more than helpful. With Miroslav sticking like glue to his side, the pilot managed to arrange for a small truck to go to the side of the plane, and then he and his colleagues started to unload the contents of the cargo hold, piece by piece. Luckily, Anna's luggage surfaced after only twenty minutes of this painful but necessary exercise. The plane was then reloaded and took off about two hours behind schedule. It is astounding, in these days of high security, to reflect on how Miroslav was able to bring Shannon Airport to a standstill in the hunt for his mother's two suitcases.

Miroslav drove Anna in his Ford Anglia from Shannon back to Waterford. By about seven in the morning, they were in Limerick City, having an Irish breakfast of sausages and eggs, and, with dawn breaking, Anna truly had the sense of being in another world. As she watched her son's adopted country roll by, she assured him once again that she and Franta were happy that he had found a new life in Ireland, and that they did not expect him ever to come back to Czechoslovakia.

He always wanted – and maybe needed – to ask his mother if she or Franta felt any anger about his leaving, and about the way he had left, but she never allowed him get to those questions. This was the past, and Anna was looking forward to a brief but happy future in Waterford with her son and his family. For the first time, she would be meeting her new daughter-in-law, her three grandsons and Betty's parents, Jimmy and Biddy. She talked to all of them in streams of animated Czech, and Miroslav sometimes – but not always – made poor translations, but nobody minded the communication gap.

In a time when Aer Lingus offers what amounts to a cheap air-shuttle service between Dublin and Prague, and when the Czech Republic and Slovakia are both members of the European Union, it is hard to conceive how unusual Anna's visit must have seemed to her Irish hosts in the early 1960s. Maybe the best way to recapture this sense of unusualness is to relate that Ireland's fledgling national television service, Telefís Éireann (now RTÉ), did a national news story on the woman from a small Czechoslovak village who had been reunited with her son in Waterford after a fifteen-year separation.

The television news crew came down from Dublin to Grange Lawn, and a bemused Anna (who spoke not a word of English) stood in the back garden as the camera filmed Miroslav's three small sons jumping on and off a garden swing that she was gently pushing. Miroslav made some comments about how much Anna was enjoying her visit, but declined to make any political observations about his or his mother's experience of Communism. The story also showed some of the neighbours clustered around the front of the house as though a film star were lurking inside.

The spot closed with some simple Cold War commentary about Anna's life under a repressive Communist government, mentioning that there had been a marginal relaxation of exit restrictions to allow short visits to family members in exile. The presenter did mention, however, that the relaxation policy did not apply to emigrants like Miroslav who had left before the Revolution and now wished to return home. But the main story was the human-interest angle of the reunion. Anna, needless to say, was astonished to see the whole thing unfold on the next evening's television news.

Here is how the story was reported in the local Waterford

newspaper, the *Munster Express*, beneath a photograph on the front page showing Anna with Miroslav and Betty and their three children:

> Behind this happy family portrait lies a story of great human interest. It is a story of a 67-year-old mother and her 42-year-old son meeting again after a separation of eighteen years. The mother, Mrs Anna Havel, is from Držkov, Czechoslovakia, in a beautiful mountainous area about a hundred miles from Prague. She is pictured here in the middle with her son Mr Miroslav Havel, industrial designer from Domov, Grange Lawn, who she last saw in 1947 ... Talking to *Munster Express* journalists, Mr Havel, who works at Waterford Glass, said that for many years his greatest wish was to have his mother come to Ireland and stay some time with him and his family ... Mr Con Dooley, marketing director of Waterford Glass, helped speed the papers and get the travel documents so that Mrs Havel could spend this holiday with her son and his family. Through Mr Dooley's intervention, the bureaucratic formalities for getting her a Czechoslovak passport were considerably shortened ... Mr Havel received a letter from the Czechoslovak police indicating that the requested permission for the trip to Ireland had been granted. This was followed by a declaration from the Irish Ministry for External Affairs that this letter could be used by Mrs Havel as an entering visa to Ireland ... A big surprise awaited Mrs Havel when she was the guest of honour at the annual dinner of the Waterford Glass company on Thursday night at Tramore's Grand Hotel. The happy meeting of mother and son was the subject of the main news bulletin on Telefís Éireann on Friday evening.

It has never been clear how RTÉ got wind of Anna's visit. Miroslav thinks that Griffin tipped off the national broadcaster, but the newspaper report shows that Con Dooley was fairly good at getting some publicity also.

Even without her spectacular media splash, however, Anna

attracted a lot of attention in Waterford. Miroslav showed her off at the factory, where she appeared immaculately dressed as always in her high-collared fur coat, and where she caused quite a commotion as 'Mr Havel's mother'. And, as the newspaper noted, Noel Griffin made her the guest of honour at the annual company dinner at the Grand Hotel in Tramore.

Anna sat next to Griffin during the dinner, with Miroslav on the other side, and Griffin gave a little speech in which he spoke of how heart-warming it was to see a mother and her son reunited after so many years. The applause was so appreciative that Griffin insisted that Anna should stand up and say a few words to the guests in Czech, with Miroslav providing his usual loosely plotted translation. She was very nervous, not having expected such an ordeal, but she did manage to say that nothing like this had ever happened to her in her life, and that she was truly proud of Miroslav's work with Waterford Glass. As Miroslav recalls, there was no time for her to pull out the little brown-covered notebook she always carried with her in Ireland, in which she had written down hundreds of everyday English words (with their pronunciations). In any event, a speech that strung together greetings like 'Good evening' with grocery items like 'bread' and 'milk' would have truly mystified her audience.

It was autumn in Ireland, a very beautiful autumn, and one of the things that Anna loved to do during her visit was to walk on the beaches at Tramore, Dunmore, Woodstown, Stradbally and Annestown – all those lovely wide sandy beaches that are strung like pearls along the County Waterford coast. More than anything, the sights and sounds of the sea gave her the sense that she was in a place far away from Czechoslovakia. She happily spent hours sitting on one of the benches along the endless Tramore seafront, listening to the roar of the sea and watching the silvery white foam of the waves. She particularly liked the sight and sound of the big waves crashing against Tramore's massive sea walls.

In his first days in Ireland, Anna had warned Miroslav in her letters to stay away from the sea. She worried about him drowning.

And she had also told him, alarmingly, that sea water 'will cause your hair to go yellow or fall out'. As Miroslav puts it, Anna came from one of the 'inner countries', devoid of sea and waves and the ceaseless noise of the ocean. Like Miroslav himself, however, when she came to Ireland she found the experience of the tides utterly beguiling and she forgot all of her earlier fears.

Because she came from a farming family, she also loved long drives in the almost absurdly green Irish countryside, and often she would step out of the car and just stare quietly at the grazing cows and sheep. She marvelled at the idea that Ireland's relatively mild winter temperatures (in comparison with the ferocity of Bohemia's late-year climate) meant that the animals would be grazing outdoors even at Christmastime.

It is hard to imagine how Miroslav and Anna must have felt when he took her back again to Shannon for the journey home, which would once again take place courtesy of Cuban international trade relations. She told him that she was happy to return, because she could see that he was happy with Betty and the boys and with his career at the glass factory. It was a huge relief to Miroslav that Anna and Betty had liked each other so much. 'She was meeting her daughter-in-law for the first time, and that was very different from looking at pictures,' he remembers.

Miroslav and Betty gave her some little souvenirs of Ireland to take back with her, and then he and his mother walked slowly together to the departure area at Shannon. Their conversation was quiet, and he knew that she was sad although she did not allow herself to cry. His mother was the kind of woman, he says, who felt things deeply inside but would never keen and wail and throw her arms around in the air in some mad ritual of despair. As they embraced in a final farewell, he told her softly that she must start thinking immediately about a second visit to Ireland, although neither of them imagined that it would take another eight years before she could get official permission to visit again.

Neither Miroslav nor Anna ever raised the question of her simply not returning to Czechoslovakia after that first visit. Anna knew that such a brazen defiance of her Communist masters would not only put Franta at risk, but would also spell the end for Miroslav's already dim prospects of ever being able to return to Czechoslovakia. She and Miroslav were well aware that another young man from Držkov, who had left for Germany about the same time that Miroslav was heading to Ireland, had cheated the government by getting his wife out on a mercy visa. He claimed that he was seriously ill, and then persuaded his wife to remain in Germany. His story was well-known in the village, and it was commonly understood that neither of them would ever be allowed to come back to Czechoslovakia again. Anna was, above all, a 'sensible woman', according to her son, and she never allowed herself to entertain thoughts of a dramatic defection to the West.

Betty, too, was deeply sad to see Anna leave, but she must have harboured some small number of mixed feelings when she reflected on Anna's incredible passion for diligently repairing every torn sock or shirt she could find in the house. Betty's housekeeping skills, as she readily agrees, certainly paled beside those of her Czech mother-in-law. The other thing that irked Betty was destined never to be resolved. Miroslav talked with his mother in rapid-fire Czech, as one can imagine, but he rarely paused to offer a translation to Betty or, if he did, she suspected that he had hugely reduced the content of the conversation. He would simply never get into that habit, and in fact often made things even worse by speaking to his mother (and later his father) in English and then to Betty in vigorous Czech. To be fair to Miroslav, his hearing problems made the role of dual-language translator a very difficult one for him.

A couple of years later, in the middle of October 1966, Franta arrived in Ireland. Unlike Anna, he was able to fly a regularly scheduled Czechoslovak Airlines service from Prague to London, connecting with Aer Lingus for the onward segment to Dublin. The Aer Lingus staff members were wonderful, Miroslav recalls. Notified by Miroslav's travel agent that an elderly Czech gentleman with no English would be arriving in London, they picked him up at the arrival gate and accompanied him through the maze of

Heathrow Airport to catch the Dublin flight.

As the Aer Lingus attendants quickly discovered, it was entirely inappropriate for the travel agent to have referred to Franta as elderly. He marched off the plane at Dublin Airport, according to Miroslav, as a 'majestic figure', and wherever he went during his time in Waterford he always had to play the 'showman'. He was totally sincere about everything he did, Miroslav remembers, but adds, slyly, that his father also needed to 'show' his sincerity so that everyone could see it. Even without the kind of television coverage that greeted Anna, therefore, Franta made his large presence felt in Miroslav's adopted country. He visited more Irish pubs in a month than Miroslav had done in nearly two decades, and he dragged his reluctant son along to every one of them, as his unofficial translator. As he knocked back the Guinness, he told tall stories as good as those of the natives, and declared that he found no cultural differences whatsoever between his country and Ireland.

On one occasion, Miroslav received a telephone call from the local Garda station to tell him that a very imposing man in a French beret, who could not understand English but kept pointing to himself and saying 'Meester Havel', was causing a commotion outside the Woolworth's department store in the centre of the city. Miroslav immediately recognised this accurate portrayal of his father, whose fondness for the beret recalls Miroslav's own display of plus-fours when he first arrived in Ireland.

Franta had taken Miroslav's new baby daughter, Elizabeth, for a walk in her pram, and was now hopelessly lost. He had been standing so long in the same spot, panicked about his predicament, that he had attracted a large crowd of curious shoppers and had also provoked a heated discussion about how to help this poor foreign man and his baby. Eventually someone had the presence of mind to call the police to intervene. Franta was amazed, he later explained after Miroslav had picked him up in the car, that a little ten-minute walk put him in the middle of the city. When Anna heard the story, she was more than surprised, since she could not recall Franta even once touching baby Miroslav's pram in Czechoslovakia.

On one particularly balmy evening, Miroslav drove his father to Tramore for a walk on the strand. Franta, like Anna, adored these moments at the seaside. Afterwards, as they strolled up toward the town, they passed a fish-and-chip shop. 'I told him to go there and have some,' Miroslav recalls. 'But of course he did not know what it was.'

'They sell potatoes,' Miroslav explained, using the Czech word *brambory*. They went in, and Franta was surprised to see people picking pieces of potato out of heaps of old newspaper. Then he noticed a whole chicken spinning slowly on a rotisserie, and fancied having the entire bird. His appetite was as powerful in his late sixties as it had been in his twenties. As they sat down together to enjoy this unusual feast, Miroslav noticed that not only did his father relish the taste of the chips, but he was also licking every chicken bone completely clean and carefully putting it back into the newspaper wrapping. The following day, in the kitchen, Franta requested a large pot from Betty, carefully opened his newspaper wrapping, threw all the bones into the pot, and proceeded to boil up a tasty chicken broth for himself. Like Anna, his memory of wartime shortages made him hate any kind of waste – every morsel of food had to be eaten or turned into something that could be eaten.

Franta's three weeks in Ireland passed by much too quickly for his liking. His favourite outing, he would later tell Miroslav, was to the fishing village of Dunmore East, where he wandered inquisitively for hours among the fishermen with their trawlers and lobster pots, sporting his beret and puffing contentedly on a large Cuban cigar. One other memory stuck with him. Like Anna, he was puzzled that farm animals seemed to have the right-of-way on country roads, a privilege which made him laugh out loud every time Miroslav had to stop the car while a herd of cows lumbered past, gazing with their big watery eyes at their Czech visitor.

Towards the end of Franta's trip, Miroslav noticed that his father was becoming, in Miroslav's words, 'little nervy'. He clearly wanted to tell his son something, but couldn't seem to find the words. Eventually Miroslav decided to broach the unspoken subject, which he had suspected very well. 'Do you want to tell me something, *Tátínek?*' Miroslav asked him, using the Czech word for father.

'I want to stay,' Franta finally responded, as Miroslav had thought he would. Franta told his son that he was tired of the Communists, tired of life at the coal mines, and that he had an overwhelming sense of freedom in Ireland. 'It is a better life here,' Franta told Miroslav.

Miroslav gently reminded his father that he had permission to come to Ireland only because Anna stayed behind, and that she would certainly be prosecuted if he did not go back. Franta agreed, sadly. If he didn't fear that Anna would be prosecuted, he told his son, he would certainly defect. In the end, although he was not at all a 'sensible man', he really could not imagine getting Anna into any kind of trouble.

When the day came for Franta to leave, Miroslav drove him back to Dublin Airport with Betty. It was very hard for Miroslav to see the old man crying as they said goodbye. He had always known, even on that notorious occasion when his father had shoved his face into the Christmas goose, that Franta's tough-as-nails exterior concealed a genuinely sentimental heart. He remembers that his father was 'sincerely crying' on that day at the airport.

After Franta had gone through to the departure lounge, Miroslav and Betty raced up to the outside viewing gallery. As they looked across the tarmac in the direction of the new Aer Lingus aeroplane gleaming in the morning sun, they could see Franta walking backwards, waving up at the gallery. He continued his backward walk-and-wave all the way up the steps and into the plane, and then he was gone.

Franta never came back again to Ireland, but he carried his memories of that visit to the end of his days. Rogue that he was, he returned home to Držkov feeling entitled to boast that he, almost alone of his fellow villagers, had travelled 'across the sea' to a foreign country. He just couldn't resist spreading the 'big news' (as he put it) that Miroslav was a multi-millionaire twice over, adding that, if his son had stayed in Czechoslovakia, he would be poor like all the unfortunate wretches who chose instead to live the Communist dream. No doubt this prattling annoyed his countrymen intensely, and Miroslav always hated his father's crazy exaggerations, but Franta was impossible to restrain.

Anna wrote to Miroslav that Franta had settled back into his usual corner in the local restaurant and was crowing to everyone that he had met all the directors of Waterford Glass. He had certainly met Griffin and Bačik. The Bačiks had had him to their home several times, and seemed relieved (Miroslav thought) that Franta did not try to blame them for Miroslav's forced exile. Instead, Franta worked himself into a lather at the dinner table, condemning the idiot Communists and their stupid government. Edith seemed to enjoy the elder Havel's rambunctious company, and Bačik himself was happy to join the Communist-bashing, telling Franta that he was finished with Czechoslovakia.

As the years passed, Miroslav recalls, Franta started to 'cool down' in his attitude to life, becoming less fixated on his old notion that money must always be his key to happiness. He even toned down his grandstanding behaviour at the village watering-holes, going sober for longer and longer periods. In so many ways, he felt cheated by history. He had all the entrepreneurial skills needed to become a very wealthy man – much wealthier than he was before the war and the Red Revolution – but the times worked against him. As Miroslav says, even the difficult years in the uranium and coal mines did not mean that his father had given up hope of a 'better kind of life', the kind of life that, for a brief moment, he must have imagined that he could still pursue in a free and capitalist Ireland.

Although Franta almost never wrote letters, he sent a flurry of correspondence to Miroslav in the last few years of his life. Among his many complaints about the discomforts of old age, he seemed most obsessed with the difficulty of getting replacement filters for his German-made electric shaver. He couldn't use razor blades because his sight was too poor. 'I have this damn machine and I can't shave myself!' he wrote to Miroslav, who spent an equal amount of time locating and sending filters to Franta.

But he did have some optimistic advice when his son turned sixty. 'Well done, Mirek,' he wrote. 'The years fifty-five to sixty are the critical years, and if something goes wrong that's when you'll know it. Now you'll be fine!' He reminded Miroslav that his youngest daughter, Julie, had arrived when Miroslav was 55. 'That proves my point,' he concluded mysteriously.

In one of his last letters, Franta reported that he and Anna went now for dinner to the local glass factory restaurant, because they couldn't cook at home any more. 'She gets tired a lot after dinner,' he wrote, 'and I put a blanket over her when she takes a nap.' Maybe Anna was right, and Franta indeed was showing a gentler side in his declining years.

Franta did not live to see Czechoslovakia lifted up from the Communism he hated. He died suddenly in 1979, at the age of 81, suffering a heart attack in the kitchen of his Držkov home. It was ten years before his namesake and distant cousin Václav Havel would go to Prague Castle to lead the Velvet Revolution.

Because of the notorious six-month Irish postal strike in 1979 (which even Franta had mentioned disapprovingly in one of his letters), Miroslav did not receive the telegram announcing his father's death on 19 June until three weeks after it happened. The shock of the news was compounded by his disbelief that nobody in the Irish post office would break the strike to get the telegram to him. And so the only son missed his father's funeral, something that still pains him. Miroslav's cousin, who sent the telegram, had been assured that delivery would occur the same day. Even as late as 1979, a telephone call from Czechoslovakia to Ireland would have been a matter of last resort.

When Miroslav wrote to his mother after Franta's passing, he made sure to bring the letter to Dublin where he gave it personally to his friend, Georges Graf, another émigré Czech. Graf had been born in Železny Brod and, after service in the French military, had chosen a diplomatic career that led to his appointment as the commercial attaché to the French Embassy in Dublin. He was flying to London the next day and promised to post the letter from there.

After Franta returned to Držkov, the possibility opened up of Miroslav's own return to Czechoslovakia. In 1968, Alexander Dubček became prime minister of Czechoslovakia. Anticipating Mikhail Gorbachev's policy of *glasnost* ('openness') by two decades, Dubček started to loosen some of the restrictions of Communism and to give Czechoslovak citizens more of a sense of civic freedom. Censorship was relaxed, and Miroslav's letters and photographs started to get through to his parents without official interception.

Miroslav, who was still doggedly writing unanswered letters to the Czechoslovak President's office, begging for a visa, sensed that a chance to go home might finally have arrived. He was in tears, therefore, on the morning of 20 August 1968, as he listened on the radio to reports of the arrival of the so-called 'fraternal heroes' to liberate his countrymen from Dubček's Prague Spring. Over the next few days, he was fascinated by the visceral reaction of the Czech people, who did not treat the self-proclaimed 'liberators' as anything other than barbarian invaders.

Once again, politics and timing had conspired against Miroslav, as they had always against his father also. He would have to wait yet another four years – a total of twenty-five years since he had stood on a Prague train platform with Rosa and Frank on that gloomy post-war day in 1947 – to see his beloved Držkov once again.

In 1972, Miroslav made what he expected to be his usual hopeless request for a visa. The response from the Czechoslovak Embassy officials in London was unusual. They demanded that he formally surrender any claim to Czechoslovak citizenship and provide a reason for doing so. In his reply, Miroslav explained that he had extended his stay in Ireland after February 1948 'to learn English a little better'. Then he had got an inner ear infection and stayed a little longer. Then the work got interesting, he met his wife, had children and stayed a little longer. Then he decided to stay permanently and become an Irish citizen. To have two citizenships, he concluded, would affect his children's application for university grants and complicate his dealings with Irish government offices.

Amazingly, the Embassy accepted this imaginative reconstruction of his life and his weak arguments about the bureaucratic disadvantages of dual citizenship. The officials in London raised none of their usual issues of treasonable or bourgeois behaviour. In a bolt from the blue, Miroslav was informed in May 1972 that he been approved for a visa to visit Czechoslovakia for three weeks. In June, he took his wife and five children on a marathon car journey across Europe, retracing the journey he had made in 1947 in very different circumstances.

Betty remembers the astonishment of the Czechs that Miroslav, an only child from a country of very small families, had brought back a vast brood of five children. (Five years later, Miroslav would became the proud father of a sixth child.) Much interest was also shown in Mirolav's oversized and luxurious British Wolseley automobile, a rare sight in a country dominated by Communist-built rattletraps. The high point of the visit was the emotional moment when Miroslav drove slowly down Držkov's main street towards his parents' house, taking his first look at the little village (and the life) he had left twenty-five years before. Although his parents never came back again to Ireland after his mother's second visit in 1970, Miroslav and members of his family visited Czechoslovakia almost every year between 1972 and 1985.

In May 1985, Anna wrote to Miroslav that her health was deteriorating rapidly. Now approaching her eighty-eighth birthday, Anna had moved from her Držkov house into one of the country's state-run nursing homes, about eight kilometres outside Jablonec. In another of those political ironies that Franta had always enjoyed, the home had formerly been a mansion owned by one of the bourgeois industrialists of the old pre-war Republic. A building that had once had forty rooms now had two hundred and forty, but the conditions there were warm and comfortable.

Anna also asked Miroslav, as she often did, to send some dollars for her nurses. Dollars in Communist Czechoslovakia were a precious commodity, since they could be used to buy Western appliances and cosmetics in the special government-operated 'Tuzex' stores. Miroslav replied that he planned to travel to Czechoslovakia in June, and that he was happy to keep sending dollars: 'I am making a lot of money,' he jokingly assured his mother.

The following month, he made good his promise and visited Anna with his daughter, Elizabeth. Above her bed, Anna still displayed her 'Socialist Worker of the Year' award, and she pointed to it with wry amusement when Miroslav and his daughter arrived. 'This is why they treat me so well,' she told them. Miroslav and Elizabeth flew back to Ireland on Friday, 21 June 1985. On Sunday morning, 23 June, Miroslav received a telephone call from the nursing home to tell him that Anna had passed away peacefully during the night. The cremation was postponed by a day to allow him time to return.

Things had changed so much in almost forty years that Miroslav was able to have his new Czechoslovak visa issued at the London Embassy after only an hour's wait. The creaking hulk of Czechoslovak Communism would be submerged forever within a matter of five years, but now Anna and Franta were both gone, and Miroslav knew that he would never again live in the country where he was born.

In November 1990, at the invitation of the Czechoslovak Embassy in Dublin, Miroslav and his daughter, Clodagh (who had studied at the Charles University in Prague), had the opportunity to meet Alexander Dubček at an Embassy reception. Dubček by then had been elected as President of the Czechoslovak Parliament, following the Velvet Revolution which overthrew the Communists in 1989, and was on a worldwide goodwill mission for the new government of President Václav Havel.

Dubček, who died in a car crash near Prague the following year, spoke excellent Slovakian, Miroslav recalls, and the two men chatted in mutually comprehensible Czech and Slovakian. 'I was waiting twenty-five years to see my country again,' Miroslav told the former Communist first secretary.

'You are not the only one,' Dubček replied wistfully. 'The sound of his voice was beautiful,' according to Miroslav. For the Czechoslovak Irishman, it was the sound of history – his own and that of his former homeland.

# An Industrial Designer at Work

Meanwhile, the story of Waterford Glass continued to evolve. By the mid-1960s, its collections were being sold in some of Ireland's best-known luxury gift stores, including Joseph Knox in Waterford and the Switzer's, Brown Thomas, and Clery's department stores in Dublin. Luxury Dublin jewellers like Weir's and West's were also stockists of the product. Waterford glassware was now so successful that the company could insist, as it never could previously, on substantial store pre-payments even before its products left the shelves.

The European and Irish markets, however, were relatively modest, and the engine of the company's growth came from its great strides in penetrating the huge American marketplace. Three-quarters of Waterford's production was now destined for the dollar market, where the company was becoming a recognised symbol of prestige. The relatively weak performance of Waterford Glass in Europe, according to Miroslav, was the consequence of entrenched manufacturers and the persistence of the Continental styles that Miroslav consciously set himself against.

Only relatively plain patterns like the 'Sheila' flat-cut suite, rather than Miroslav's preferred wedge-cut patterns, seemed to resonate with the very traditional Europeans. A breakthrough in those circumstances, particularly by an upstart 'foreign' company that had been in existence for barely twenty years, would have been hard to achieve. In the United States, in contrast, the kaleidoscope of nationalities tended to level the commercial playing field, and Waterford's special appeal to the Irish-American community was its trump card.

The company's biggest stroke of good fortune in the United States was the link that Con Dooley forged with John Miller, the chief buyer for the crystal-glass department at the colossal B. Altman's store in New York City. Miller, despite his job title at Altman's, was by no means a connoisseur of luxury crystal. A short, stocky, former American footballer, notorious for his quick temper and salty language, he was indeed an odd choice to become the principal US representative for this exquisite and delicate new product from the old country. His wife, Barbara, a much gentler soul, was an importer of cheap but cute Mexican glass bathroom accessories.

Yet Miller had what Con Dooley and the other Waterford sales team could never have had – an insider's hard-headed command of the American retail marketplace. Miller liked what Dooley had to show him, but he also knew that a great product needed a savvy marketing strategy. After he became President of Waterford Glass Incorporated in 1960, he grabbed onto Dooley's parade of Irish names (Lismore, Sheila and the like), and started to push the 'Irishness' of Waterford Glass. Waterford, which had previously used agents to reach the American market, put Miller in charge of direct sales and distribution to stores throughout the United States.

Miller's sales jaunts across the Land of Freedom became part of company lore. He knew every important glass and crystal buyer in the country. He even came up with the slogan 'Collect Waterford' which is credited with coaxing Americans to acquire not only every glass in one of Miroslav's suites, but also multiple suites. Waterford paid Miller a handsome percentage of its US turnover and he became a very rich man. Enjoying the status of being so closely identified with Ireland's most famous brand name, he ran Waterford Glass Incorporated in style, from a handsome office and showroom suite located in the middle of New York City's most fashionable boulevard, Fifth Avenue.

Miller quickly started to deal directly with Miroslav, always pushing for new designs for the spiralling US marketplace. In the late 1970s and through the mid-1980s, in the wake of his Kennedy Centre triumph, Miroslav made frequent visits to Miller's Fifth Avenue operation. Number 225 Fifth Avenue housed a wholesale merchandise mart for the finest gift, tabletop and home décor manufacturers and distributors from all over the world, and Miroslav, never shy about such things since his earliest visit to Orrefors, loved to wander around his competitors' showrooms to 'spy' on their newest ranges.

He particularly relished dropping by the numerous Bohemian glass showrooms, but, like a good John le Carré protagonist, he preserved his anonymity or even sometimes gave a false identity. 'But it was both ways – they also came to visit and spy in our showroom,' he remembers. Although the Miller showroom was closed several years ago, 225 itself soldiered on until January 2005, when, in a typical American business story, its roster of upscale tenants shifted en masse to a new address at West 34th Street.

Miroslav found himself straying outside his areas of expertise in this effort to help Miller. He designed a special carton to contain the crystal, which is still in use today. When Noel Griffin found out that Miroslav was now designing the company's packaging, he reportedly told one of his colleagues that 'Mr Havel is probably the only craftsman in the world who is an expert in every single aspect of crystal production from the drawing board to the packing box!'

And Miroslav did the trademark on the packing box, too. Not long after Miller took over the US operation, he pressed Miroslav to create a 'mark of quality' that would emphasise that Waterford Glass was not an English product. So Miroslav did some doodling to create a distinctive Waterford trademark that Miller could exploit in the United States (see photograph 15, the original sketch of Miroslav's proposed trademark). Under US law, the trademark had to include a written quality assurance that the product was mouth-blown and hand-cut in the Republic of Ireland.

Miroslav had always liked the coat of arms of the city of Waterford, and he started trying out some designs incorporating some of its elements. He rejected the lion rampant, which is such a conventional feature of many coats of arms. But he very much liked the somewhat cartoonish dolphin that stands on the right side of the central shield of the coat of arms. In a flash of inspiration, Miroslav made the dolphin's curvy body, rather than its head, the central image of the mark. Substituting a stylised head would give him the space he needed to insert the required quality assurance. At the top, therefore, he replaced the mammal's head with a crown, symbolising the ultimate in quality ('You cannot be more than a king,' he explains), and above the crown he placed a sunburst pattern which incorporated the legal language of quality. On the curve of the dolphin's body, he put the words, 'Made in the Republic of Ireland'. Finally, at the foot of the mark, he wrapped the dolphin's tail backwards around a shamrock, and inside the shamrock he put the name of the company in Gothic lettering.

As Miroslav points out, it was a totally 'free' and original design, quite unlike the European glass-makers' fixation on religious symbols such as churches and crucifixes. He was a little peeved that the Waterford directors also asked some Continental designers to invent a trademark. He remembers one rival effort which comprised an unlikely combination of a rugby ball and a silhouette of a glass blower. This design reflected Ireland's emerging prowess in the sport of rugby but had little to do with Waterford's products.

In any event, Miroslav's logo was chosen as the most appropriate (see photograph 16). It was a remarkable example of graphic compression, forcing all those words onto a distinctive but tiny green-and-gold sticker affixed to the bottom of each authentic piece of Waterford. The design has been simplified a bit, responding to changes in the legal requirements, and the changes are a source of minor bemusement to the original artist. Miroslav observes that the present version, created at the expiration of the original registered mark in 1987, depicts a sea-horse rather than a dolphin (see photograph 17). 'Visibly, the new designer did not know I had drawn a dolphin,' he says. To Miroslav, this change of species also represents an anatomical impossibility – the tail of a sea-horse points forward while in the revised trademark version it still curves backward.

Miller pressed Miroslav not only on marketing designs. He now regarded Waterford as his chief livelihood and was determined to make sure that the products coming out of Johnstown (and later Kilbarry) would appeal to the sometimes quirky tastes of American consumers. They also had to be good enough for volume production, because the giant American market, as Miroslav recalls, was always dominated by an obsession with volume. 'There was no point to design something that was beautiful and nice but not something we could produce in volume,' he says, a little regretfully.

Miroslav, who by the late 1960s had total control of the Waterford design process, found himself developing special features for the US market. Miller was demanding, and Miroslav inevitably had to play the role of the artist-turned-industrial designer. A good example was Miller's reaction to the size and shape of Miroslav's designs for whiskey glasses. The glasses sold in the United States, but evidently not well enough for Miller's relentless ambitions. On one of Miroslav's visits to 225 Fifth Avenue, Miller criticised his whiskey glasses as simply too dainty for the American bourbon-swigging market. Americans, he told his Czech-Irish designer, loved the patterns and weight and shine of his glasses, but preferred to drink their whiskey on the rocks. A successful American whiskey glass should therefore accommodate at least three cubes of ice (or 'three squares of ice,' as Miroslav puts it). 'Oh, and by the way, Miroslav,' Miller added helpfully. 'These cubes are a standard size.'

It was obviously costly to tailor design and production to specific markets, but America was a commercial law unto itself for Waterford Glass. Miroslav did indeed create a new design concept that widened and shortened his traditional whiskey glass in a way that he felt could probably be used in all markets. He even had his assistant, Frances Cahill, test the new design by making ice cubes to the size specified by Miller. Frances's ice cubes were a novelty in a country which consumed its alcoholic drinks at room temperature.

The revamped Waterford whiskey glass achieved great recognition in the United States, justifying the increased cost.

Miller and Dooley masterminded one other marketing ploy that remains one of Waterford's best ideas. Taking their cue from Bačik's early practice at Ballytruckle of giving little awards for local sporting events as a way to generate goodwill and interest, they magnified this idea a thousandfold into a full-scale assault on the multi-billion dollar, media-saturated American professional sports industry. Miller worked the phones and cajoled the organisers of dozens of big-ticket events in baseball, football, golf and horse-racing to present Waterford Glass trophies in their winners' circles.

Waterford Glass, unlike, for example, its now much smaller European rivals, had the manufacturing capacity to turn out these one-off crystal trophies in tandem with its normal production runs of decanters and suites and giftware for the mass market. And Waterford also had the special advantage of having the world's most versatile glass designer. Responding once again to the demands of the sales and marketing gurus, Miroslav developed yet another professional specialty – the design and execution of massive crystal sports trophies. The free publicity earned by Miroslav's trophies in the United States was incalculable. Dooley told him that it was the single most effective marketing concept the company had ever developed.

Product placement at big sports events gradually led to crossover benefits when celebrity endorsements followed in the arts and entertainment field. Just as the Penroses had built old Waterford's reputation by cultivating the custom of the Anglo-Irish nobility, the revived Waterford reached out to the modern nobility of Hollywood stars and sports personalities. Part of the Lismore pattern's early popular success, in fact, came about because singer Bing Crosby bought a complete Lismore suite as a wedding anniversary gift for his wife, Kathryn.

Crosby's choice launched waves of glowing media attention. The singer remained a loyal Waterford Glass fan, and, prior to his sudden death on a golf course in 1977, he and Kathryn visited Miroslav's design departments at Johnstown and Kilbarry on several occasions.

One of Miroslav's first big trophy commissions was for the Bing Crosby Celebrity Pro-Am Golf Tournament in Pebble Beach, California. An engraved portrait of the singer adorns the huge perpetual trophy (see photograph 18). At its height, the Crosby tournament was the second-biggest US sporting event after the football Super Bowl. Miroslav also welcomed Crosby's friend, Fred Astaire, whose sister had married into the family that owned Lismore Castle in 1970. Astaire was at the factory 'every second day', according to Miroslav, and felt a special affinity for the famous crystal suite named after his sister's historic County Waterford residence.

The trickle of celebrities visiting the Waterford Glass factory and Waterford's New York City showroom had become a torrent by 1980. Miroslav was especially happy to greet sports superstar Muhammad Ali in New York in the autumn of 1984 (see photograph 19). And he recalls how the Waterford Glass name even piqued the interest of American political leaders. House of Representatives Speaker Thomas ('Tip') O'Neill was a regular visitor to the factory in the mid-1970s, and at one time, Miroslav recalls, 'the whole American Senate was buying Waterford crystal.' Con Dooley, watching all of this with the eye of a master salesman, made sure to exploit the celebrity curiosity in Waterford Glass as part of his million-dollar US advertising budget.

In 1965, as the American market began to boom, Noel Griffin had finally approved Miroslav's new design department as the nerve centre of the Waterford production process. A few years later, when the factory moved to its new Kilbarry facility, Griffin made sure that Miroslav and his designers and engravers were housed in a fancy suite of roof-level studios. But Griffin also made a proposal to his newly designated 'Chief Designer' that somewhat unnerved Miroslav.

Miroslav had always held his position on the basis of written contracts, first with Bačik in 1951, and later with Griffin from 1954. His 1951 contract guaranteed him £750 a year plus bonus, and in 1954 he got a £100 raise. These were respectable salaries, a lot better than Communist pay scales (although hardly in the multi-millionaire class, despite Franta's boasting). Sometimes Miroslav must have wondered if being forced to stay in Ireland would really be such a terrible thing. It was not the general practice at the time for senior management to have written contracts, but it is obvious from reading Miroslav's contracts that the reason he was treated differently was because he was in possession of important company trade secrets – his designing skills and his knowledge of Waterford's manufacturing processes. The contracts included a 'non-compete clause' which restricted him from joining a competitor in the Republic of Ireland (there weren't any in the 1950s and 1960s), or indeed becoming a competitor himself, for at least two years after he ceased to work with Waterford Glass. While employed with the company, he was prohibited also from being 'concerned or interested directly or indirectly, except as an employee of the company, in the business of glass or glass products.'

Griffin nevertheless decided in 1965 that Miroslav should be treated in this respect no differently from the executives who ran the business side of Waterford Glass. He said to Miroslav that 'from now on, Mr Havel, you will deal with me personally – there will be no more contracts.' Griffin's gesture was intended positively, but he must have forgotten his earlier grasp of Miroslav's natural insecurity after years of stateless exile. As the factory boosted its output, its success and its revenues, Miroslav felt under increasing pressure to create workable designs that would satisfy even difficult people like John Miller. He had a wife and young family, and felt constantly at risk for any blame that might attach to designs that didn't catch fire in the marketplace. And technical demands always had to be taken into account. As production grew, some of his more complex patterns clearly had to be dropped because they were simply too slow to produce. All of those factors made Miroslav initially uneasy about Griffin's 'no contract' proposal, but he recalls now that Griffin 'never let me down'.

Griffin's determination to deal 'personally' with Miroslav was not destined always to improve the nature of their communications. Indeed, Griffin suspected (according to some of Miroslav's former colleagues) that his top designer was sometimes happy to use his hearing and language problems as a convenient way to ignore instructions from the many executives now running Waterford Glass. On one occasion in the early 1970s, Griffin asked Miroslav to drive to Farmleigh House near Dublin, the seat of Lord Iveagh of the Guinness family, to supervise installation of a new chandelier. Miroslav pulled up in front of the great house in his Ford Cortina, now in a seriously dilapidated state after several years of being punished by Miroslav's all-clutch driving style. Lord Iveagh was delighted with the chandelier installation, but telephoned Noel Griffin to complain that the chief designer of Waterford Glass was driving a dangerous wreck. Griffin summoned Miroslav into his office and (so Miroslav thought) ordered him to get a new car. Miroslav was grumpy in response, but he did go out and buy a Fiat 124 estate, also a modestly-priced car like the Cortina.

A month later, an executive from the Dublin Austin-Morris dealership came into Miroslav's office waving the keys of a beautiful new Austin Princess. Griffin had apparently tried to tell Miroslav in their earlier meeting that he would be getting the unusual perk of a company car (besides Griffin himself, almost no-one at Waterford Glass had a company car in those days). But Miroslav had been only half-listening to Griffin, his mind focused on some new design project, and he had no idea that Griffin had actually promised him this benefit. He refused to accept the keys of the Princess and ordered the dealer to take it away immediately. 'I cannot afford this car and I don't know why you are trying to make me take it,' he shouted. Back at Griffin's office, the whole thing was sorted out. Miroslav got a company car and he sold the Fiat just three weeks after he bought it. After that, Griffin told Terry Murphy, a member of the design department, to sit in on his meetings with Miroslav so that future misunderstandings would not arise. However, Miroslav quickly told Murphy that he should have better things to be doing with his time and Griffin never made the suggestion again.

Although Miroslav was now officially named Waterford's chief designer, for many years previously he had been semi-officially considered as having that title. And, indeed, for Miroslav, the official nature of his title, and recognition of his design department, hardly changed his life at the factory at all. He still dashed around in his white coat, swinging through the blowing and cutting departments, keeping an eye on production standards, working closely with the craftsmen on new designs or the production of special pieces.

He never isolated himself from the production line – that was how he had started in Bačik's little Ballytruckle operation, where he even helped out in the exhausting physical process of blowing the molten glass. Although, as mentioned earlier, he encountered union opposition on demarcation issues, at heart he remained a production man until his retirement. Next to his design department, he was also supervising a growing team of specialist engravers, and he often found himself sitting at an engraving wheel, working along with his team.

Miroslav had the technical capacity to design, blow, cut, engrave and sculpt glass, and he saw a knowledge of all of these processes as essential to his work as Waterford's master designer. His working philosophy at Waterford Glass was that his designs would be useless if they could not be produced commercially on the factory floor. As a designer, he needed to know the subtleties of the blowing process and the sizes of the cutting wheels. He had to 'go into the shop', as he puts it, armed with his sketches and ready to experiment with the blowing and cutting of single test pieces to see if a production run would be feasible. And that slow ritual of trial and error was true for every item in the Waterford catalogue.

So, Miroslav Havel, designer of crystal, of trademarks, and even of cartons, saw himself throughout his career at Waterford Glass as an industrial designer. He was a man of practical ideas who happened also to be a creative artist. He had trained at Umprum as an artist, but designing for industry added the complexity of creating a product that not only could be economically produced but that enough people would also actually like.

A freelance artist – and Miroslav knew many of the successful Czech freelancers who went to places like Steuben Glass in the United States – can create anything he or she wants, hoping that it will have success, but ultimately without responsibility to a public audience. A freelancer can, in an artistic sense, be 'crazy', he says – like his late contemporary, Stanislav Libenský, who was noted for his monumental coloured-glass sculptures that were often created through support from public commissions in Czechoslovakia and in the United States. Whereas Libenský could (and did) wax poetic about the spiritual and aesthetic qualities of glass, its power 'to evoke the process of birth, growth, movement, change, and distortion', Miroslav had to keep his gaze on what Con Dooley could sell to the marketplace. When he started at Waterford, he was under immediate pressure because his foremost responsibility was creating products that would be good enough to generate jobs for all of the company's growing band of employees.

And he was working in a city where there was very little heavy industry other than the iron foundry and Goodbody's sack-making factory, so the economic pressure on his skills was even more intense. He knows that some commentators do not consider industrial design to be art, because the products are produced and reproduced in huge quantities, but he is in no personal doubt that all of his production design work at Waterford was an intrinsically artistic experience.

Thus, Miroslav had the capacity, sustained over four decades, to evolve a design ethos that managed to resolve the paradox of a genuine handmade product developed for a mass marketplace. The whole industry, like all industries competing in the cost-and-price frenzy of the modern economy, has scaled back the amount of handcraft that can be tolerated while still making some money. Mass production of pressed glass has become the norm. Machinery and computers have entered every stage of the production process.

Con Dooley always assured Miroslav that Waterford Glass would remain distinctive because it would always be produced as though Miroslav himself were personally shovelling the ingredients into the furnace and putting the fine vertical wedge-cuts on a Lismore wine goblet. The company pushed this image, but it was economically unsustainable.

Miroslav recalls that the first machine installed at Waterford Glass was used to press chandelier arms to avoid the problem of thickness variations that had always plagued and slowed down production. But in Miroslav's time there was never any attempt to, as he says, 'semi-press' glass that would then be finished by hand, which of course would have meant a return to the process used in the early Bačik days at Ballytruckle. Despite his sometimes sceptical view of the unions, he was glad as an artist that they were so vocal about not replacing Waterford's teams of highly qualified craftsmen with all kinds of clever but inauthentic machinery.

Miroslav was always keenly aware of the ongoing debate in the glass industry about the contrast between pressed and handmade crystal. 'Pressed glass', a phrase he uses almost with contempt, infuses the molten glass into multiple pre-made moulds which, when the glass hardens, yield near-perfect replicas of the inside walls of the moulds. It can even duplicate the characteristic diamond patterns of cut crystal. But pressed glass produces a blunter and duller finish than hand-cut crystal, and the expert eye can sometimes spot tell-tale seams – the after-print of the mould. Pressed glass, however, consumes many fewer man-hours and is, as a consequence, considerably cheaper than mouth-blown crystal.

Moreover, Miroslav concedes that pressed glass, which was popular in France, Germany and Sweden even when Waterford Glass was just beginning its revival, avoids certain technical problems of hand-crafted glass, including variations in stem thickness. Even flat cuts can be pre-pressed onto these perfect stems. The most contentious aspect of the debate, as he learned at numerous European glass conferences, concerned pieces that showed elements of both processes. If a jug is blown by the traditional method, and the handle is automatically attached by a machine, is the jug a genuinely hand-made article?

In the spirit of conferences, of course, no absolute conclusion was ever reached. Every representative of every factory had a different view, no doubt all informed by practices in their home plant. But Miroslav acknowledges how pressed-glass technology has advanced so much in the past fifty years or so that it is extremely hard for the average consumer to tell the difference from the hand-made product.

Even the old problem with visible seams has been vanquished. He states his conclusion in emphatic terms: 'I will say that when you look on the table, and you see two glasses, one fully hand-made and the other moulded or pressed, you will think that the machine-made article is perfect.'

And it's not just a question of how manufacturing processes had to become more cost-effective. As Miroslav looks back, he is very aware of the changing tastes and fashions that affect someone who chooses industry over the studio. In an RTÉ television interview in 1991, the interviewer confronted him with a couple of very direct questions, asking 'Are Waterford Glass's designs too elaborate and isn't the glass too heavy?'

Miroslav, now in retirement and not so nervous about tough questions, was unruffled. He gave an astute industrial designer's response, noting that Waterford's market ambitions made the elaborate designs inevitable. 'We wanted to get that unique sparkle, and you have to make heavy glass to get it. So we never tried to produce thin glass, and we had too many cutters, several hundred of them, and you cannot do heavy cuts on thin glass.'

Waterford Glass, in other words, was both the beneficiary and to some extent the victim of a clear design philosophy. To make high-quality decorated crystal, it needed a heavy product. The success of its heavy product required hiring many teams of cutters. With many teams of cutters, it had to continue making a heavy product. No doubt, that philosophy presented new challenges to the executives who took over Waterford after Miroslav's retirement and faced a slackening in demand. But Miroslav used his talents to steer Waterford Glass into the success that made its name.

Miroslav addressed the fashion issue, too. It is not merely coincidental that the English language has the phrase 'the glass of fashion'. Waterford was the glass of fashion for most of the second half of the twentieth century. As noted earlier, Miroslav recognises that white wine glasses now dominate the marketplace, and how it is the fashion to drink wine from big glass 'bowls' (the oversized, bubble-shaped glasses that are everywhere nowadays). Recent shifts in social etiquette have allowed the wine bottle to return to the dining table, despite wine-makers' support for the benefits of decanting wines. Decanters, once described fancifully as 'wine's cosmetic', have now become ornamental relics.

Even the art of engraving has fallen victim to economic pressures, because it has become difficult to find a cost-effective way to market detailed hand-made engravings that may take three or four days to execute for each piece. During Miroslav's years at Waterford, engravings other than those for special commissions required that one person executed the piece, and then up to ten engravers copied it. This practice naturally limited the difficulty of the design to the standard of the least accomplished engraver in the group. It was, in effect, another compromise between art and industrial design. Today, computer-aided sandblasting, which cuts away the glass by directing abrasive sands in a stream of compressed air, provides a much more cost-effective system for transferring patterns to glass. It has essentially replaced engraving in the mass market.

As he looks back, Miroslav is certain that the Waterford Glass company that emerged in Ireland in the 1960s was probably not the company that Charles Bačik had imagined, even when he was casting around for investors in the bad old days at Ballytruckle. 'I think what Mr Bačik wanted,' Miroslav reflects, 'was a small factory making exquisite special pieces, with maybe two hundred persons maximum working there.' Bačik, in other words, wanted to fuse the artistic and the industrial in the way that the Corning/Steuben corporation has been able to do in the United States. He overlooked the fact that Steuben art glass has always been generously subsidised through sales of applied products like Corning's Pyrex kitchenware.

Things might have turned out that way, Miroslav supposes, except that Dooley and Miller unleashed such a phenomenal demand in the United States that the industrial side took over, expensive patterns had to be dropped, and Waterford Glass, by necessity, became a mass operation, backed by an artist-turned-industrial designer who understood the compromises he needed to make. The United States market transformed Waterford Glass into a giant multi-faceted enterprise, producing everything from delicate thimble-sized liqueur glasses to mammoth stateroom chandeliers.

However, from Miroslav's standpoint as an artist, there were substantial professional upsides to all of this industrial success. The biggest upside was his opportunity to do special commissions and some of his own experimental creations, and therefore to enjoy some of the benefits of cross-subsidisation which he admired at Corning/Steuben. But there was another upside that he found enjoyable, at least for a while. As the Waterford name and reputation spread across the American continent, attention naturally turned to the designer of this highly desired product. In another marketing innovation that has remained a core component of Waterford's US presence two decades later, John Miller persuaded Dooley to allow Miroslav, as Waterford's master designer, to make personal appearances in North America at retail stores specialising in Waterford Glass. The itineraries from 1982 to 1987 covered over thirty cities in the United States and Canada. They were arranged and supervised by Miller's Irish-American executive assistant, Áine Kelly.

Miroslav wrote a long letter to his mother from every one of the string of super-luxury hotels in which he stayed. Despite being billeted at such celebrated palaces as the Pierre in New York and the Beverly Rodeo in Beverly Hills, Miroslav always complained to Anna about the tasteless American food. Only American ice cream impressed him, and then it had to be Howard Johnson's. His only positive culinary report came when he went to the Vašatov Czech restaurant in New York in April 1984, where he enjoyed traditional Bohemian helpings of pork, potato dumplings and sauerkraut.

Still, these trips gave Miroslav (and Betty, who always accompanied him) an exposure to American corporate extravagance. Miroslav enjoyed these opportunities to meet the consumers of his life's work, but was always astounded at how little the retail public seemed to know about the most basic elements of the manufacture and decoration of crystal glass (or of any kind of glass, for that matter). However, his natural sense of humour never deserted him, even in the white heat of his marketing blitzes. He remembers an appearance in Dallas in 1983 that occurred during a media controversy, played up by Waterford's rivals, about the quality of the glass being produced at the new factory in Kilbarry. Miroslav was not pleased, therefore, to read the full-page advertisement in the *Dallas Morning News* announcing his appearance at the Sanger Harris department store. 'Miroslav Havel can blow, cut, sculpt, paint, and engrave as well as design,' the ad ran. 'And he can also answer every question you have about Waterford Crystal!'

Miroslav was terrified that he would be peppered with tough questions at the customer presentation, and more anxious still that his eccentric English would make things even worse. So he came up with the idea that Betty would stand up at the presentation to ask him, as though she were an ordinary shopper, to comment on whether Waterford Crystal, at its current price points, represented good value for money.

Betty was just as nervous as Miroslav about this strange assignment. But she rose to the occasion, even faking a slight American twang to be more convincing. Miroslav, in turn, faultlessly delivered his prepared answer to Betty's question as though he had just thought of it. He was so relaxed after his performance that he didn't even mind when Áine Kelly forced him to watch while the executive chef at the local Hyatt Regency attempted to turn a block of ice into Waterford's intricate 'Boat Bowl' period piece.

At the presentation, Miroslav was standing in front of a series of huge photographs of what appeared to be a gallery of Waterford blowers, engravers and cutters at work on their celebrated products. The middle photograph seemed to be of the magnificent new Waterford Glass factory itself. All of the factory's modern circumstances were visible. The blowers were on raised platforms beside a circle of furnaces in a lofty hall, looking for all the world like trumpeters raising their pipes in fanfare. Another photograph showed brightly lit airy bays, with row upon row of cutters at work at benches with electric-driven but hand-operated cutting wheels.

In fact, all of the photographs had been left behind by a German glass company after its own presentation on the previous day.

Miroslav requisitioned them for his appearance, on the theory that nobody in his audience, given the low level of knowledge the public seemed to have about how glass was made, would be likely to detect or appreciate any physical difference between one glass factory (and its craftsmen) and another.

# A Gallery of Special Pieces
# and a White House Moment

For Miroslav, the most emotionally rewarding consequence of Waterford's US commercial success was that the company finally had the financial flexibility to indulge his artistic gifts through special commissions. Miroslav freely admits that these commissions were propelled by the marketplace, again making him responsible to a public (albeit a very specialised public) for his creative output. But the idea that the production floor could, in effect, subsidise unique studio creations was something he had always found impressive about the Corning/Steuben operation in New York, and he was delighted that the same opportunity now existed for him at Waterford.

This chapter describes some examples of Miroslav's artistic works which show his diverse repertoire of skills as a crystal engraver, cutter and sculptor. These works are from the same hand that produced the commercial triumphs of the entire range of Waterford's retail catalogue, including Lismore and Colleen and the other suites, but they allow an opportunity to appreciate Miroslav as a great studio artist as well as the industrial designer that he was for over forty years.

Had Miroslav spent his career entirely as a studio artist, he would no doubt have emulated his master and mentor at Umprum, Professor Štipl, by pursuing glass sculpting. Štipl always encouraged

Miroslav to focus his energies on sculpture, the most challenging of the glass crystal arts. If he had remained in Czechoslovkia, he might have even joined Štipl after the war in developing Štipl's new design studio in Prague.

In glass sculpture, the artist is neither cutting nor engraving an existing piece, but taking an unformed solid block of crystal and carving it, using the same spinning copper wheels of the cutter and engraver, into a new creation that springs solely from the combination of the artist's imagination and technical talents. The level of craft involved is so demanding, and the risks of failure so huge, that it is hard to imagine that blocks of glass can be sculpted by spinning copper wheels in the way that we instinctively appreciate that blocks of marble or stone can be chiselled by the hands of the traditional sculptor. 'It is not like tapping at the glass with a chisel,' Miroslav says. 'But the principle is the same, since you are trying to transfer a shape into some material.' Instead of changing chisels, the glass sculptor changes wheel sizes. At Umprum, Miroslav worked extensively in marble and sand sculpture, but his skills in crystal sculpture were honed in Ireland. Sculpture of all kinds died out for many years under the Communists, unless it was for the greater glorification of Lenin and Stalin. In a sense, therefore, he feels that Ireland gave him this opportunity to develop skills that he might have been unable to use in Czechoslovakia.

Creating glass sculpture in Ireland was ironic, too, because neither Ireland nor Britain had any tradition of the kind of 'art glass' that Miroslav intended to do. He spent many solitary nights at the Ballytruckle and Johnstown factories, after the day's production had been completed, sitting at the engraving and cutting tables and practising his craft on blocks of glass prepared for him by his friends in the blowing shop during their lunch or dinner breaks.

Miroslav's range of sculpted, cut or engraved commissioned pieces is impressive. But it all began with his chandeliers. Waterford Glass and its designer were accepting special commissions from as early as the mid-1950s, especially after Miroslav re-invented the crystal chandelier. But he recalls that his first major international commission came in 1965, when the Guinness family invited him to design sixteen chandeliers to be hung along the central nave of Westminster Abbey in London. The cathedral was celebrating its 900th anniversary, so this commission attracted a huge amount of attention (see photograph 21).

The Westminster chandeliers, each comprising eight thousand separate pieces of crystal, are now so much a part of the London scene that they even appear on souvenir postcards. The drops used in the chandeliers were unusually large (23 centimetres), and created some difficult technical challenges at the Johnstown factory. They were blown as sticks of glass, but a long stick of glass cools much more quickly at either end than in the middle, causing the piece to bend. Much glass was wasted in perfecting ways to keep the entire stick cooling at the same rate. After the success of the Westminster commission, the British Parliament asked Miroslav to design a suite of plain drinking glasses with cut stems. Miroslav engraved each bowl of the glasses with the Parliament's coat of arms.

Quite different from the Westminster chandeliers, but no less striking, is the chandelier Miroslav designed for and installed in the President's Lounge of the John F. Kennedy Centre for the Performing Arts in Washington, DC, in 1971 (see photograph 22). The commission included four large sconces or wall brackets which are mounted on the walls surrounding the chandelier. The chandelier and sconces were specially ordered by Jacqueline Kennedy Onassis. Miroslav had shown Mrs Onassis a scale model of his Westminster chandeliers when she visited the Johnstown factory during her Woodstown holiday in 1967.

The Kennedy chandelier is three metres in diameter and weighs approximately 500 kilos. It is supported by three massive metal rims from which are suspended over 4,000 separate pieces of crystal, lighted with 116 bulbs. The metal in the rims is of a type that is used in building aircraft. It is light and strong, but far too expensive for regular commercial use in chandeliers. Miroslav obtained the metal through Aer Lingus, and worked with Aer Lingus mechanics to assemble the rims. He spent a week in the Kennedy Centre in

Washington to complete the installation of the chandelier.

The Kennedy project was the reason for Miroslav's first trip to the United States, in late April 1971, and also for his first exposure to the tough US immigration and labour laws. He was told on arrival at the Centre that he was prohibited from touching a single piece of the chandelier as it emerged from four big boxes shipped from Waterford. He was supposed just to stand and give assembly instructions to a team of American workers at the Centre. For someone like Miroslav, temperamentally incapable of trusting anyone but himself to do the right job, it was a very frustrating experience. It will hardly come as a surprise that he broke the American law several times every single day.

The highlight of his stay in Washington, he told a *Dallas Morning News* journalist reporting on the Kennedy chandelier, was a chance to sample every one of the thirty-two flavours of the famous Howard Johnson's American ice cream. Staying at the Howard Johnson Hotel, he asked the staff to put a carton of each flavour in his room refrigerator. He noticed that the same journalist, in his newspaper story, described the revival of Waterford Glass 'following the civil war between England and Ireland'. Even with his shady knowledge of Irish history, Miroslav knew that such a statement couldn't be accurate.

Two other chandeliers deserve mention. The first is a replica of one of the Imperial Russian Romanov chandeliers which Miroslav created at the request of the Romanoff Restaurant in Beverly Hills, California, in 1954 (see photograph 23). The restaurant was redoing an original room in the grand imperial style, and had some pictures of one of the old Russian chandeliers. Miroslav worked entirely from these pictures, and the finished product elegantly displays his ability to execute almost any design in lead crystal.

This chandelier is obviously like nothing in the Waterford catalogue. It is not even a typical chandelier, since it is purely ornamental and has no lights. Two design features were especially challenging to reproduce – the central motif of the crown jewels of the Romanovs, and the four interconnected 'R' symbols that form the base of the work. A complete 'R' is visible no matter where the viewer is positioned underneath the chandelier. Although the six-foot tall and six-foot wide piece hangs so delicately that it resembles a huge glistening snowflake, there is a good deal more metal in the structure, Miroslav says, than the picture suggests.

The other notable chandelier, dripping crystal buttons and drops, will be familiar to many Irish people and tourists who have entered the lobby of Dublin's Shelbourne Hotel in St Stephen's Green (see photograph 24). A signature feature of this piece is its crown motif perched at the very top.

Crystal aeroplanes became another Miroslav speciality. In 1974, the French government requested a scale model in crystal of the Concorde aircraft, and sent Miroslav actual blueprints from the manufacture of the original. Miroslav had an instinctive mathematical talent for developing scale reproductions. Many of his sketches for projects like the Concorde have dozens of mysterious calculations along the margins, including even the dreaded sigma symbol of differential calculus ($\sum$).

The sleek aerodynamic profile of the Concorde emerged almost entirely from a single block of glass after Miroslav spent months sitting patiently at his spinning copper wheels. The only feature that was separately blown was Concorde's unique tail. The finished piece, a stunning replica in exact scale, was presented to the Chairman of Air France on the inaugural flight of Concorde from Paris to Rio de Janeiro (see photograph 25).

Miroslav also created a scaled miniature of the private jet owned by Jack Moseley, the aviation-obsessed chairman of United States Fidelity and Guaranty Insurance Company (USF&G), one of America's largest insurance franchises. The USF&G commission (see photograph 26) arose because chairman Moseley flew his Falcon jet to a landing field in Mallow, County Cork, and then took a day trip to see the Waterford Glass factory. Impressed by Miroslav's Concorde, Moseley sent pictures of his precious jet aircraft to Miroslav (no blueprints this time), and Miroslav created a scale replica, mounted on a crystal pedestal that is engraved with the

USF&G corporate insignia. The scaling was much larger than the Concorde.

For the Moseley commission, Miroslav instructed the blowing room to create three blocks of crystal. The longest block he carved into the fuselage, engines and tail wings, and the two shorter blocks were each transformed into one of the wide lateral wings. He then slotted these wings into the fuselage section and secured them with special resins. Another slot connected this unique model aeroplane to its crystal pedestal, which Miroslav shaped and cut in a twisting, spiralling motif that gives the impression of forward motion, an aeroplane in flight.

The Falcon model is replete with little engraved details (the nationality and registration number of the plane, the name of the company, even the cockpit and passenger windows and the engine turbines). If this work had been done with a pressed mould, Miroslav points out, the viewer would notice a great deal of uniformity in the glass thickness. Pressed glass leads to 'rounding' of the finished elements, whereas in his hand-crafted version, the wings, for example, taper to a thin hard edge just as in the real aircraft.

The finished crystal jet was unveiled at a special dinner, at USF&G's headquarters in Baltimore, Maryland, in October 1986. Miroslav and Betty were in attendance. Miroslav recalls an unsettling moment when Jack Moseley's wife, Pat, used just a little too much force to pull the cloth off the piece to unveil it, causing the plane to wobble dangerously on its pedestal. She appeared to have no idea where the glass was sitting under the cloth. Luckily, her husband's beautiful new toy jet came to rest before a bad omen was created, not to mention great embarrassment to the table of twenty-four city and corporate dignitaries.

Such is the power of USF&G in Baltimore that Mayor William Donald Schaefer not only attended the dinner, but also issued a special proclamation declaring 17 and 18 October 1986, to be 'Miroslav Havel Weekend' in Baltimore. On the Sunday of his weekend, Miroslav presented the Waterford trophies for the first running of the Maryland Million steeplechase championship.

Popes and monarchs and sports heroes were also part of Miroslav's commission portfolio. As a good convert to Catholicism and a friend of bishops, Miroslav was pleased to receive a request in 1976 from Bishop Michael Russell of Waterford, to create a very unusual paperweight and pen-holder to be presented to Pope Paul VI at the canonisation ceremony for the Irish martyr, Blessed Oliver Plunkett, on 12 October 1976 (see photograph 27).

The paperweight, which stands 15 centimetres high, was blown as a single piece in the shape of the ancient St Patrick's Bell. Miroslav cut and engraved its decoration, including the papal coat of arms of Paul VI on the front, and the distinctive papal tiara that appears on top. Bishop Russell apparently kept the gift a secret from his fellow prelates, producing it from under his cassock while the Irish bishops were gathered in an intimate audience with the Pope. The photograph of the occasion shows the visible astonishment of the late Archbishop Dermot Ryan of Dublin at Bishop Russell's episcopal oneupmanship.

A second papal assignment followed in 1980, when Miroslav created a similar paperweight for Pope John Paul II (see photograph 28). The piece was commissioned as a gift to the Pope from the Polish community in Britain (see photograph 29 showing Miroslav's original sketch for this paperweight).

For the 1978 visit to Ireland of Queen Margrethe of Denmark, Miroslav designed an exquisitely cut vase with a drop-shaped front panel on which he engraved the Queen's special signature (see photograph 30). With the help of the Danish Embassy in Dublin, he discovered that the Queen had a flamboyant personal signature, a highly stylised 'M', which she had used on the covers of a series of children's books that she authored.

In the sports world, Miroslav designed and engraved a beautiful trophy with a scalloped crown, which the Wimbledon Lawn Tennis Association commissioned for the centenary of ladies' tennis at Wimbledon, to celebrate tennis champion Billie Jean King's record number of tournament victories (see photograph 31). For golfing legend Sam Snead he created a unique personal trophy (see photograph 32). The design of the tall pedestal, from which the bowl can be removed, contains twenty-four crystal 'pouches' into which Snead could pop his numerous golf championship medals.

The 1976 *Daily Express* Cheltenham Triumph Hurdle Championship trophy is one of many horse-racing trophies that Miroslav designed (see photograph 33). He thinks that it is one of the loveliest of his Waterford trophies. It is an effective combination of rich wedge-cutting on the lid and bowl and perfect flat cuts along the broad and graceful stem. The stem, which resembles a shimmering cascade of clear water, allows the bowl to appear suspended in space.

The scale and intricacy of these large sports trophies is illustrated by two pictures showing the USF&G golf trophy before and after the wedge-cutting of the bowl and the final polishing of the entire piece (see photographs 34 and 35). Photograph 34 captures the moment when Miroslav is discussing the completed flat cuts on the stem with a USF&G official who was visiting his roof-top studios at Kilbarry. The bowl of the trophy, as the picture shows, is still in its post-blowing state prior to application of decorative cuts.

Other sports trophies departed from this traditional trophy vocabulary. A good example is Miroslav's mounted tennis racket sculpture, created for the Stuttgart 'Golden Racket' competition (see photograph 36). The racket strings are an optical trick caused by matching rows of cuts made on one side of the piece with rows cut in a different direction on the other side. Another example, appropriate given the earlier reference to the American football Super Bowl, is Miroslav's football-shaped trophy commemorating the triumph of the San Francisco 49ers in Super Bowl XIX (see photograph 37). Despite its apparent unity of form, this trophy was actually blown as three separate pieces. And a final example is a crystal golf ball and Number 9 club-face commissioned by Tony Jacklin and his wife to honour the performance of German golf superstar Bernhard Langer in the 1989 Ryder Cup (see photograph 38). This was one of Miroslav's last special commissions before his retirement.

Miroslav also excelled in portraiture, probably the most

challenging branch of representational engraving. As mentioned earlier, for an Irish television tribute to comedian and musical star Maureen Potter in 1978, Miroslav shaped a six-sided block of crystal on which he engraved the faces of Ms Potter's two young sons, then aged about 11 or 12 (see photograph 39). The piece was requested by Gay Byrne, Ireland's leading television presenter, for a special edition of his *Late Late Show*, celebrating Ms Potter's fortieth year on the boards of Dublin's Olympia Theatre. At the moment of the presentation, as Byrne described 'this exquisite piece designed by Miroslav Havel', the camera swung directly to Miroslav (accompanied, strangely enough, by his solicitor, John Cooke), who was in the studio audience and appeared startled by the sudden attention.

Miroslav was inwardly pleased, however, with the art of Ms Potter's crystal. He had finally conquered the 'cherub' problem that he had encountered many years before in Frank Bouček's little cutting-shop in Mála Skála. Children are very hard to portray on glass, because their faces are so smooth and wrinkle-free that it is difficult to engrave any strong features – precisely why Miroslav's cherubs of 1939 were so inadequate.

Miroslav focused his design on the Potter boys' heads, which he posed together but looking in different directions from one another. He used his drawing skills to concentrate on the shape of the boys' noses and their relatively long hair as the dominant characteristics of his design. The line of the nose gives a central strength to each of the portraits. And the bottom of each hairline is delicately scratched to give a neat finish to the boys' then-fashionable mop-tops. The overall impression is classical and timeless. As Miroslav commented later, 'Thank God I managed to make the boys look much younger than Maureen!' Pam Collins, the *Late Late Show*'s senior researcher, later sent Miroslav a gift of one of the lavish new reproductions of the Book of Kells that had just been published in Ireland.

Throughout his career, Miroslav produced many experimental crystal pieces that either never went into production or were simply done as part of his personal artistic mission. Before closing this chapter with a discussion of his favourite commissioned piece, we will look at a few selected creations from what Mairead Dunlevy, writing in the *Irish Arts Review* in 1997, called 'the Miroslav Havel collection'.

Miroslav's oval bowl (see photograph 40) actually went into production briefly, but it proved too expensive to maintain as a regular catalogue item. The piece has such a specialised shape that it had to be blown as a regular round bowl and then painstakingly cut into its dramatic swooping oval shape. The lovely horizontal cut vase (see photograph 41), on the other hand, is one that he never intended for production. Given Waterford's union-mandated separation between wedge and flat cutters, he thought that the technical complexity of the piece, which subtly combines the two types of cut, would create too many demarcation issues.

The very abstract statute of the Virgin Mary (see photograph 42) was cut from a single block of crystal and shows Miroslav's growing comfort with the challenges of using deep winding cuts to imitate the folds of drapery, a skill he would use most effectively in his Statue of Liberty piece discussed below.

Miroslav's red jug (see photograph 43) was a rare venture into coloured glass after his early abandoned experiments, but it is technically very interesting as an example of his versatility. He made this piece in 1954 by 'casing' or enveloping the blown crystal shape with melted coloured glass. He then cut deep circular and vertical patterns through the coloured glass to expose the white crystal underneath. The play of the circular patterns is vividly magnified through each circle. The superb handle, thicker on the bottom than on the top, is actually counter-intuitive to good utilitarian design. A jug filled with water is fairly heavy, and, when the jug is held by the handle, the strain is outwards at the upper connection and inwards at the lower, so the greater strength should be at the top of the handle. Here, however, Miroslav was happy to discount this piece of commonsense physics in favour of a more appealing design.

Among other pieces in the Miroslav Havel Collection are his 1981 vase with a free-flowing design rendered in polished and unpolished surface tones (see photograph 44); a 1984 bowl, showing a naturalistic design of a fish swimming through water, and enhanced by deep prismatic wedge cutting, suggesting fleeting motion (see photograph 45); continuing the aquatic theme, 1985 sculptures of a fish (see photograph 46) and a sailboat (see photograph 47), each carved from solid blocks of crystal; a 1980 bowl, with ball-wheel cutting on the body and large diamonds below, hand-polished by Miroslav with ash-wood and felt (see photograph 48); a 1980 vase, cut and polished into vertical lobes, and then wedge-cut (see photograph 49); and a striking 1981 stem vase, where the flat surface facing the observer reflects the deep cutting on the other surfaces (see photograph 50).

And there are whimsical pieces, like the Indian snake charmer vase (see photograph 51), where the engraved design of the well-upholstered charmer is in complete harmony with the teardrop shape of the vessel. Other pieces of whimsy include his Cinderella slipper (see photograph 53) and trilby hat (see photograph 54). The slipper is not a blown piece. It was extracted from the same shaping moulds that were used to make the curving arms of Waterford's chandeliers.

The hat was actually made as a curiosity to anchor an exhibition on the history of hats at Bloomingdale's department store in New York. Although it may be whimsical, Miroslav recalls how difficult it was to imitate in hard crystal the soft turns of the brim. The hat was blown as a single piece, and the turns were made (after much experimentation) by quickly taking the blown glass off the blower's pipe and gently shaping it with a set of tongs. At the exhibition, the hat was floodlit in the middle of a vast array of real gentlemen's headwear. It was the only sparkling hat in the bunch.

A final example of whimsy, the armadillo (see photograph 52) was a sample Miroslav made for a Waterford Glass sales representative in Texas, where the armadillo is a popular state symbol and also a major nuisance. Again, it is made from a solid block of crystal and Miroslav used many small copper engraving wheels to mimic the effect of the small mammal's shell. Miroslav took a little biological liberty with the design, since he admits that he has no idea whether the creature can actually turn its tail forward as it is doing in his piece. To have allowed the tail its full extension would have been risky – the long tapering tail would be likely to snap off because the piece would be so front-heavy.

The commission of which Miroslav is most proud is his crystal scale replica of the Statue of Liberty, which the then Taoiseach, Dr Garret FitzGerald, presented on behalf of the Irish people to US President Ronald Reagan on St Patrick's Day 1986, the year of the Statue's centennial celebrations (see photograph 55). The Statue had been renovated at a cost of $60 million and would re-open on 3 July 1986, with a new museum in its base. Miroslav's replica is now on permanent display in the museum.

This was the second time Miroslav had been asked to design a commemorative piece for an Irish prime minister to present on a major American occasion. Exactly ten years previously, on St Patrick's Day 1976, former Taoiseach Liam Cosgrave celebrated the US Independence Bicentennial with a Waterford Crystal presentation to President Gerald Ford. That piece was a soaring oval-shaped trophy, with rich wedge-cutting, which Miroslav engraved with a portrait of George Washington (see photograph 56).

The 1986 Statue of Liberty commission appealed to Miroslav from several standpoints. First, he was delighted to be asked once again to design something for the traditional St Patrick's Day presentation by the Irish leader to the US President that wasn't, as he puts it, 'a big bowl filled with the shamrocks'. Second, the replica presented several design problems that truly tested his glass-sculpting skills and the production processes at the factory.

The first prototype, which Miroslav was trying to sculpt from a single large block of crystal, disintegrated half-way through the sculpting process because of tension flaws. The block of fine crystal had cooled too fast after it came out of the furnace and was therefore, in effect, not perfectly 'baked'. In technical terms, the piece had not fully annealed. With only three months left to the presentation, Miroslav had to start all over again. Fearing another sudden disintegration, he decided that this time he would sculpt Liberty's head, crown and the tablet in her left hand from separate smaller blocks of glass. Using special resins, he would then attach these separate carved pieces to the main body of the statue.

Miroslav remembers that the design of his Liberty piece was not his paramount concern – the elements of the statue were a given, after all. Rather, his biggest challenge was the intense and time-consuming process of carving every detail onto his crystal blocks. He remembers one particular technical obstacle that consumed him more than any other. Since glass is transparent, the front and back sides of the great flowing draperies of Liberty's dress would naturally be visible at the same time through the body of the statue, causing distracting reflections from front to back and back to front. Miroslav painstakingly ensured that the folds of the dress would be precisely the same on the front and back of the statue, with each fold on the front matching exactly a fold on the back, thereby creating a unified appearance through the sculpture. Miroslav was delighted with the result, which he thought looked much more like the actual statue than if he had tried to make a perfect replica.

The base of the statue was blown separately and Miroslav cut the same designs onto the base that he noticed in pictures of the real Statute of Liberty. Using special industrial glues, Miroslav then bonded all of the elements together into a single piece of crystal 61 centimetres tall. The whole process from initial sketches, including the wasted work on the block that disintegrated, took eight months.

For Miroslav, the most appealing aspect of the Statue of Liberty commission was the opportunity it gave him to step out from behind the curtain at Waterford Crystal and to be part of a presentation ceremony for one of his creations. This opportunity was unexpected. His main task in flying to the United States in March 1986 was not to be involved in the presentation but just to ensure the safe transit of the statue.

Even that not-so-distant year can be seen today as a much more innocent time. Miroslav was unhindered by the mild security checks when he boarded his Aer Lingus flight to New York, and his United

Airlines connection to Washington, DC, with the crystal replica of the American Statue of Liberty tucked carefully inside his carry-on bag. It certainly seems odd, looking back, that the Irish government's gift to the American President was carried to Washington in Miroslav's luggage. 'They left it on my neck,' Miroslav recalls now with some amusement. But he took his responsibility very seriously. He even slept in his hotel bedroom with the statue at his side.

All of this good care was ultimately rewarded, however. When he arrived in the US capital city, he learned that Waterford Crystal's public relations guru, Chris Hartman, had arranged for him to join the President and the Taoiseach immediately after the official presentation ceremony on the South Lawn of the White House. On the morning of St Patrick's Day, a limousine picked Miroslav up at his hotel and delivered him to the White House. He was still holding his precious Liberty in a tight grip. At the White House, Miroslav surrendered the statue to a White House aide and was ushered into a waiting area near the welcoming dais erected on the South Lawn. He could clearly see President Ronald Reagan in the distance greeting the Prime Minister of Canada – he assumed it was the Canadian premier because the lawn was festooned with maple-leaf flags. Suddenly the Canadian flags vanished and the Irish tricolour appeared everywhere around the dais. Miroslav was amazed by the crispness of the changeover.

Garret FitzGerald made the presentation and the President accepted it. The Taoiseach also handed the President a big Waterford bowl filled with shamrocks, so tradition was not completely violated. Then Miroslav was escorted by a Marine officer to a spot just behind the dais, at the edge of a gravel pathway that cuts through the lawn, where he awaited the arrival of the two political leaders. The officer showed him exactly where to stand so that the cameras, already lined up alongside the pathway, would catch the best angles of the moment. 'We never take a bad picture of the President,' he was frostily informed.

A few minutes later, Reagan and FitzGerald were at Miroslav's side and the cameras were clicking furiously. It was truly a glorious moment in his life, standing on the White House lawn with the President of the United States and the Taoiseach, both of them having just admired a superb specimen of his Czech-Irish craftsmanship. What would Anna and Franta have thought? Franta, surely, would have dined off the story for decades, and probably would have found a way to write himself into it.

The official White House pictures of the moment capture Miroslav's happiness very well. His ramrod-straight posture and gesticulating hands give the distinct impression, in fact, that he is the person greeting the two politicians and not the other way around. 'I did not bend, I match him!' Miroslav recalls, referring to the always well-postured Reagan. At the moment of the picture that appears in this book (see photograph 57), Miroslav wryly suggests that he was describing to the two political leaders 'how perfectly I cut the Statue!'

The conversation on the South Lawn was amiable. The President told Miroslav how much he admired the crystal Liberty that had just been presented to him, and that he was already thinking how best to put it on display for the public. He would probably put it in the new museum in the Statue's base. Then, showing his characteristic ease with the personal, Reagan switched gear and observed that both he and Miroslav were wearing identical hearing-aids, commenting on how well his aid always seemed to work. As Miroslav wondered whether he should compliment the hearing abilities of the President of the United States, Dr FitzGerald entered the conversation to make some nice remarks about Miroslav's work, as though (according to Miroslav) he had known the Waterford chief designer for years instead of just a few minutes.

Finally, the President turned to Miroslav before walking back to the Oval Office. 'By the way, Mr Havel, where are you from?' he asked, obviously detecting a trace of non-Irishness in Miroslav's voice.

'I am from Ireland, Mr President,' was Miroslav's firm reply, made even more appropriate by the presence a few inches away of the Irish prime minister. Reagan smiled, not quite believing that any Irishman would ever sound like (or, for that matter, be named) Miroslav Havel.

After the President left, Miroslav and Dr FitzGerald stayed together for an inside tour of the White House, including the private room where the White House stores gifts that are given to the President. Since very few items are kept by departing Presidents for their personal use, the room is a treasure-palace, filled with extravagant gifts from sheikhs and oil magnates and government leaders from all over the planet.

Miroslav noticed in particular a crystal ashtray that he had engraved back in 1961, an earlier gift of the Irish government to the first Irish-American President, John F. Kennedy. Kennedy always kept the ashtray on his desk in the Oval Office. Miroslav drew Dr FitzGerald's attention to his craftsman's signature, 'Havel, 1961', which was barely perceptible on the underside of the piece.

Almost at that very moment, the door burst open and Vice-President (later President) George H. W. Bush came in to greet the visitors and to boast that he had just learned of the birth of his newest grandchild. The commotion of Bush's unexpected arrival ended Miroslav's opportunity to show the Taoiseach some other examples of Waterford Glass from the Kennedy era, including engravings he had done of the President's portrait. Miroslav's great day in Washington concluded with a dinner, hosted by Dr FitzGerald, at the Irish Embassy.

# Parting Reflections

As Miroslav puts it, 'When I came to Waterford in 1947, I was poor little fella, I saw absolutely nothing here, and it shook me hard ... what I will do? I was ready to design some little things and go home, and I was suddenly faced with making a decision of importance that I hardly knew anything about.'

The burden he undertook at Waterford Glass was immense for someone who was still pursuing his graduate courses in glass-making and who was barely in his mid-twenties when he arrived in Ireland. He had a few books on glass-making techniques and even a handful of sample cutting wheels that he had tucked away in his little suitcase, but otherwise he started in Ballytruckle with an empty slate.

What Miroslav Havel eventually accomplished in Waterford, alongside Charles Bačik and Con Dooley and Noel Griffin and the many pioneering craftsmen and craftswomen of the Waterford Glass company, was the invention of a world brand name that became as big as Corning or Orrefors or any of the other great powerhouses of crystal glass. They created a new Waterford Crystal tradition. Indeed, when he spoke at the European Domestic Glass Congress in 1986, on the eve of his retirement, Miroslav felt that he shocked his audience with the information that the Kilbarry operation employed (and the figure was very precise) 3,430 people. It was unprecedented in the glass industry to have a huge 3,000-person operation dedicated to traditional mouth-blowing and hand-cutting practices. Waterford has a unique place in industrial history for its blending of mass production and high art.

Driven by its appeal to Americans, the company sustained a pace of output that, at its peak in the mid-1970s to the mid-1980s, was twice as large on a per-shift basis as any of its European competitors. In that era, Waterford Glass was regularly cited as Ireland's most successful industrial company, a Nirvana of proud teams of masters and apprentices, limitless overtime opportunities, and a worldwide market presence (with 28 per cent of the US market alone) that allowed the products almost literally to sell themselves. Waterford Glass became a public company in 1966, and after 1970 it started a series of acquisitions that gave it a broader base of commercial activities beyond lead crystal. But, for Miroslav, there only ever was one company – the glass factory that he and Charles Bačik had launched in a builder's shed in that long-ago autumn of 1947.

When Miroslav looks back, he is proud of his special commissions, but he understands that these commissions were appreciated by just a handful of patrons. He is more pleased, he says, that he was also able to use his skills to produce a galaxy of crystal suites and glasses and giftware that continues to delight millions of consumers. 'This may have pleased me more, it was a lot of thinking in that,' he remembers.

Miroslav's youngest son, Mirek Jr, continues the glass-decorating tradition at Albert S. Smyth jewellers in Timonium, Maryland, USA. Smyth, established in 1918, is the largest single-store jewellery and fine arts business in the United States. Mirek trained as a copper-wheel engraver under his father at the Kilbarry factory and in 1990 he was assigned to the Waterford Glass warehouse in New Jersey to open the company's first off-site engraving operation. Mirek had some nice commisions in New Jersey. He engraved a crystal memento that President Bill Clinton gave to heads of state around the world to celebrate the Millennium. Ironically, one of the recipients was the President of Ireland. He also engraved a presentation given to William Shatner, alias Captain

James T. Kirk of the *Star Trek* television series, by the US National Trekkies Association.

After twenty-three years with Waterford, Mirek joined Smyth in December 1999. In 2001, Smyth director Buzz Getschel launched a private-label range of crystal (coincidentally adopting the same 'Miroslav Havel Collection' designation used in the *Irish Arts Review*), based on designs Miroslav had made exclusively for Smyth in his retirement. The crystal is manufactured in Poland using traditional blowing and cutting processes. At 79 years of age, Miroslav got a big kick out of this new co-operative venture with his son, and enjoyed returning for a few years to his designing table.

Miroslav made his last visit to the United States in 2001 to sign examples of his new work at the Smyth store. It was the first time that he and Mirek Jr had appeared together at a public signing, although each of them had done many of these events for Waterford. Mirek reports that many of his American customers are surprised to learn that their favourite Waterford patterns were designed in the past sixty years and not 200 years ago. They are even more shocked to learn that the designer of Lismore, the pattern selected by over 23,000 American brides in 2000, is still living in Waterford City.

For Miroslav, those achievements – from his reunion with Charles Bačik in that little builder's shed in Ballytruckle to a place of honour on the South Lawn of the White House – were earned at the great personal cost of leaving his homeland, his parents and the woman he might well have married had he stayed. I can scarcely imagine his sadness as he read the letters from Franta and Anna as they aged in loneliness so far away from him.

Yet, Miroslav's story is different from the stories of tens of thousands of young Irish men and women who were forced to leave Ireland for opportunities in Britain, the United States and Australia. He did not have to leave Czechoslovakia in 1947. He was not a displaced refugee like many of his German and Eastern European colleagues who came to Waterford. His parents were prosperous, and, even after his father's fall from grace under Communism, the family still lived a decent life. He was a graduate of a famous glass school and of Czechoslovakia's finest academy for decorative arts. He went to Ireland for a post-war summertime adventure, and somehow destiny and the chance events of history would keep him in that tropical paradise for the rest of his days.

Miroslav no longer designs or decorates crystal glass. Sometimes, when I am visiting my home in Waterford City, I look across the kitchen and watch him while he sits on his little stool, patiently cutting every ounce of fat from the meat he will use in one of the stir fries he likes to cook. In those moments, I can catch just a glimmer of the extraordinary intensity that I remember from his great designing years, that same habit of pushing his tongue slightly out between his lips in profound concentration, and those sharp and focused and always twinkling eyes of the Maestro.

Only his hands betray his age – those beautiful steady hands that now tremble just a little and bear some of the telltale marks of weaker circulation. But I know that these are the same hands that once created the most celebrated crystal patterns in the world, and some of the most beautiful glass sculptures and engravings of our time. This has been Miroslav Havel's story of his long and interesting journey from a little village in Bohemia, and I feel privileged to have been able to write it.